INSIDERS' GUIDE®

QUICK ESCAPES

Quick Escapes®
washington, d.c.

getaways from
the nation's capital

SIXTH EDITION

John Fitzpatrick
and
Holly J. Burkhalter

Revised and Updated by Evan Balkan

INSIDERS' GUIDE®

GUILFORD, CONNECTICUT
AN IMPRINT OF THE GLOBE PEQUOT PRESS

The prices, hours of operation, and other details listed in this guidebook were confirmed at press time. We recommend, however, that you call establishments before traveling to obtain current information.

To buy books in quantity for corporate use
or incentives, call **(800) 962–0973**
or e-mail **premiums@GlobePequot.com.**

INSIDERS' GUIDE®

Photo credits: pp. 1, 55: courtesy Virginia Tourism Corporation; p. 4: courtesy Shenandoah National Park; p. 19: courtesy Virginia Division of Tourism; p. 30: courtesy Richard T. Nowitz/Metro Richmond Visitors & Convention Bureau; p. 42: courtesy Virginia Division of Tourism; pp. 63, 115: courtesy Tim Tadder/ Maryland Office of Tourism; p. 67: courtesy Annapolis & Anne Arundel County Conference and Visitors Bureau; p. 76: courtesy Michael Ventura/Maryland Office of Tourism; pp. 100, 165: courtesy Terry Way/Commonwealth Media Services; pp. 121, 160: courtesy Steve Shaluta Jr./West Virginia Division of Tourism; p. 127: courtesy Evan Balkan; pp. 173, 209, 224: courtesy Pennsylvania Office of Travel and Tourism; p. 184: courtesy Jeffrey Hixon/Commonwealth Media Services; pp. 219, 235: courtesy Delaware Economic Development Office; p. 249: courtesy Cape May Chamber of Commerce.

Text design by Nancy Freeborn
Maps by M. A. Dubé © Morris Book Publishing, LLC

ISSN 1541-5198
ISBN 978-0-7627-4434-3

Manufactured in the United States of America
Sixth Edition/First Printing

To Grace and Josie

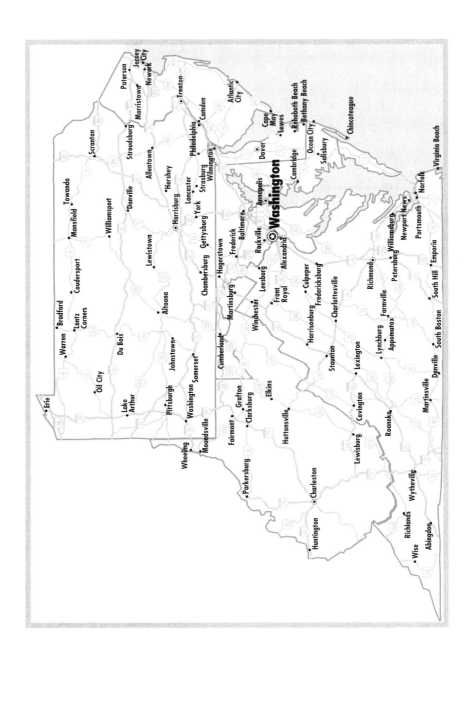

CONTENTS

DELAWARE AND BEYOND ESCAPES.... 219

INTRODUCTION

There are many advantages to living in the Washington, D.C., area. One of them is that our nation's capital is located within easy driving distance of some of the most spectacular scenery and most enjoyable vacation spots in the United States.

For example, a three-hour drive east takes you to the Atlantic Ocean, where you can revel in the busy beach scene or walk for miles along the surf, alone except for the wild beach ponies. Three hours north is Pennsylvania Dutch country, where horse-drawn buggies, handheld plows, Mennonite and Amish women in somber dresses and bonnets, and handmade quilts fluttering on clotheslines are common sights. Straight west takes you to the mountains, abounding with great hikes, orchards where you pick your own apples and berries, and cozy country inns. Head south and you're in the land of colonial and Civil War history.

All this and much more is included in *Quick Escapes Washington, D.C.,* a narrated travel itinerary that will be useful to both locals and visiting tourists. Our twenty-one escapes include a mix of urban and rural, with great dining, shopping, and sightseeing in such cities as Philadelphia, Pittsburgh, and Richmond, as well as hiking in West Virginia's parks, sailing on the Chesapeake Bay, bicycling on the Eastern Shore, and beachcombing at Assateague Island.

Here's how to use this book: The chapter heading lists the activities that are included in the itinerary. When you've found an activity you're interested in, read through the whole chapter. In each chapter, we tell you what's special about the destination; explain how to get there; and describe the restaurants, lodgings, and sights that we've planned for you. Once you've made a decision on a destination for your quick escape, be sure to make reservations for lodgings, restaurants, and other activities (such as white-water rafting) that require them. In fact, it's always a good idea to call ahead when you're planning a jaunt: Hours of operation and prices of admission change, and restaurants change their menus or sometimes close. We've included Web addresses (when they were available) for attractions and lodgings as well as a listing of Web sites to help you plan your trip.

In planning weekend escapes, we have used the following formula:

First, most chapters include a mix of indoor and outdoor activities, from hiking, swimming, and skiing to shopping, antiquing, museumgoing, and visiting historic homes and gardens.

Second, we've included a mix of well-known must-sees as well as off-the-beaten-track finds of our own. For example, the Williamsburg chapter provides a detailed itinerary for seeing the best of the famous reconstructed colonial area. But we've added some great new restaurants that most tourists don't know about, and we've also included a bike ride around lovely Jamestown Island—a pleasure that many visitors fail to take advantage of.

Third, in case you're staying longer than a weekend, or want a variation, each chapter includes a "There's More" section of additional sights and attractions. And there's a calendar of Special Events full of local seasonal and annual events, with numbers to call for precise dates and details.

Fourth, the overnight accommodations we have selected are mostly small private inns or bed-and-breakfasts. (If you have a favorite chain motel or hotel, you can always call its toll-free number to find out the nearest location.) We've avoided chain restaurants, too, and searched out one-of-a-kind local favorites, most of them in the moderate price range. Other Recommended Restaurants lists alternatives, some inexpensive and others more costly.

Fifth, a word about restaurant prices: "Inexpensive" means less than $7.00 for lunch and coffee and less than $12.00 for dinner and beverage; "moderate" means $7.00–$15.00 for lunch, $12.00–$25.00 for dinner; "expensive" means $15.00–$30.00 for lunch, $25.00–$50.00 for dinner; "very expensive" means more than $30.00 for lunch, more than $50.00 for dinner.

Finally, we have tried to include activities that everybody will enjoy—friends, children, and grandparents. Some weekend itineraries are especially kid-friendly, such as the trip to Colonial Williamsburg and Busch Gardens in Virginia, and others are obviously more adult-oriented, such as the visit to the mansions and formal gardens of the Brandywine River Valley. But every weekend includes things that everybody will like: fresh air, beautiful scenery, and great food.

Oh, yes. There's one more thing. We break for doughnuts whenever possible. Have a great time!

VIRGINIA
ESCAPES

Shenandoah National Park

Scenic Skyline Drive / 2 Nights

Shenandoah National Park is considered by many to be among the premier national parks in America. It is, by anyone's reckoning, a national treasure.

The park sits astride the beautiful Blue Ridge Mountains, which are spectacular 365 days a year. In fall the ridge is aflame with color. In winter snow and ice glisten from every branch. In spring the budding trees turn a misty pale green, and high summer brings a dark green velvet cloak to the mountains.

- ☐ National park
- ☐ Scenic mountain drive
- ☐ Hiking
- ☐ Apple orchard
- ☐ Picnicking
- ☐ Gourmet dining

You'll see exposed rock faces, tunnels of trees, high ridges dappled with light and shade, and banks of wildflowers. With its 280 square miles of forest and mountains, the park is home to some 200 species of birds, as well as deer, bobcats, bears, groundhogs, and other creatures. You're sure to see some of them on the two long hikes included in this itinerary.

Winding through the park is the beautiful 105-mile-long Skyline Drive, which offers glorious views of the Shenandoah River in the deep valley to the west and the lush piedmont terrain to the east. Much of Skyline Drive, which stretches from Front Royal on the northern end to Waynesboro on the southern end, is on top of the ridge, and you can see for miles in every direction. Every turn and twist (and there are many!) brings a new and breathtaking vista into view.

Best of all, Shenandoah National Park has more than 500 miles of trails, nearly all of them accessible from Skyline Drive. You can walk a short loop to see a waterfall or pack a picnic lunch and go the distance with a 10-mile hike. Indeed, if you wanted to, you could hike all the way down the mountain chain on the Appalachian Trail, which runs the length of the park.

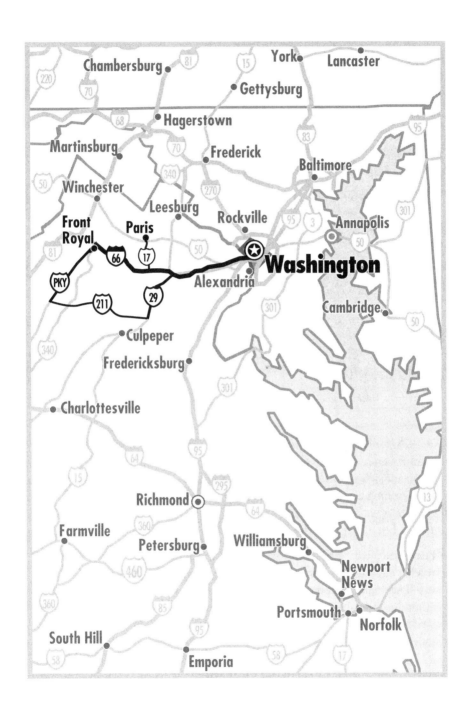

View from Buck Hollow Overlook, Shenandoah National Park

This quick escape to rural Virginia takes full advantage of both the spectacular scenery of Skyline Drive and the unparalleled hiking possibilities in Shenandoah National Park. You'll dine and relax at a different country inn each evening as you watch the sun set over the Blue Ridge Mountains.

Day 1 / Afternoon

Leave late afternoon or after work on a Friday to get an early start on the weekend. Your first destination is the tiny town of Paris, Virginia, where you'll have dinner and spend the first night. Paris is about 50 miles west of Washington on U.S. Highway 50. If you prefer, you can take Interstate 66 west about 50 miles to exit 23, and then take U.S. Highway 17 north 7 miles to Paris.

If it's late summer or early fall and you get an early enough start, consider a short detour to **Hartland Orchard** (Belle Meade Lane, Markham;

540–364–2316; www.hartlandorchard.com), where you can pick your own or buy a basket of apples to snack on throughout the weekend. Hartland is easy to find from I–66. Take exit 18, turn right (north) on Virginia Highway 688, and then immediately left on Virginia Highway 284 (Belle Meade Lane); it's only about a mile from the interstate, and there are signs. (From the more scenic US 50, you'll have to take US 17 south 7 miles and Virginia Highway 55 west 5 miles to get to VA 688. Cross under the interstate and proceed north as above.) At the orchard, you can stock up on Jonathans, Red or Golden Delicious, Granny Smiths, Fuji, Gala, or a half dozen other varieties of apples. You can also buy pumpkins, peaches, cherries, and blueberries in season; cider; jelly; and honey for weekend picnicking and snacking, and for the drive home. Open daily 8:00 A.M. to 6:00 P.M.

DINNER: **The Ashby Inn & Restaurant,** 692 Federal Street, Paris (200 yards west of the intersection of US 17 and 50 on Virginia Highway 701); (540) 592–3900 or (866) 336–0099; www.ashbyinn.com. The Ashby has won accolades for the beauty of the facility and the splendor of its menu, which changes daily but always includes homemade bread and desserts, mouthwatering fresh seafood and game entrees, and produce and herbs from the inn's garden. The Ashby Inn also has one of the best wine selections in the Mid-Atlantic region. Open for dinner Wednesday to Saturday 6:00 to 9:00 P.M.; reservations necessary. Expensive.

LODGING: The Ashby Inn is located in a tiny corner crossing of Paris, and the nineteenth-century dwelling and nearby schoolhouse, which houses four extra suites, have been meticulously restored, expanded, and decorated. Antiques, worn Oriental rugs, old quilts, dark rich colors on the walls, and old prints and paintings can be found in every room. In addition, each room has a wonderful view of the surrounding countryside and mountains. Rooms are $115–$185, and the big, beautiful suites (each with its own fireplace) are $215–$250. There is a 20 percent surcharge added on October weekends.

Day 2 / Morning

BREAKFAST: The Ashby Inn serves a full breakfast with fruit, cereal, and something luscious from the oven.

After breakfast, head for **Front Royal.** Go 7 miles south on US 17, then go 17 miles west on I–66 and 4 miles south on U.S. Highway 340. If you plan on picnicking, there are a half dozen places in Front Royal where you can stop and pick up provisions for a picnic lunch at the park. The best is **J's Gourmet,** 206 South Royal Avenue (US 340). There you can get the likes of a trout mousse with cucumber sandwich, fresh salads, sweets and savories, and a decent bottle of wine. Phone in advance (540–636–9293; www.jsgourmet.com), and your provisions will be ready when you arrive. Open Monday through Saturday 11:00 A.M. to 3:00 P.M.

After you've picked up lunch, cross the street to the **Royal Oak Bookshop,** 207 South Royal Avenue; (540) 635–7070; www.royaloak bookshop.com. The Royal Oak has been in business for more than twenty-five years and has five pleasant rooms crammed with new and used books, posters, and prints. Open Monday, Friday, and Saturday 10:00 A.M. to 6:00 P.M., Thursday 10:00 A.M. to 8:00 P.M.; and Sunday noon to 5:00 P.M.

The northernmost entrance to **Shenandoah National Park** is on US 340 just south of Front Royal. Get on Skyline Drive there and plan to spend the entire day in the first 30 miles of the park and **Skyline Drive.** Both the park and the drive are open 365 days a year, weather permitting; call (540) 999–3500 or visit www.nps.gov/shen. The entrance fee is $10 per car December to February, $15 March to November. Save your receipt, because the admission is good for a week. It's free if you have a $20 annual "Shenandoah Pass," a National Park Pass, a Golden Eagle Passport, a Golden Access Passport, or a Golden Age Passport.

The National Park Service personnel at the Front Royal entrance station will give you a free map, a brochure describing the park and Skyline Drive, and a publication called the *Shenandoah Overlook* that tells you the times all facilities are open and lists special events in and around the park.

Don't resist stopping at the **Shenandoah Valley Overlook** at mile 2.8. There you have a panoramic view of the Shenandoah Valley to the west and 40-mile-long Massanutten Mountain, which divides the Shenandoah River into two forks that meet near Front Royal.

Stop at the **Dickey Ridge Visitor Center** at mile 4.6 to see exhibits describing the geology, flora, and fauna in the park. If you're planning any serious hiking, you should buy a copy of the Potomac Appalachian Trail Club's *Circuit Hikes in Shenandoah National Park* or one (or more) of their detailed trail maps. Also talk with the park personnel at the visitor center. Park staff members will help you plan a hike and let you know if any of the trails have been washed out by rain or are undergoing repair.

Across the road from the visitor center is the **Fox Hollow Nature Trail,** a short 1.3-mile loop trail that takes you past an ancient cemetery, rock fences, and the rock foundations of several ruined buildings. Until the 1920s when the Commonwealth of Virginia purchased the land and gave it to the federal government to create Shenandoah National Park, this area was populated by farmers. The gently sloping nature trail roughly follows the farm road the Fox family traveled to go to market before there was a paved road in the area.

As you drive south on Skyline Drive, you'll be climbing steadily for the first 20 miles or so from an elevation of about 600 feet near the entrance at Front Royal to nearly 3,400 feet at Hogback Overlook. Then the road dips up and down over Hogback Mountain, through Elkwallow Gap, over Neighbor Mountain, through a couple of hollows, up over Pass Mountain, and, finally, down again at Thornton Gap without a billboard in sight. It's as pretty a drive as you'll ever take.

Plan to stop at several of the overlooks and waysides. There's nearly always a vista or some close-in scene worth a photograph. Remember to watch the road carefully as you drive. You'll be sharing it with hikers, bikers, deer, an occasional bear, and rubbernecking drivers.

LUNCH: At **Elkwallow Wayside** at mile 24.1, there are tables where you can eat a picnic lunch. There's also a snack bar that sells soup, sandwiches, chips, and drinks. The snack bar is usually open weekdays 9:00 A.M. to 5:30 P.M. and weekends 9:00 A.M. to 6:30 P.M. from mid-April through early November; (540) 999–2253. Inexpensive.

Afternoon

Set aside the whole afternoon for a strenuous hike with breathtaking views; you're going to climb the **Little Devils Stairs.** Drive back north 5 miles from Elkwallow Wayside to **Little Hogback Overlook** between mileposts 19 and 20. Park there, walk north a half mile along the roadside, cross Skyline Drive, and look for a fence gate leading to the Keyser Run Fire Road going south and east down the mountain. Follow the fire road 1 mile to the Little Devils Stairs Trail; halfway there, you'll pass beneath Little Devils Stairs Overlook, where cars are parked at the top of a steep cliff to your right.

When you reach the trail marked by blue blazes on the trees, leave the road, turning left (to the right is the Pole Bridge Link Trail), and descend Little Devils Stairs. The descent is quite steep; in the first mile or so of the trail, you'll go from an elevation of more than 2,600 feet to an elevation of 1,100 feet.

The "stairs" are enormous boulders and chunks of the mountain that broke off and tumbled down eons ago. You'll feel like a mountain goat as you scramble from rock to rock, sliding and slipping as you go. A stream, Keyser Run, parallels the trail almost the whole way; take frequent breaks and sit on a log or a boulder by the stream to give your legs and knees a rest.

When you've reached the bottom of Little Devils Stairs after about 2 miles, you'll know you've had a hike! At that point, you will have come to the edge of the park; the boundary is marked by signs, and you'll see a parking lot where hikers from outside the park leave their cars while they climb up the stairs.

Now for the moment of truth. You can turn around and climb up the Little Devils Stairs, or you can walk past the parking lot to the Keyser Run Fire Road and stroll up the gravel road all the way back to Skyline Drive. Walking up the fire road adds a mile or so to the 8-mile hike, but it will be easier on your muscles. Either way, allow at least four hours for the entire circuit.

When you're "hiked out," get back in your car for a 12-mile drive south to **Thornton Gap.** Exit from Skyline Drive and Shenandoah National Park (save your receipt for admission the next day) onto U.S. Highway 211 west, and follow it 9 miles to Luray. In Luray, pick up U.S. Highway 340 Business south and drive 6 miles. Turn left on Virginia Highway 624. After a half mile, turn right onto Virginia Highway 626 (Hawksbill Park Road). Your evening destination is a quarter mile on the right.

You will be dining and staying over at **Jordan Hollow Farm Inn,** 326 Hawksbill Park Road, Stanley; (540) 778–2285 or (888) 418–7000; www.jordanhollow.com. The inn is known for its gracious hospitality and its beautiful views of the Shenandoah Mountains.

DINNER: The Farmhouse Restaurant at Jordan Hollow Farm Inn combines traditional home-style cooking and fancy New American cuisine with an emphasis on local produce. You can start with their signature crab dip with garlic toast and follow it with pistachio-encrusted rack of lamb with rosemary Dijon cream sauce. Moderate to expensive.

LODGING: The Jordan Hollow Farm Inn has six guest rooms and eight luxury suites. The rooms are homey and beautifully furnished; most have fireplaces, whirlpool baths, and private porches. The suites have a two-person thermomassage spa in the bedroom and a separate sitting room/anteroom. Rates: $143–$190 a night; $190–$250 double occupancy.

Day 3 / Morning

BREAKFAST: The Jordan Hollow Farm Inn serves a big breakfast, which is included in the price of the room. It's likely to feature ham and eggs or pancakes, and fruit and fresh-baked pastries. Fuel up, because you have another good hike ahead of you.

After you've had breakfast and packed up your car, reenter Shenandoah National Park at Thornton Gap and head south 20 miles to **Big Meadows.** This morning, you'll hike from Big Meadows to **Rapidan Camp** and back, a 10-mile trek that takes in some of the loveliest features of the park, including streams, waterfalls, boulders, and spectacular views.

Park at Big Meadows Wayside just south of milepost 51. Cross Skyline Drive diagonally to Rapidan Road, a gravel service road with a chain across its entrance. As you hike down the road through the meadow and into the woods, keep your eyes open for deer, which frequently graze there. You'll also see plenty of wildflowers, and strawberries and blueberries when they're in season.

Rapidan Road descends from an elevation of more than 3,600 feet to about 2,500 feet through a series of three gentle switchbacks over a 5-mile stretch. After a mile or so, you'll pass the yellow-blazed Mill Prong Horse Trail on your right, and after another mile or so the blue-blazed Upper Dark Hollow Trail on your left; ignore both and stay on the gravel road another 2-plus miles until you reach the narrow Rapidan River and an intersecting gravel road heading uphill to the right. Follow this road up the hill 0.7 mile, crossing the bridge over Mill Prong Stream. Once you've crossed the bridge, you're at the halfway point on your hike.

You'd turn right on the yellow-blazed Mill Prong Horse Trail to head back, but before you do, take a few minutes to walk around **Rapidan Camp,** a small fishing camp built as a summer retreat by President Herbert Hoover.

To return, take the Mill Prong Horse Trail along the stream (notice the waterfall) 0.8 mile to the blue-blazed Mill Prong Trail, which goes straight as the horse trail heads right. Follow Mill Prong Trail 1 mile and turn right onto the Appalachian Trail (marked with white blazes on the trees). Take it 1.7 miles back to Skyline Drive. Turn right and head back to Big Meadows.

Until recently, Camp Hoover (as it was then known) was reserved for the exclusive use of top government officials and their friends. Rapidan Camp is now open to the public, and free guided tours of Hoover's retreat are provided by the National Park Service at 9:00 A.M. and 1:30 P.M. five days a week (Thursday to Monday) from Memorial Day through October.

If you're an early riser, you can time your 10-mile hike to link up with the 9:00 A.M. guided tour of the camp; you'll find both the history lesson and the renovation effort fascinating. Later risers can shorten the hike by 50 percent by parking at the lot at milepost 52.8 and following the Mill Prong Trail directly to the camp. (Directions and a map are available at the park's visitor centers.)

Or, if you prefer, you can sign up at the **Byrd Visitor Center** (open daily April through November) at Big Meadow or by phone for a van ride to the Rapidan Camp tour. The combined van ride and tour take nearly three hours. Advance reservations are strongly advised since the van can accommodate only a dozen people. Call (540) 999–3283.

LUNCH: When you complete the hike to Rapidan Camp and back and you are completely hot, tired, and sweaty, cool off and have lunch at **Big Meadows Lodge.** There is a casual restaurant where you can get sandwiches and full meals at moderate prices. At Big Meadows, you can also bone up on park history, geography, and biology at the Byrd Visitor Center, or stop in at the gift shop and pick up some Appalachian crafts.

Afternoon

After lunch, take one last scenic swing on Skyline Drive before leaving for home. You'll especially like the drive back from Big Meadows to Thornton Gap. You will be breezing through the highest points in the park, and the traffic is always lighter going from south to north.

If you still have energy to spare, just north of Big Meadows at **Dark Hollow Falls** is a 70-foot waterfall about three-quarters of a mile from the parking area. And 8 miles farther north at mile 42.6 is **Whiteoak Canyon,** a popular spot near the highest point in the drive where you can take a 5-mile hike and see six waterfalls and a beautiful stand of hemlocks.

Exit from the park at Thornton Gap and return home via US 211 east 35 miles to Warrenton, U.S. Highway 29 north 13 miles to the interstate, and I–66 east about 30 miles to Washington.

There's More

Horseback Riding. Shenandoah National Park has stables at Skyland; (540) 999–2210. One-hour or two-and-a-half-hour rides available; reservations necessary. Rates: $20–$42. A fifteen-minute pony ride for children is $3.00. All rides are available May through October.

Canoeing. The Front Royal Canoe Company, located on US 340 about 3 miles south of Front Royal, rents canoes, kayaks, rafts, and inner tubes from April through October for use on the Shenandoah River. Expect to pay about $40 for a canoe or $16 for a tube for a ninety-minute rental; a half-day rental doesn't cost much more. (540) 635–5440 or (800) 270–8808; www.frontroyalcanoe.com.

Washington, Virginia. Delightful village with upscale art galleries, antiques stores, cabinetmaking studios, and a pleasant museum.

Luray Caverns. Very popular commercialized natural cavern that features a one-hour tour, a huge "stalacpipe" organ that plays real music, a forty-seven-bell carillon, and a car and carriage museum. A restaurant, motel, and golf course are also on the premises. Located on US 211 about 9 miles west of Shenandoah National Park; (540) 743–6551 or www.luraycaverns.com. Open seven days a week year-round at 9:00 A.M.; closing time varies with the season. Admission is $17.00 for everyone over age thirteen and $8.00 for children seven to thirteen. Children six and under are admitted free.

Special Events

March. Annual Spring Arts and Crafts Show. Area artists display and sell their works in Harrisonburg. (540) 434–0005.

May. Wildflower Weekend in Shenandoah National Park. Naturalist tours and lectures, photo exhibits, and, of course, the flowers. (540) 999–3500.

June–July. North American Butterfly Association Count. Volunteers are invited to spend a day counting the butterflies in an assigned section of Shenandoah National Park or the immediate vicinity. (540) 999–3282.

August. Hoover Days. Tours, historical talks, refreshments at Hoover's summer home (Rapidan Camp—located in the park) and in surrounding towns. (540) 999–3500.

December. Annual Bird Count. Volunteers are invited to spend the third Sunday in December counting the birds in an assigned section of Shenandoah National Park or the immediate vicinity. (540) 999–3282.

Other Recommended Restaurants

Washington

The Inn at Little Washington, Middle and Main Streets; (540) 675–3800; www.theinnatlittlewashington.com. One of the best restaurants in the country—of the "you have to go there at least once in your life" type. Menu changes daily, but everything is prepared from the freshest local ingredients. Very elegant, very romantic, very expensive.

Flint Hill

Four and Twenty Blackbirds, U.S. Highway 522 and Virginia Highway 647; (540) 675–1111; www.fourandtwenty.com. Lovely, casual-chic restaurant in an old home with fireplace, lace curtains, and antique furniture; specializes in New American cuisine, with Italian, Thai, and Southwestern tones. Expensive.

Sperryville

Appetite Repair Shop, just off US 211; (540) 987–9533. Good place to get a burger and onion rings, a deli sandwich, chips, fruit, and a candy bar for a picnic or for the road. Inexpensive.

Front Royal

Villa Giuseppe's Italian Restaurant, 865 John Marshall Highway; (540) 636–8999. Traditional, family-oriented Italian restaurant serving spaghetti, lasagna, and veal dishes that are popular with locals. Moderate.

Stadt Kaffee Cafe and Restaurant, 300 East Main Street; (540) 635–8300. Traditional, family-oriented German restaurant serving sauerbraten, schnitzel, and apple strudel. Moderate.

Stanley

Best place for doughnuts: D.R. Quick Shop Bakery, 714 East Main Street; (540) 778–1982. Your choice: glazed, cake, cinnamon . . . and they open between 3:30 and 5:00 A.M. for early birds. If they run out of doughnuts, they'll make them up fresh for you within fifteen minutes. Call ahead for large orders.

(For other restaurants see the listings under Other Recommended Lodgings.)

Other Recommended Lodgings

Shenandoah National Park

Shenandoah National Park has two lodges, one at Skyland and one at Big Meadows; (540) 743–5108 or (800) 778–2851. Both have comfortable guest rooms, great views of the Shenandoah Valley, and restaurants on the premises. Rates: $64–$184. You can also rent a rustic cabin in the park (the Lewis Mountain Cabins); cabins are set up for housekeeping but have no stoves. Rates: $74–$119. There are campgrounds at Mathews Arm, Lewis Mountain, Loft Mountain, and Big Meadows. Campsites cost $14 at Lewis Mountain and Loft Mountain and are on a first-come, first-served basis. You can reserve a site at Big Meadows ($19) by calling (800) 365–2267 and giving SHEN as the four-letter designator when prompted. Back-country camping is permitted throughout the park; the required permit is free. There are also six locked cabins in backcountry areas of the park rented through the Potomac Appalachian Trail Club for $25 a night; (703) 242–0693.

Woodstock

The Inn at Narrow Passage, U.S. Highway 11, about 3 miles south of Woodstock; (540) 459–8000 or (800) 459–8002; www.innatnarrowpassage .com. Log inn that has been a stopping place for travelers for 250 years; completely restored with gleaming floors, air-conditioning, and a huge limestone fireplace. The inn has twelve guest rooms with private baths. Large country breakfast by the fire. Rates: $115–$165.

Syria

Graves' Mountain Lodge, County Road 670; (540) 923–4231; www.graves mountain.com. Hilltop lodge located about 1 mile from the pedestrian entrance at the base of Shenandoah National Park's Whiteoak Canyon Trail and Old Rag Mountain Trail, two of the park's most beautiful and popular trails. There are thirty-eight rooms in the lodge; the $72.00–$126.50 per person daily charge includes all meals. There are also nine cabins that accommodate up to fifteen people; the cabins (which sleep two to ten people and have cooking facilities) rent for $133 to $254 a day without meals. The dining room's fried chicken, country ham, and rainbow trout dinners are first-rate.

Washington

Bleu Rock Inn, US 211; (504) 987–3190 or (800) 341–2538; www.bleu rockinn.com. Pleasant, newer country inn with five guest rooms, all with private baths and balconies with views of the mountains. Complimentary afternoon sherry; orchards to stroll through before you retire. Excellent restaurant serving French and American cuisine on premises. Rates: $155–$220, including breakfast.

Strasburg

The Hotel Strasburg, 213 South Holliday Street; (540) 465–9191 or (800) 348–8327; www.hotelstrasburg.com. A renovated century-old Victorian hotel with seventeen rooms and twelve suites, some of which have Jacuzzis. There is also an excellent restaurant on the premises. The $83 to $180 room charge includes breakfast.

Front Royal

Killahevlin, 1401 North Royal Avenue; (540) 636–7335 or (800) 847–6132; www.vairish.com. Antique-filled Edwardian mansion with Irish pub on the premises. All guest rooms have whirlpool baths, telephones, and working fireplaces. Large breakfasts; complimentary coffee and soda available all day. Rates: $155–$255.

Sperryville

The Conyers House Country Inn and Stable, 3131 Slate Mills Road; (540) 987–8025; www.conyershouse.com. Elegant old country store made into an inn. Seven guest rooms with lovely antiques, private baths, and cozy fireplaces; full country breakfast. Six-course, four-wine, candlelight dinner available upon reservation. A two-hour cross-country horseback ride can be arranged for $50 a person. Rates: $150–$300; dinner for two is an additional $175.

For More Information

Shenandoah National Park, 3655 US 211 East, Luray, VA 22835; (540) 999–3500; www.nps.gov/shen.

Shenandoah Valley Travel Association, P.O. Box 1040, Dept. SNP, New Market, VA 22844; (540) 740–3132 or (800) 847–4878; www.visitshenandoah.org.

Front Royal Visitors' Center, 104 East Main Street, Front Royal, VA 22630; (540) 635–3185 or (800) 338–2576; www.frontroyalchamber.com.

Charlottesville

A Presidential Neighborhood / 2 Nights

They were the best of friends. They rode to each other's neighboring plantations to play chess, lent one another skilled servants, and bought each other's furniture when one or another of them was hard up for cash. They also succeeded each other as the third, fourth, and fifth presidents of the United States of America.

Thomas Jefferson, James Madison, and James Monroe lived within 30 miles of one another in the rolling foothills of the Blue Ridge Mountains. It was quite a neighborhood. And it is your destination on this perfect weekend escape to Charlottesville and its environs.

☐ Three presidential homes

☐ University of Virginia

☐ Antiques

☐ Music festival

☐ Vineyards

It is said that Charlottesville is "Mr. Jefferson's town." And, indeed, his imprint is everywhere. Just above the city is Monticello, the plantation home that he designed and lived in until his death. And Charlottesville itself is dominated by another of his architectural creations: the University of Virginia, considered by some to be the most beautiful college campus in America.

Yet every aspect of Jefferson's life was influenced and enriched by his beloved neighbors, James Madison and James Monroe. Madison was the brilliant young Virginian who crafted the Constitution, as well as many of the famous Federalist Papers, which became the basis for the form of government America has today. He was a close political collaborator of Jefferson, as well as a warm friend, and served the third president as his secretary of state.

The third member of the trio, James Monroe, studied law with Thomas Jefferson and served both Presidents Washington and Jefferson as minister to France. And it was his famous Monroe Doctrine that drew a

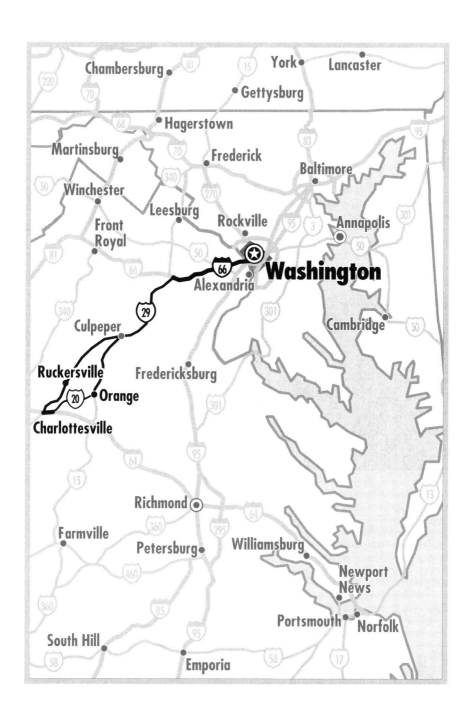

line in the sand with Europe by prohibiting any encroachment in the Western Hemisphere.

The three friends were truly "men of the Enlightenment," and evidence of their voracious appetites for philosophy, foreign language, agricultural pursuits, engineering inventions, and, most of all, public service is everywhere.

The best way to explore their neighborhood is by touring their three great homes. Each tour offers a very different experience of the past. At Jefferson's Monticello you will see the home much as it was when he lived there. The vegetable gardens are planted with the crops he raised, and tour guides quote from his writings. A visit to Madison's ancestral home at Montpelier, by contrast, is like joining an architectural dig, where devoted historians and archaeologists are "looking for Mr. Madison" beneath the changes wrought by two centuries of subsequent owners. James Monroe's more modest Ash Lawn–Highland Plantation is not just a lovely historic home, but also a working farm, as well as a favorite spot for evening concerts, plays, and operas.

Your weekend escape also includes two nights at a beautiful downtown Charlottesville inn, a sampling of the city's first-rate restaurants, a tour and wine tasting at one of Virginia's best vineyards, a stroll through artists' workshops, and shopping for antiques.

Day 1 / *Afternoon*

Charlottesville is 120 miles southwest of Washington. Depending on traffic, the trip can take anywhere from two to three hours. Plan a late afternoon or after-work departure so you can get there by dinnertime. From Washington take Interstate 66 west about 35 miles to Gainesville (exit 43). Then head south on U.S. Highway 29 for 87 miles. About 10 miles before you get to Charlottesville, begin looking for your dinner stop, which is located 1 mile past Charlottesville Airport Road. Turn left on Virginia Highway 1520 and head east about a mile to the restaurant.

DINNER: The Silver Thatch Inn, 3001 Hollymead Drive (434–978–4686 or 800–261–0720; www.silverthatch.com), has three intimate dining rooms in a house that dates from the Revolution. (The original structure, which has been added to, was built by Hessian soldiers fighting in the war.) It is a totally charming place, and the New American cuisine will help you unwind from the drive and begin to enjoy your weekend. The menu features several interesting dishes. A typical appetizer would be Thai green-curried shrimp tossed with diced tomato, green onions, and fresh lime. From there proceed to the daily meat, seafood, and vegetarian specials. Typical specials are Jamaican jerk pulled pork served over jasmine rice with roasted pepper, mango salsa, and fried plantains; grilled salmon fillet with a julienne of vegetables and a roasted tomato aioli; and homemade lemon and thyme fettuccine with asparagus and mushrooms in a lemon, caper, and butter sauce. The Silver Thatch has a full-time pastry chef and is renowned for its desserts, so linger after dinner for coffee and a treat. Expensive.

After dinner, continue south on US 29 to town. Avoid the bypass, and take Business Route 29 (Emmet Street) to Business Route 250 (West Main Street). Turn left, and follow Main Street downtown to South Street, a short one-way street heading east into the historic area. Look for two yellow houses, one with a large wraparound veranda. This is your lodging for the night. Pull into the parking lot, and head for the red door at the back of the larger building.

LODGING: **200 South Street Inn** is indeed located at 200 South Street; (434) 979–0200 or (800) 964–7008; www.southstreetinn.com. The inn consists of two buildings, both of which have been completely restored. It is old-fashioned and very romantic. Many of the nineteen rooms and suites have whirlpools and fireplaces; all have high ceilings and private baths and all are furnished with English and Belgian antiques. Rates: $130–$270 a night; two-night minimum on spring and fall weekends.

Day 2 / Morning

BREAKFAST: 200 South Street Inn serves a very nice complimentary continental breakfast of fruit and rolls. Order an early-morning wake-up call, and ask at the same time for a 7:00 A.M. breakfast; breakfast usually begins at 8:00 A.M., but the inn's friendly staff will be happy to accommodate you.

You need to get an early start on your first full day in Charlottesville because the lines at **Monticello** form early and only get longer. If you get there by 9:00 A.M., however, you can join a tour and enter the home with no more than a fifteen-minute wait.

Monticello is located on Virginia Highway 53, 3 miles southeast of Charlottesville. It is perched high on a mountaintop that offers a dazzling view of the surrounding countryside and the Blue Ridge Mountains. Start your tour at the Monticello Visitors Center, on Virginia Highway 20 South

Monticello, near Charlottesville

at Interstate 64; (434) 984–9822; www.monticello.org. There you can purchase tickets to enter Monticello at $14.00 for adults and $6.00 for children six to eleven. Children under six are admitted free. Monticello is open
daily 9:00 A.M. to 4:30 P.M. from November through February, 8:00 A.M.
to 5:00 P.M. from March through October, closed Christmas. At the visitor center, you can also purchase a combined Monticello/Ash Lawn–
Highland/Michie Tavern admission ticket for $24.

The house tour at Monticello takes about fifty minutes and offers a
superb look at Jefferson and his times. Guides are clearly devoted to the
preservation of his memory and proudly describe his formidable intellect
(he could read in seven languages), his genius as a self-taught architect,
his love of gadgets, his prowess as a horticultural scientist, and his skill as
a violinist.

At the same time, there is no attempt to skim over the fact that
Jefferson was also a typical slave owner, who treated the men and women
he owned no better and no worse than others of the period. A separate
hour-long outdoor plantation-life tour provides abundant information
about the lives of slaves at Monticello, including those, like Sally Hemings,
who were particularly close to the Jefferson family.

If you got an early start at Monticello, you should be able to beat the rush for lunch at historic **Michie Tavern,** just down the hill from Monticello at 683 Thomas Jefferson Parkway; (434) 977–1234; www.michietavern.com. The tavern is a beautiful eighteenth-century inn that offers its own tour. Once serving travelers on a stagecoach route in the 1780s, Michie Tavern is steeped in history. Guests who explore the house from ballroom to wine cellar will see wonderful artifacts, displays, and furnishings from the period. There's a fun general store on the premises full of Virginia specialties for sale. Open daily 9:00 A.M. to 5:00 P.M.; last tour at 4:20 P.M. The tour costs $8.00 for adults and $3.00 for children six to eleven; children under six are admitted free.

LUNCH: The Ordinary at Michie Tavern offers famished guests a very hearty colonial meal, specializing in fried chicken, black-eyed peas, and apple cobbler. Happily, the service is buffet so the wait is short, and the seating for hundreds is divided up into adjoining, wood-beamed dining rooms. The buffet lunch is $13.50, $9.30 for youth twelve to fifteen, $6.75 for children six to eleven. Children under six eat free. But you'll get a $1.00 discount on your Michie Tavern tour admission if you lunch there.

Afternoon

After lunch, a 3-mile drive east on VA 53, then south on Virginia Highway 795 (follow the signs), takes you to **Ash Lawn–Highland,** the home of James Monroe, located at 1000 James Monroe Parkway, Charlottesville; (434) 293–9539; www.monticelloavenue.org/ashlawn. Open daily 9:00 A.M. to 6:00 P.M. March through October, 11:00 A.M. to 5:00 P.M. November through February. Admission is $9.00 for adults, $8.00 for seniors, $5.00 for children six to eleven. Children under six are admitted free.

Ash Lawn–Highland, which is now owned by the College of William and Mary, is not as grand a structure as Monticello. But a tour there is nearly as interesting an experience as Monticello itself, and it is much less crowded.

The grounds, boxwoods, great trees, and gardens are very beautiful. The house is full of Monroe memorabilia, and each has a story to go with it. After the short, well-presented guided tour, take time to roam about the grounds and gardens. You'll see and hear cattle lowing in nearby meadows on the farm and the screech of a peacock in the garden. On summer evenings, Ash Lawn–Highland is a favorite place for music and theater lovers to bring a picnic supper and enjoy opera or a concert under the stars. (See Special Events.)

Back in town, visit the **McGuffey Art Center,** 210 Second Street Northwest; (434) 295–7973; www.mcguffeyartcenter.com. At this schoolhouse-turned-artists'-collective, you'll find forty local artists at work in their studios and galleries. The center has sculpture, fiber, clay, paintings, prints, photographs, and more, and a gift shop where the artists' works are for sale. If kids are restless, they can play in a park adjacent to the art center while their parents peruse the artwork inside. Open Tuesday to Saturday 10:00 A.M. to 6:00 P.M., Sunday 1:00 to 5:00 P.M.

A stroll through the downtown pedestrian mall on Main Street takes you past more than a hundred local shops and two dozen eateries. Be sure to stop for an ice-cream soda at **The Hardware Store Restaurant,** 316 East Main Street; (434) 977–1518 or (800) 426–6001; www.hardwarestore restaurant.com. This is a really fun collection of boutique stores housed within an old converted hardware store, which has a very nice casual restaurant in it.

When you return to your inn, relax in the deep rockers on the veranda or sit in the pleasant library and sip the complimentary wine.

DINNER: Your dinner destination is the **Shebeen Pub and Braai,** 247 Ridge/McIntire (in the Vinegar Hill shopping center, a couple of blocks from the downtown pedestrian mall); (434) 296–3185; www.shebeen pub.com. Shebeen serves South African fare including ground nut stew (think ratatouille) over basmati rice, spicy Peri-Peri chicken, and calamari in a sweet chile marinade. You can also get traditional pub fare like fish and chips or a delicious shepherd's pie made with ground lamb. If you opt for a late dinner, you may catch some live entertainment while you dine. Moderate.

LODGING: 200 South Street Inn.

Day 3 / Morning

BREAKFAST: After you finish your coffee at the inn, drive west on Main Street for a mile or so to the **University of Virginia** campus. The mighty Rotunda, with its brick courtyard and statue of Jefferson, dominates the center of the campus. Walk around it and enter the long greensward between the Rotunda and Cabell Hall. On each side of the park are Jeffersonian buildings, and the whole campus has a feeling of peace and dignity. The university offers free historical tours five times a day, except mid-December to mid-January. Call (434) 924–7969 to arrange one.

LUNCH: Charlottesville is full of great restaurants for Sunday brunch. One favorite is the funky **Southern Culture Cafe and Restaurant,** 633 West Main Street; (434) 979–1990; www.southernculturerestaurant.com. The food is wonderful, the check surprisingly small, and the atmosphere pleasant and casual. Southern Culture offers its specialty scrambled eggs with tiny crab cakes or smoked salmon—both are delicious. The tiled floors, comfy booths, and friendly wait staff make this a great Sunday spot. Moderate.

Afternoon

As you drive out of Charlottesville, take time to stop at **Oakencroft Vineyard,** about 3 miles west of US 29 on Virginia Highway 654 (Barracks Road). You can tour the winemaking rooms and have a chat with the wine masters at the gift shop, who will urge you to try five or six different wines. Oakencroft, while not the largest vineyard in Virginia, is one of the finest; its Country White was selected by the Reagan White House for the president to take to the Gorbachev summit in 1986. Open daily 11:00 A.M. to 5:00 P.M. April through December and weekends January through March. (434) 296–4188; www.oakencroft.com.

Your next destination is **Montpelier,** the estate of James Madison, which is located a scenic 25 miles northeast of Charlottesville on Virginia Highway 20; (540) 672–2728; www.montpelier.org. Open daily 9:30 A.M. to 5:30 P.M. April through October, 9:30 A.M. to 4:30 P.M. November through March. Admission is $11.00 for adults, $10.00 for seniors, and $6.00 for children six to twelve. Children under six are admitted free.

Montpelier is the least dramatic and the least seen of the three presidential estates (tourists are relatively few), but in many ways it is the most interesting of them all. It has been a museum only since 1987, and a dedicated team of archaeologists, curators, preservationists, and grounds staff are, as they put it, attempting to bring back Mr. Madison to the house.

The crux of the problem is that, because of the gambling debts of Madison's stepson, Montpelier was sold shortly after the ex-president's death in 1849. Since then, it has had six private owners, and they all felt obliged to put their own dramatic stamp on the original building. The du Ponts, for example, who owned the home for most of the last century, enlarged it to twice its size and installed elaborate Victorian furnishings and woodwork throughout. Earlier owners rampaged throughout Montpelier, moving walls, building staircases, replacing eighteenth-century mantels, and so on.

Mr. Madison and his wife, Dolley, almost got lost in the process, but today you can see the effort in progress to bring them back. When the restoration is complete in 2008, the mansion will be reduced from its current fifty-five rooms to the twenty-two-room home of the Madison family. After your tour and the mini history lesson, you are free to roam about the beautiful grounds and garden at Montpelier for as long as you like. It is a lovely spot, high on a hill with a stunning view of the rolling countryside around it.

When you leave Montpelier, you might want to make one last stop in the area. Take VA 20 back south 8 miles to Virginia Highway 33, turn right, and follow VA 33 west 7 miles until it intersects with US 29 at **Ruckersville.** There you will find a couple of large antiques complexes, each with dozens of small stalls bursting with old stuff. The shops are a gold mine of modestly priced furniture, jewelry, books, china, silver, pictures, and all sorts of wonderful junk. You can wander to your heart's content—there's no pressure to buy. You can't miss **Greene House Shops** (434–985–6053) and **Country Store** (434–985–3649) on opposite corners of the highway intersection.

Return to Washington on US 29 north and I–66 east. It should take about two hours.

There's More

Virginia Discovery Museum. Small, interactive children's museum with permanent exhibits featuring puppets, arts and crafts, computers, magnets, bees, and, of course, Thomas Jefferson. Located at the east end of the downtown mall; (434) 977–1025; www.vadm.org. Open Tuesday through Saturday 10:00 A.M. to 5:00 P.M., Sunday 1:00 to 5:00 P.M. Admission is $4.00 per person.

Heritage Repertory Theatre. University of Virginia's professional summer theater, which has been performing at Culbreth Theater for more than twenty years; (434) 924–3326; www.virginia.edu/drama.

Barboursville Vineyards and Ruins. Ruined remains of a great home designed by Thomas Jefferson. Now home to a fine vineyard, located at 17655 Winery Road, Route 777, Barboursville; (540) 832–3824; www.barboursvillewine.com. Open for tastings and sales, Monday through

Saturday 10:00 A.M. to 5:00 P.M., Sunday 11:00 A.M. to 5:00 P.M. Tours on Saturday and Sunday noon to 4:00 P.M.

Canoeing and Tubing on the James River. Day or overnight trips on the James River by canoe, raft, or inner tube. Offered by James River Runners, 10082 Hatton Ferry Road, Scottsville; (434) 286–2338; www.james river.com. A four-hour tube ride will cost you $17 a person. Call for other prices.

Special Events

March. James Madison Birthday Celebration. Music and events at Montpelier. (540) 672–2728.

June–August. Ash Lawn–Highland Summer Festival of the Arts. Internationally recognized opera festival, plus musicals, choirs, country music on the lawns of the Monroe estate. (434) 293–9539.

July. Independence Day Ceremony at Monticello. Naturalization of new citizens, patriotic music, and speeches. (434) 984–9822.

Annual African American Cultural Arts Festival. Art exhibits, food, entertainment, games for kids in Charlottesville's Booker T. Washington Park. (434) 979–0582; www.cvilleafrican-amfest.com.

October. Virginia Film Festival, at the University of Virginia. (434) 982–FEST; www.vafilm.com.

Other Recommended Restaurants

Charlottesville

C&O Restaurant, 515 East Water Street; (434) 971–7044; www.cando restaurant.com. The modest exterior belies the offerings. This has been one of Charlottesville's top restaurants for years. The bistro features innovative beef, chicken, and seafood dishes. Moderate to expensive.

Blue Bird Cafe, 625 West Main Street; (434) 295–1166; www.bluebird cville.com. Casual cafe, popular with UVA students and faculty; good pasta, vegetarian selections, and sandwiches; patio dining in season. Moderate.

The Boar's Head Inn's Old Mill Room, U.S. Highway 250 West; (434) 296–2181; www.boarsheadinn.com. Myriad of excellent regional specialties in a restored 1834 gristmill. Expensive.

Tastings, in the downtown parking garage at Fifth and Market Streets; (434) 293–3663. Restaurant and wine bar. The cuisine is traditional European and American, with an emphasis on seafood and local produce. Moderate.

Best places for doughnuts: If you must eat chain-store doughnuts, there are only two brands to consider, and Charlottesville has them both. In fact, it may be the only city in the Mid-Atlantic that does. So conduct your own taste test. There is a Spudnut shop at 309 Avon Street (434–296–0590), and it sells the real thing: doughnuts made with potatoes. The almost-as-good challenger, Krispy Kreme Doughnuts, has a shop at 1805 Emmet Street; (434) 923–4007.

See additional restaurant listings under Other Recommended Lodgings.

Other Recommended Lodgings

Charlottesville

Silver Thatch Inn, 3001 Hollymead Drive; (434) 978–4686 or (800) 261–0720; www.silverthatch.com. Very nice 200-year-old inn with seven period rooms, all with private baths and some with fireplaces. Continental-plus breakfast. Guests can use adjacent swimming pool and tennis courts. Rates: $155–$190.

The Boar's Head Inn & Sports Club, US 250 West; (434) 296–2181 or (800) 476–1988; www.boarsheadinn.com. Large, 170-room country resort hotel complete with tennis courts, pools (indoor and outdoor), saunas, golf, and squash courts. Rates: rooms, $188–$325; suites, $375–$675.

Clifton, the Country Inn, 1296 Clifton Inn Drive (7 miles from downtown); (434) 971–1800 or (888) 971–1800; www.cliftoninn.net. Manor house built by Thomas Jefferson's son-in-law has fourteen guest rooms and suites, all with private baths and fireplaces; swimming pool, heated spa, tennis courts. Breakfast and dinner available. Rates: $225–$495, plus service charge and tax; dinner extra.

The Inn at the Crossroads, US 29 at Virginia Highway 692, about 9 miles south of town; (434) 979–6452 or (866) 809–2136; www.cross roadsinn.com. Five guest rooms and one cottage, all with private baths. Spacious grounds with fantastic views; full country breakfast. Rates: $119–$189.

Scottsville

High Meadows Vineyard Inn, VA 20 about 17 miles south of Charlottes-ville; (434) 286–2218 or (800) 232–1832; www.highmeadows.com. Superb small inn with twelve guest rooms and fifty acres of gardens and lawns. Country breakfast and complimentary local wine in the afternoon. Rates: $199–$375. If you stay at the inn, you should treat yourself to dinner at its first-rate restaurant.

Orange

Willow Grove, 14079 Plantation Way; (540) 672–5982 or (800) 949–1778; www.willowgroveinn.com. Manor house in rural Orange County with five guest rooms, all with private baths; lots of antiques, acres of country-side. Willow Grove is on a modified American plan: Dinner and a large breakfast are included in the $295–$450 room price.

For More Information

Charlottesville/Albemarle County Convention and Visitors Bureau, 600 College Drive, P.O. Box 178, Charlottesville, VA 22902; (434) 977–1783 or (877) 386–1102; www.charlottesvilletourism.org.

Orange County Visitors Bureau, 122 East Main Street, Orange, VA 22960; (540) 672–1653 or (877) 222–8072; www.visitocva.com.

Richmond

Old South, New South / 1 Night

Richmond, Virginia, with its Confederate war heroes posed triumphantly on Monument Avenue, its antebellum mansions, towering magnolias, and languid accents, is as traditionally Southern as a mint julep. At the same time, a visit to Richmond reveals sights you might not have expected from the one-time capital of the Confederacy. The new galleries and restaurants of funky Shockoe Slip and a museum that illuminates the history of Richmond are also part of this beautiful old city. A quick escape to Richmond offers visitors a great opportunity to explore both the old South and the new South in one weekend.

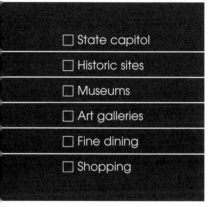

- ☐ State capitol
- ☐ Historic sites
- ☐ Museums
- ☐ Art galleries
- ☐ Fine dining
- ☐ Shopping

Richmond's landmarks tell the story of the city's extraordinary place in American history. There is the neoclassical Virginia State Capitol, designed by Thomas Jefferson, where the legislature met in 1785 and still does today. A mile or so east is Saint John's Church, where Patrick Henry made a speech that became the battle cry of the American Revolution: "Give me liberty or give me death!" The White House of the Confederacy, where its president, Jefferson Davis, lived, is here, as is the home of the nation's first female African-American banker, Maggie Walker.

Richmond is a fairly easy city to navigate, but there is an enormous amount to do and see in just a few short days. Accordingly, try to organize your visit along geographic lines, so you can explore the maximum number of attractions with a minimum of wear and tear.

Day 1 / Morning

Richmond is about a two-hour drive from Washington on Interstate 95 heading south. An 8:00 A.M. start will get you to Richmond by 10:00 A.M., in time for a full day of fun. To reach your first destination, take exit

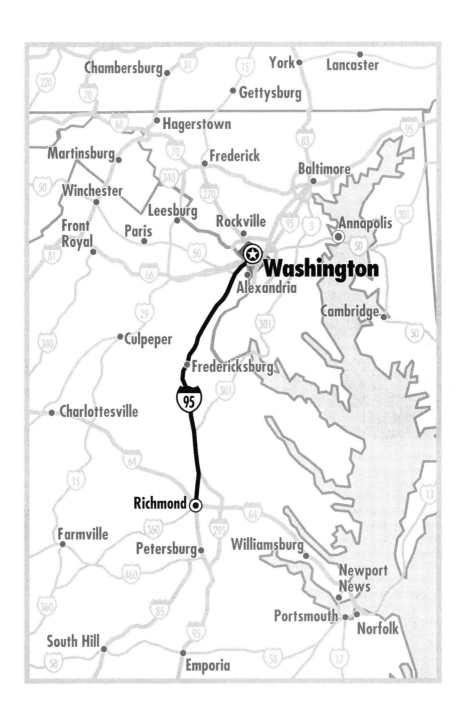

74C off I–95 and drive east (left) on East Broad Street about 1 mile to **St. John's Church,** 2401 East Broad Street; (804) 648–5015. St. John's sits high on a hill in the middle of a churchyard cemetery shaded by huge trees. Some of the gravestones date from the 1700s, and most are so old that they're crumbling.

On March 23, 1775, during a meeting of the Second Virginia Convention, Patrick Henry rose to support the raising of a Virginia militia with the words:

> Is life so dear or peace so sweet as to be purchased
> at the price of chains and slavery? Forbid it, Almighty
> God. I know not what course others may take, but as
> for me, give me liberty or give me death!

You can tour the church (which has been in use for more than 200 years) Monday through Saturday 10:00 A.M. to 3:30 P.M., Sunday 1:00 to 3:30 P.M. At 2:00 P.M. on summer Sundays, Patrick Henry's famous speech is reenacted.

Before lunch, spend an hour or so strolling in nearby Shockoe Bottom and Shockoe Slip, adjoining neighborhoods in Richmond's old warehouse district that artists, restaurateurs, and small-shop owners began flocking to about a decade ago. You'll certainly want to spend some time perusing the upscale shops in Shockoe Slip.

LUNCH: A fun place for lunch is the **Europa Mediterranean Cafe and Tapas Bar** in the heart of Shockoe Slip, which guarantees that no more than forty-five minutes will elapse from the time you take your seat until the time you get your check, or your lunch is free. You can get a cup of white corn bisque, a salad or pasta, and a sandwich for less than $10. The sandwiches are special: The tuna sandwich includes steamed tuna, caramelized onions, roasted fennel seeds, and dill mayonnaise on multi-grain bread; the vegetarian panini consists of portobello mushrooms, red peppers, roasted garlic goat cheese, red onions, and spinach. Located at 1409 East Cary Street; (804) 643–0911; www.europarichmond.com. Moderate to expensive.

Afternoon

After lunch, head for the downtown historic area, where your first destination is the **Valentine Richmond History Center,** 1015 East Clay Street; (804) 649–0711; www.richmondhistorycenter.com. The Valentine special-

Richmond skyline

izes in the economic, social, and cultural history of Richmond, and it prides itself on having one of the largest costume and textile collections in the nation. The tour of the adjoining 1812 **Wickham House** complements the extensive collections through an in-depth look at one family over time. Open Tuesday through Saturday 10:00 A.M. to 5:00 P.M., Sunday noon to 5:00 P.M. Admission to the museum and the Wickham House is $7.00 for adults, $6.00 for seniors, $4.00 for children age seven to twelve, and $1.00 for children three to six. Children two and under are admitted free.

A short 2 blocks away is your next destination, the **Museum of the Confederacy,** 1201 East Clay Street; (804) 649–1861; www.moc.org. Open Monday to Saturday 10:00 A.M. to 5:00 P.M., Sunday noon to 5:00 P.M. Admission is $10.00 for adults, $7.00 for seniors and students. Children under three are admitted free. For an additional $3.00 ($2.00 for students), you get a tour of the **White House of the Confederacy** next door, where Jefferson Davis lived during the Civil War. At the museum, don't expect a Confederate flag-waving tribute to the slave-owning South; instead you'll get an absorbing account of the South's role in the Civil War. Although the facility is small enough to tour in an hour or so, the collection of Civil War letters, weapons, photographs, flags, uniforms, newspapers, paintings, and documents could easily capture the attention of anyone with even a passing interest in the Civil War for much longer.

As you continue your tour of the area on foot, don't miss the **Virginia State Capitol,** located at Capitol Square about 3 blocks south of the museums; (804) 698–1788. It is as grand and gracious as you would expect. In the rotunda is the Washington statue that is said to most resemble America's first president. Outside is another statue of George Washington flanked by other famous Virginians. You can tour the capitol free of charge from 9:00 A.M. to 5:00 P.M. weekdays, 10:00 A.M. to 4:15 P.M. Saturday, and 12:30 to 4:15 P.M. Sunday.

Before you finish your walking tour of the downtown area, make a stop at the **Maggie Walker National Historic Site,** 110½ East Leigh Street; (804) 771–2017; www.nps.gov/malw. Open Monday through Saturday 9:00 A.M. to 5:00 P.M.; donations are requested. Walker, an African American who was paralyzed and used a wheelchair for much of her life, was the first woman in America to found a bank. She and her family lived in the twenty-two-room house on Leigh Street from 1904 to 1934. The National Park Service, which maintains the site, shows an inspirational ten-minute film about Walker's life and conducts guided tours of the house.

Four blocks from the Maggie Walker House is the **Black History Museum and Cultural Center of Virginia,** an expanding facility designed to display the economic, social, and cultural life of Virginia's African Americans from colonial times to the present. It's located on Clay Street at St. James Street, (804) 780–9093, and is open Tuesday through Saturday 10:00 A.M. to 5:00 P.M., Sunday 11:00 A.M. to 5:00 P.M. Admission is $5.00 for adults, $3.00 for seniors, and $2.00 for children under age thirteen.

After your day of sightseeing, check into your "digs" for the night— the **Linden Row Inn,** 100 East Franklin Street; (804) 783–7000 or (800) 348–7424; www.lindenrowinn.com. This lovely seventy-room hotel in a restored block of row houses belongs to the Historic Richmond Foundation, and the flawless attention to period details reflects it. The larger rooms have 12-foot-high ceilings and heavy crown molding. The guest rooms and common parlor are furnished with antiques (except for the renovated, modern bathrooms). The Linden Row Inn's $99–$169-per-night rates would be reasonable even without the complimentary continental breakfast; afternoon wine, cheese, and fruit served in the parlor; and free use of the pool and gym at the nearby YMCA.

DINNER: Stay at the Linden Row Inn for dinner. The small dining room, which seats only thirty-six guests, caters mainly to the inn's guests and offers traditional American and Southern favorites. Expect to see steak, lamb chops, crab, salmon, pasta, and at least one vegetarian offering on the menu of the day. Moderate.

LODGING: Linden Row Inn.

Day 2 / Morning

BREAKFAST: After a light breakfast at Linden Row Inn, head south on East Fifth Street a few blocks toward the James River. Your destination is **Canal Walk,** which parallels the river for more than a mile.

You can easily kill an hour or two strolling along the canal, enjoying the spectacular views of the James River rushing by small tree-covered islands and large boulders. Thirty-three circular bronze plaques set up at irregular intervals are chock-full of information about Richmond and the canal. The National Park Service staffs the **Richmond Civil War Visitor Center** along the canal, and you can pick up general tourist information there as well. Located in the Tredegar Iron Works at Fifth and Tredegar Streets; (804) 771–2145. Open daily 9:00 A.M. to 5:00 P.M.

You can also take a half-hour boat ride down the canal for $5.00 for adults, $4.00 for seniors and students five to twelve; children under five are admitted free. Inquire at **Richmond Canal Cruises,** (804) 788–6466; www.richmondriverfront.com.

After your canal stroll, head for **Maymont,** a beautiful, thirty-three-room mansion set on one hundred acres overlooking the James River. Tours of the mansion are available Tuesday through Sunday noon to 5:00 P.M. by reservation; the suggested donation is $4.00. The grounds—which include a Japanese garden and an Italian garden; a children's farm with sheep to pet; wildlife habitats for birds, beavers, and bison; a turtle pool; and several aquariums—are a free public park operated by the city of Richmond. Tram rides of the grounds are available from noon to 5:00 P.M. Admission is adults, $3.00; children twelve and under, $2.00. Horse-drawn carriage rides are available, only on Sunday afternoon. The grounds are open daily from 10:00 A.M. to 5:00 P.M., often later in the summer. Maymont is located at 2201 Shields Lake Drive (off Hampton Street); (804) 358–7166; www.maymont.org.

BRUNCH: For a late Sunday brunch, there's no better place than the century-old **Jefferson Hotel** at Franklin and Adams Streets; (804) 788–8000 or (800) 424–8014. Its eye-popping, navy blue–walled Palm Court Lobby has a life-size marble statue of Thomas Jefferson and a 35-

foot-high Tiffany stained-glass ceiling. Two flights of steps will take you to the Jefferson Rotunda, where brunch is served. The Jefferson boasts that the rotunda, with its stained-glass ceiling, dozens of wide marble pillars, dark red walls, and heavy oil paintings, was the model for the staircase setting in *Gone with the Wind,* and you can well believe it.

Brunch itself is an awesome buffet with everything from just-made omelettes to fresh seafood. There's a meat-carving station, an enormous dessert table, and acres of fresh fruit and breads. Because the Jefferson brunch is so popular (on Easter they serve upwards of 700), be sure to make a reservation well in advance. Brunch, which is easily a day's worth of food, costs about $38 for adults and $20 for children.

Afternoon

After brunch, head for the **Virginia Museum of Fine Arts.** From your first sight of the 7-foot-long golden rabbit in the entranceway, you'll know this is a special museum. It has the largest art collection in the southeastern United States, including works by Monet, Renoir, Degas, and Picasso. It also has one of the best Art Nouveau and Art Deco collections in the country, a fine array of African art, a priceless Fabergé collection of jeweled eggs and other objects from the Russian court, and a gallery of "British sporting art." Your first visit will only whet your appetite for several return trips.

The Virginia Museum of Fine Arts is located at 200 North Boulevard; (804) 340–1400; www.vmfa.state.va.us. It's open Wednesday through Sunday 11:00 A.M. to 5:00 P.M. The suggested donation is $5.00 for adults, and there is sometimes a supplemental charge for special exhibits. Don't put off stopping at the great museum shop until the end of the day, because it sometimes closes a few minutes before the museum does.

Follow your visit to the museum with a driving tour of Richmond's **Fan District,** a beautiful residential area of Victorian row houses located between Cary Street and Monument Avenue on the west side of town. Its large, eclectic selection of restaurants and boutiques testifies to the diversity of the Fan District neighborhood, which is home to old money, new money, students, and much of Richmond's art community.

Or go a few blocks farther west on Cary Street to **Carytown,** where some of the best of Richmond's shops can be found in 10-plus blocks on Cary Street between Boulevard and Thompson Streets. You can find everything from antique jewelry to Latin imports to artist-designed lawn furniture to Junior League used clothing. Gifts, beads, books, flowers, galleries, espresso, antiques—if you like to wander, gawk, and shop, Carytown is for you.

You can't leave Richmond without a short drive along **Monument Avenue,** the tree-lined and monument-studded boulevard that serves as the northern boundary of the Fan District. You'll enjoy seeing the enormous old Southern mansions (with double- and triple-decker porches) on both sides of the street. Until recently, the only statues on Monument Avenue honored Confederate war heroes. Now, the tennis great (and Richmond native) Arthur Ashe has joined their ranks.

At the end of your day, allow two hours for your return trip to Washington via I–95.

There's More

John Marshall House. Restored home of America's most famous chief justice of the Supreme Court and the father of the concept of judicial review. Located at 818 East Marshall Street; (804) 648–7998; www.apva.org/marshall. Open Tuesday through Saturday 10:00 A.M. to 4:30 P.M., Sunday noon to 5:00 P.M. Admission is $10.00 for adults, $7.00 for seniors and children. Children three and under admitted free. Ticket includes admission to Valentine Richmond Historical Center, 1812 Wickham House, and Monumental Church, all within the state capitol neighborhood.

Children's Museum of Richmond. A nice stop for the three-to-twelve crowd. The arts studio and hands-on science exhibits are favorites, as is the simulated cave. Located at 2626 West Broad Street; (804) 474–2667; www.c-mor.org. Open Tuesday through Saturday 9:30 A.M. to 5:00 P.M., Sunday noon to 5:00 P.M. Admission is $7.00 for everyone over one year old.

Richmond National Battlefield Park. Richmond was the capital of the Confederacy, its supply center, and the site of seven major battles. Information about all the Civil War sites in the area is available at the Tradegar Iron Works Visitor Center, Fifth and Tradegar Streets, which is operated by the National Park Service. Open daily 9:00 A.M. to 5:00 P.M. No admission charged; (804) 771–2145; www.nps.gov/rich.

Edgar Allan Poe Museum. Worth a visit just to see the Raven Room, with its several dozen illustrations of Poe's most famous poem. Located at 1914 East Main Street; (804) 648–5523 or (888) 213–2763; www.poe museum.org. Open Tuesday through Saturday 10:00 A.M. to 5:00 P.M., Sunday 11:00 A.M. to 5:00 P.M. Admission is $6.00 for adults, $5.00 for seniors and students. Children under six are admitted free.

Special Events

March–April. Easter at Maymont. Easter egg hunt, egg rolling and tossing, music, pony rides, puppet shows, craft activities. (804) 358–7166.

April. Historic Garden Week. Part of a statewide series of April garden
tours, but Richmond's gardens are special. (804) 644–7776.

June–August. Summer Music Concert Series at the Virginia Museum of
Fine Art. (804) 340–1400.

December. Christmas Open House. Tour of historic homes in the Fan
District. (804) 254–2550.

Other Recommended Restaurants

Sam Miller's Warehouse Restaurant, 1210 East Cary Street; (804) 644–
5465; www.sammillers.com. Top choice for beef and seafood. Moderate to
expensive.

The Dining Room at the Berkeley Hotel, 1200 East Cary Street; (804)
780–1300 or (888) 780–4422; www.berkeleyhotel.com. Quiet, gracious,
hotel restaurant with regional American, continental, and—sometimes—
Asian or African offerings. Hard to beat for either lunch or dinner.
Expensive.

La Grotta, 1218 East Cary Street; (804) 644–2466; www.lagrottaristorante
.com. Comfortable, upscale Italian restaurant in the Shockoe Slip district.
Seafood, veal, quail, pasta, and heavenly salads. Expensive.

The Hard Shell Restaurant, 1411 East Cary Street; (804) 643–2333; www
.thehardshell.com. Casual seafood and sandwich favorite in Shockoe Slip;
raw bar, patio dining, and jazz brunch on Sunday. Moderate.

Strawberry Street Cafe, 421 North Strawberry Street; (804) 353–6860;
www.strawberrystreetcafe.com. Popular eatery in the Fan District. Long
on atmosphere, with antique mirrors, stained glass, candles and flowers on
the tables, and a salad bar of fresh fruit and vegetables sitting in an antique
bathtub. Pasta, potpie, and pub fare. Great for lunch, dinner, or weekend
brunch. Moderate.

The Tobacco Company Restaurant, Twelfth and Cary Streets; (804)
782–9555; www.thetobaccocompany.com. Former tobacco warehouse in
Shockoe Slip district, renovated and decorated in eclectic style. Popular

with locals and tourists. Contemporary Southern menu. Dancing in the downstairs club. Moderate to expensive.

Lemaire Restaurant, Franklin and Adams Streets; (804) 788–8000; www .jeffersonhotel.com/dining_lemaire. The Jefferson Hotel's premier restaurant, serving Southern and Pacific Rim cuisine at its best; also great for afternoon tea. Expensive.

The John Marshall Martini Kitchen and Bubble Bar, 101 North Fifth Street; (804) 783–1929; www.thejohnmarshall.com. Fifty different martinis and champagne cocktails on the menu; steak, seafood, regional fare; "Havana" cigars for sale at the bar. Moderate.

Third Street Diner, Third and Main Streets; (804) 788–4750. Open twenty-four hours a day, seven days a week. Breakfast anytime, dinner anytime. Long waits during the lunch hour. Ideal stop for doughnuts and coffee. Inexpensive.

Other Recommended Lodgings

The Jefferson Hotel, Franklin and Adams Streets; (804) 788–8000 or (800) 424–8014; www.jeffersonhotel.com. Grand old luxury hotel with refurbished guest rooms, twenty-four-hour room service and concierge, restaurants on the premises, and complimentary use of a health spa across the street. Rates: $195–$250 for rooms, $335–$1,600 for suites.

The Massad House Hotel, 11 North Fourth Street; (804) 648–2893; www .massadhousehotel.com. Downtown European-style hotel with sixty-four redecorated rooms, all with private baths. Rates: $75 for a room, $85 for a two-room suite.

Berkeley Hotel, 1200 East Cary Street; (804) 780–1300 or (888) 780–4422; www.berkeleyhotel.com. Luxury hotel in historic Shockoe Slip area of town. Fifty-five well-appointed rooms; restaurant on premises. Rates: $190–$205; Governor's Suite, $675.

Commonwealth Park Suites Hotel, Ninth and Bank Streets; (804) 343–7300 or (888) 343–7301; www.commonwealthparksuites.com. Elegant forty-nine-suite European-style hotel conveniently located on Capitol Square. Rates: $79–$169 per suite.

The Hotel John Marshall, 101 North Fifth Street; (804) 783–1929. Recently renovated and reopened Richmond landmark, built in 1929 and host to three presidents and many entertainers (including Elvis, who usually rented a whole floor). Pleasant, convenient, historical, sometimes funky. Rates: $119–$159.

For More Information

Metro Richmond Convention and Visitors Bureau, 405 North Third Street, Richmond, VA 23219; (800) 370–9004; www.richmondva.org.

VIRGINIA ESCAPE FOUR

Williamsburg

History's Only Half of It / 2 Nights

Williamsburg, Virginia, is a favorite destination of Americans as well as many international visitors. You can see why with just one visit. The flawlessly reconstructed colonial town (once the capital of Virginia) is a delight, with its beautiful gardens, nearly 300-year-old architecture and furnishings, and reenactments of daily life in colonial times by staff in period costume.

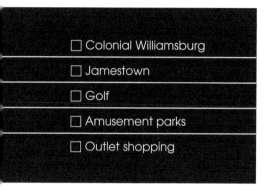

- ☐ Colonial Williamsburg
- ☐ Jamestown
- ☐ Golf
- ☐ Amusement parks
- ☐ Outlet shopping

Less than a three-hour drive south of Washington, Williamsburg has so much to do and see that you'll want to make your escape an annual one. The fact is, Williamsburg offers new pleasures every time you visit. You could easily spend a week in the colonial area alone. Then there is the natural beauty of the land to explore, along the James and York Rivers. And, if you like to shop, you've come to the right place. With hundreds of thousands of tourists visiting Williamsburg every year, shopping malls have sprung up around the outskirts of the city like mushrooms after rain.

One of the first things you'll notice when you arrive in Williamsburg is how popular it is with people of all ages. There are elderly folks in wheelchairs, young families with babies in backpacks, and energetic walkers with their handsome hounds on leashes by their sides. There's plenty for school-age kids to learn and explore, and when they tire of the history lessons, the very modern Busch Gardens amusement park is nearby.

Williamsburg has some of Virginia's best restaurants and lodgings, if you're celebrating a special occasion. And for families on a budget, the area is saturated with inexpensive places to stay and eat.

Day 1 / Morning

If you leave before 8:30 A.M., you can make it to Williamsburg in time for lunch at a fun and historic tavern, and still beat the crowds (which are

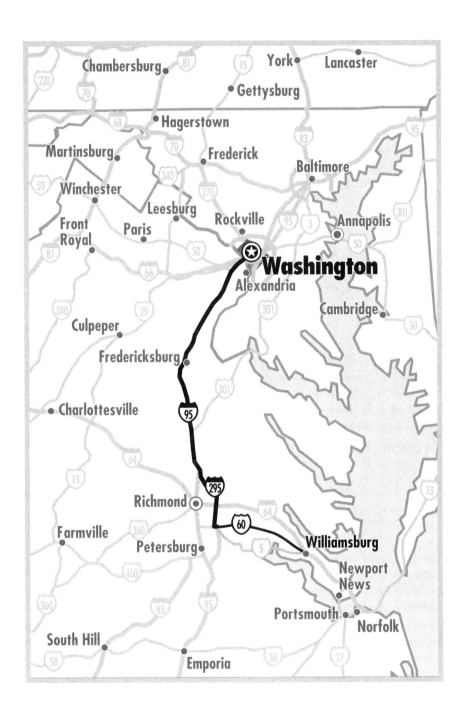

huge during summer weekends). Drive to Williamsburg via Interstate 95 south, Interstate 295 (the Richmond Beltway), and U.S. Highway 60 east. US 60 avoids the worst of the Williamsburg and beach traffic on Interstate 64, and you'll enjoy the Virginia woods and farms on each side of the road.

When you arrive in Williamsburg, follow the signs to the **Colonial Williamsburg Visitor Information Center.** There are plenty of parking places there but very few in the colonial area itself, so leave your car at the visitor center and do your touring of the historic area on foot or on the buses that swing by in a loop around the area every twenty minutes or so.

At the visitor center you can buy tickets for those attractions that require them and see a thirty-five-minute film on Colonial Williamsburg. Be sure to pick up the publication *Visitor's Companion,* which has lots of information about special events.

A word about price: Williamsburg is priceless, but it's not cheap. General admission for one day is $34 for adults and $15 for children ages six to seventeen; children under six are admitted free. However, adults can purchase a Freedom Pass—covering general admission for a full year—for $59; child's Freedom Pass, $29. The Independence Pass, which is good for admission to Williamsburg's museums and special events as well, costs $75 a year for adults and $38 for children. Most of the attractions in Colonial Williamsburg are open daily from 9:30 A.M. to 5:00 P.M., although several attractions stay open later in summer months. Call (757) 229–1000 or (800) HISTORY, or visit www.history.org, if you have questions about what's open when.

LUNCH: Chowning's Tavern is part of the historic area, and it has been rebuilt to look like Josiah Chowning's 1766 tavern. In the evenings, the wait staff dresses in period clothes and entertains with songs, ballads, and games. The lunch menu features traditional barbecue—pulled pork, beef brisket, and chicken—from 11:30 A.M. to 5:00 P.M. Located on Duke of Gloucester Street at Queen Street; (757) 229–2141 or (800) 447–8679. Moderate.

Afternoon

After lunch, stroll through the colonial area. There, you'll notice dozens of restored homes and shops on each side of Duke of Gloucester Street. You'll see an apothecary, a blacksmith, a silversmith, a shoemaker, a milliner, and many more shops. At each one, guides in period dress either explain their craft or actually engage in it. Be sure to stop at one of the most interest-

ing of Williamsburg's historic sites, **Bruton Parish Church,** which has
been in continuous use since 1715 and has seen a lot of history. Stroll
through the old churchyard, where ancient stones mark the graves of
Williamsburg's most prominent citizens.

The two major public buildings in Colonial Williamsburg are the
Capitol and the Governor's Palace. Both are interesting from architectural
and historical perspectives, and both have hour-long guided tours.

The **Capitol,** finished in 1705, was the political center of Virginia
for eighty years. There, in the House of Burgesses and in the Council,
Patrick Henry, Thomas Jefferson, and others honed their oratorical and
legislative skills.

The **Governor's Palace,** built in 1722, was an extraordinary achievement for colonial days, when life was hard and houses were modest. The
palace served as the home for seven royal governors and for the first two
governors of the Commonwealth of Virginia: Patrick Henry and Thomas
Jefferson. Make sure you walk through the formal garden (with a boxwood
maze), which may be seen without a ticket.

As you wander through the colonial town, take time to visit the side
streets and byways. There are lovely gardens in back of the restored colonial
homes, sheep and horses grazing in fenced pastures, and lots going on outdoors. Outside the magazine and guardhouse, for example, cannons are
occasionally fired. Horse-drawn carriages jingle up and down the roads, and
colonial brick makers and ironmongers can be seen at work. Keep your
eyes open for outdoor stalls, where wonderful gingerbread cookies are sold.
They are perfect with a cup of hot cider on a chilly autumn afternoon.

DINNER: Plan to have dinner at **The Trellis,** a popular and highly
acclaimed restaurant in the Merchants Square area featuring contemporary
cuisine with a seasonally changing menu, excellent wines, and nationally
famous chocolate desserts. Located near the colonial area at 403 Duke of
Gloucester Street; (757) 229–8610. Expensive.

After dinner, you might like to sample some of Williamsburg's many
evening activities. There is an excellent chamber music series at the public library, and historical musical events, plays, and dances are regularly
scheduled at 7:00 and 8:30 P.M. at the Governor's Palace. There are also
candlelight choral services at Bruton Parish Church.

LODGING: When you've explored Colonial Williamsburg thoroughly,
head for **Williamsburg Sampler Bed and Breakfast,** at 922 Jamestown
Road, approximately a mile southwest of the colonial area. This stately

Governor's Palace

brick home has four rooms filled with antiques, quilts, and cabinetwork made by the proprietress. Despite the fact that the Williamsburg Sampler has received national acclaim, it is definitely affordable. (Rooms are $150 to $180, including breakfast.) But make reservations well before your trip; the Sampler is justifiably popular. (757) 253–0398 or (800) 722–1169; www.williamsburgsampler.com.

Day 2 / Morning

BREAKFAST: Enjoy a "skip-lunch" breakfast of fruit, waffles, and sausage prepared by the friendly innkeepers at the Williamsburg Sampler.

After breakfast, return to Colonial Williamsburg to catch some of the exhibits and historic homes and shops that you missed on your first day in town.

Or consider as an alternative a visit to the **DeWitt Wallace Museum of Decorative Arts,** a gallery that displays more than 10,000 items of English and American decorative arts and special exhibits from the fascinating **Abby Aldrich Rockefeller Folk Art Museum.** The Wallace Museum is located at the corner of Francis and South Henry Streets; (757) 220–7724. Open daily 11:00 A.M. to 5:00 P.M.

You might also like to poke around the pleasant shops at **Merchants Square,** a collection of about forty locally owned and run stores selling everything from clothes and furniture and jewelry to local hams and peanuts and gourmet chocolate. Many of the shops specialize in Williamsburg reproductions, like pewter mugs and historical needlework.

LUNCH: As lunchtime nears, make your way to **The Cheese Shop,** at 410 Duke of Gloucester Street in Merchants Square; (757) 220–0298. There you can gather provisions for a picnic lunch, including great cheese, fancy salads, biscuits with thinly sliced country ham, a bottle of wine, and a selection of pastries for dessert. Inexpensive.

Then pick up your car and head for Jamestown, a fifteen-minute drive on the **Colonial Parkway.** The speed limit on the lightly traveled parkway, which stretches 23 miles from Jamestown through Williamsburg to Yorktown, is 35 to 45 miles an hour, and it's a bikers' and joggers' paradise. So take your time, drive carefully, and enjoy the splendid view of the James River. If you picked up sandwiches in town, you can picnic at one of the pull-offs along the river or at the picnic tables near the visitor center at Jamestown Colonial Historical Park.

Afternoon

Jamestown was the original landing place for Virginia's first permanent English colonists. Though the settlement did not flourish—it succumbed to Indian attacks, disease, and bad luck, and the survivors later moved to Williamsburg—Jamestown today has many fascinating remnants from those earliest times in colonial America.

Jamestown Settlement features indoor galleries and outdoor exhibits telling the story of Jamestown. There are full-size replicas of the three ships that carried the colonists—*Susan Constant, Godspeed,* and *Discovery*—which you can board and tour. Costumed interpreters will tell you all about Pocahontas, John Smith, the Powhatan Indians, and James Fort. Open daily 9:00 A.M. to 5:00 P.M. except Christmas and New Year's Day. Admission is $11.75 for adults and $5.75 for children six to twelve; children under six are admitted free. (757) 253–4838 or (888) 593–4682; www.historyisfun.org.

Jamestown Colonial National Historical Park, administered by the National Park Service, has a visitor center where you can view many exhibits on Jamestown's early life. You can, for example, see the stone foundations from the seventeenth-century buildings and the original church tower that dates from the 1640s. One particularly nice attraction is the reconstructed 1608 glassmakers' shed, where you can watch glassblowers at work making cups, pitchers, candlesticks, and vases. All the products on the premises are for sale at very reasonable prices.

One of the best ways to see Jamestown is by bicycle. (See There's More for where to rent bicycles.) What little traffic there is all goes one way in the 5-mile loop around the island. And you can see the natural beauty of marshy wetlands or the James River from almost every vantage point. Biking or walking is a great way to see the various historic sites easily as well as see and hear the birds and other wildlife. And however you get around Jamestown Island, you won't be battling the enormous crowds that surround the Williamsburg attractions. Open daily 8:30 A.M. to 4:30 P.M. Admission is $8.00 for adults, but visitors under seventeen are admitted free. Senior citizens with a National Parks Golden Age Pass get in free. (757) 229–1733; www.nps.gov/colo.

DINNER: After you've explored Jamestown and freshened up at your bed-and-breakfast, drive a couple of miles east to the Kingsmill area of town for dinner at one of Williamsburg's nicest restaurants, **Le Yaca.** This innovative French restaurant is warm and inviting, with fresh flowers everywhere and a fireplace in the middle of the restaurant complete with a lamb roasting on a spit. Le Yaca specializes in lamb and seafood—try the wonderful bouillabaisse—but its appetizers and salads alone are worth the trip. Desserts, too, are spectacular. If you're really hungry, opt for the "seven-course degustation" menu. Located at Village Shops at Kingsmill, US 60 just east of Colonial Williamsburg; (757) 220–3616. Expensive.

LODGING: The Williamsburg Sampler.

Day 3 / Morning

BREAKFAST: After breakfast at the Williamsburg Sampler, take your pick of the hundreds of things still available to do in the Williamsburg area. You might tour beautiful **William and Mary College,** located right next to the historic colonial area. It is the second-oldest institution of higher education in the United States. Of particular interest are the Wren Building, built in 1695, and the Joseph and Margaret Muscarelle Museum of Art, which contains several works by old masters; neither charges admission.

If you are interested in golf, Williamsburg has several great courses. **Kingsmill Resort's River Course** is one of the stops on the PGA tour, and its Arnold Palmer–designed **Plantation Course** is as beautiful as it is challenging. Kingsmill's **Woods Course** is also spectacular; (757) 253–3906. Colonial Williamsburg runs the **Golden Horseshoe Gold Course,** designed by Robert Trent Jones, and the **Golden Horseshoe Green Course,** designed by his son Reese Jones; (757) 220–7696. **Ford's Colony Country Club** has two scenic Dan Maples–designed courses; (757) 258–4130. Also popular are the **Colonial Golf Course,** designed by Lester George and Robert Wrenn (757–566–1600), and the **Williamsburg National,** a Nicklaus Design Associates course (757–258–9642). Expect to pay $50 to $175 for eighteen holes of golf and cart rental in the Williamsburg area.

For families with children there's **Busch Gardens,** a fabulous amusement park built around old-world European theme villages. It features more than thirty rides (including the Griffon, which features a 200-foot, ninety-degree straight freefall; the popular Alpengeist and Apollo's Chariot roller coasters; and Escape from Pompeii, a thrill-packed boat ride during which you dodge volcanic "lava"), several Broadway and country music theaters, and kid-oriented food. It's located just off US 60 east of town; (800) 343–7946; www.buschgardens.com. The park is open weekends from late March through mid-May, daily in summer, and Friday through Monday during September and October. The park opens at 10:00 A.M. and closes between 6:00 P.M. and midnight, depending on the season. Admission is $52 for everyone over age six, $45 for children three to six; children under three get in free.

The Busch Gardens folks also operate **Water Country USA,** one of the largest water theme parks in the Mid-Atlantic. The whole family can brave the nearly 50-foot-high Big Daddy Falls and race through white-water falls, pools, geysers, and showers in a 7-foot-wide tube. Teens and preteens love Rampage, and the Aquazoid—a raft ride during which you careen through a pitch-dark tunnel. Little ones can play in Kid's Kingdom or Cow–A–Bunga. Everyone enjoys Hubba Hubba Highway, three and a half acres of floating fun, the park's largest attraction. Located east of town just north of I–64's exit 242; (800) 343–7946; www.watercountryusa.com/water_country/va. Open daily at 10:00 A.M. mid-May through Labor Day and some weekends in May and September. The park closes between 6:00 and 8:00 P.M. depending on the season. Admission is $31 to $38, depending on age and time of day. At Busch Gardens and Water Country USA, multiple-day tickets and combination tickets are available.

LUNCH: A good choice for a late lunch of soup, salad, and sandwiches is **Seasons Cafe,** 110 South Henry Street; (757) 259–0018; www.seasons ofwilliamsburg.com. Wooden booths, decorative trompe l'oeil walls, a family-friendly menu with delicious burgers and onion rings, and good service make Seasons a favorite. It serves a terrific Sunday brunch buffet, too. Moderate.

Afternoon

Save your final Williamsburg afternoon for shopping. Perhaps the most popular shopping spot is **The Pottery,** a vast network of discount and outlet stores housed in thirty sprawling warehouses on 200 acres. The budget prices and wide selection bring busloads of shoppers looking for everything from inexpensive Christmas decorations to cookware to clothing. The best deal at The Pottery, though, is the pottery itself. Just outside the main building is an acre of terra-cotta pots and saucers in all sizes at bargain-basement prices. The Pottery is located on US 60 west in Lightfoot, Virginia, about 5 miles from downtown Williamsburg; (757) 564–3326. Open daily except Christmas. Hours vary by season.

Other popular shopping choices include Village Shops at Kingsmill, US 60 east, which has pleasant art studios, boutiques, and cafes; Patriot Plaza, 3044 Richmond Road, home to Dansk, Villeroy and Boch, and other upscale outlets; Prime Outlets at Williamsburg, 5715 Richmond Road, which has more than eighty name-brand clothes, shoes, and accessory outlet stores; and the Williamsburg Outlet Mall, 6401 Richmond Road, Lightfoot, where you can find clothes, toys, home furnishings, and gift stores. Most malls and shops listed are open seven days a week, and most stay open late in summer.

Your return trip home via US 60, I–295, and I–95 will take between two and three hours.

There's More

Yorktown Victory Center and Battlefield. Start at the Victory Center, a museum that tells the story of America's struggle for independence through exhibits, sight and sound presentations, a documentary film, and living history. Then head for the battlefield, starting at the National Park

Service Visitor Center, where the land and naval battles are presented through a series of multimedia exhibits. You can take a self-guided tour of the battlefield or an excellent ranger-guided tour, during which you'll climb the redoubts and see the cannons that helped Washington and Lafayette defeat Cornwallis and his British troops. Located on the York River, 12 miles east of Williamsburg on Virginia Highway 238 (but the Colonial Parkway is the scenic way to drive there). The Victory Center is open daily from 9:00 A.M. to 5:00 P.M.; (757) 887–1775 or (888) 593–4682. Admission is $8.25 for adults, $4.00 for children six through twelve; children under six are admitted free. Yorktown National Battlefield is also open daily from 9:00 A.M. to 5:00 P.M., and often later in summer months. Admission is $5.00 for everyone seventeen and older; others are admitted free. (757) 898–2410; www.nps.gov/yonb.

Berkeley Plantation. Berkeley Plantation, a 1726 mansion overlooking the James River, was home to Benjamin Harrison, a signer of the Declaration of Independence and three-term governor of Virginia; his son William Henry Harrison, the ninth president of the United States; and his great-grandson Benjamin Harrison, who served as the twenty-third president. Berkeley has several other claims to fame. The first Thanksgiving was celebrated there (two years before the Pilgrims arrived in Massachusetts), "Taps" was composed there during the Civil War, and bourbon was "invented" and first distilled at Berkeley in 1621. Berkeley is located on Virginia Highway 5 near Charles City; (804) 829–6018 or (888) 466–6018. Open daily (except Christmas) 9:00 A.M. to 5:00 P.M. Admission is $11.00 for adults, $7.50 for teenagers, and $6.00 for children six to twelve; children under six are admitted free.

Other James River Plantations. In addition to Berkeley, there are several other plantations along VA 5 worth a visit. Sherwood Forest Plantation, once the home of President John Tyler, has the nation's longest frame house; (804) 829–5377. Westover is considered by many to be the nation's premier example of Georgian architecture. The grounds are open to the public year-round, but the house is open only for five days, in April during Virginia's Historic Garden Week; (804) 644–7776. Shirley Plantation, a beautiful eighteenth-century Queen Anne building with a unique flying staircase, has been in the same family for nine generations and is the oldest plantation in Virginia; (804) 829–5121. Admission is charged at each plantation. For more information visit www.jamesriverplantations.org.

Used Books. For a real treat, seek out Bookpress, an off-the-beaten-track shop selling out-of-print and rare books and beautiful antique prints, maps, and drawings. Located at 1304 Jamestown Road; (757) 229–1260. Open only by appointment.

Bicycle Rental. Bikes Unlimited, 759 Scotland Street (757–229–4620), and Bikesmith of Williamsburg, 515 York Street (757–229–9858), both rent bikes for $10 to $16 a day.

Special Events

April. Historic Garden Week. Statewide garden show. In Williamsburg there are special tours of the gardens in the historic area. (804) 664–7776.

May. Jamestown Landing Day. Celebrates the founding of America's first permanent English colony. (757) 898–2410.

July. Independence Day. Patriotic speeches and fife-and-drum music followed by fireworks. (800) 447–8679.

October. Occasion for the Arts, Merchants Square. Invitational arts and crafts show, Virginia's oldest. (757) 258–5587.

December. Grand Illumination in Williamsburg. Kicks off a series of eighteenth-century-style holiday celebrations in the colonial area. (800) 447–8679.

Other Recommended Restaurants

The Williamsburg Lodge Bay Room, South England Street; (757) 229–2141. Convenient spot for moderately priced regional fare and a crowd-pleasing Sunday brunch from 9:00 A.M. to 2:00 P.M.

Giuseppe's Italian Cafe, 5601 Richmond Road; (757) 565–1977. Bright, cheery, and casual. Pasta, smoked chicken antipasto, individual pizzas, fantastic lentil soup. Inexpensive to moderate.

Old Chickahominy House, 1211 Jamestown Road; (757) 229–4689. Plantation-style breakfasts and lunches featuring country ham and bacon. Antiques and reproductions for sale on premises. Moderate.

Cities Grille, 4511-C John Tyler Highway; (757) 564–3955. New American and traditional entrees, extensive wine list, and friendly bistro ambience make this a favorite of locals. Moderate to expensive.

Berrett's Seafood Restaurant and Raw Bar, 199 South Boundary Street; (757) 253–1847. Merchants Square restaurant with full meals inside; seafood, salads, and sandwiches at the patio raw bar. Moderate.

The Whaling Company, 494 McLaws Circle (just off US 60 east near Busch Gardens); (757) 229–0275. Traditional and contemporary seafood dishes in a pub setting. Moderate.

Padow's Hams and Deli, 1258 Richmond Road; (757) 220–4267. Huge deli-style sandwiches, potato salad, coleslaw, ice-cream sodas. Eat in or takeout. Inexpensive.

Chez Trinh, 157 Monticello Avenue (in the Williamsburg Shopping Center); (757) 253–1888. Rice paper rolls, pho, pork with black bean sauce, Hanoi curry chicken, and more Vietnamese delights. Inexpensive.

Indian Fields Tavern, 9220 John Tyler Drive, Charles City (on VA 5 west of Williamsburg); (804) 829–5004. Worth the thirty-minute drive for the tavern's combination Smithfield ham and crab-cake special and the Sally Lund bread that could double as dessert. Moderate.

Best place for doughnuts: Williamsburg has two dozen pancake houses but no true doughnut bakery. Either do what most people do and settle for a "short stack," or head for Ukrop's Supermarket, where the doughnuts are quite good. Located in the Monticello Marketplace, west of town on Monticello Avenue extension; (757) 564–0455.

Other Recommended Lodgings

Magnolia Manor, 700 Richmond Road; (757) 220–9600 or (800) 462–6667; www.magnoliamanorwmbg.com. Elegant four-bedroom bed-and-breakfast close to town. In the morning, after you nosh on homemade cinnamon buns, you'll be served a huge breakfast on china, crystal, and sterling silver that might include shirred eggs with apple-cured bacon and hash browns, or cranberry and pecan pancakes and fresh sausage. Rates: $195–$215.

Williamsburg Manor Bed and Breakfast, 600 Richmond Road; (757) 220–8011 or (800) 422–8011; www.williamsburg-manor.com. Beautiful Georgian manor near historic area with antiques, Oriental rugs, guest parlor, garden, six guest rooms with private baths. Large country breakfast served. Rates: $119–$169.

Applewood Bed and Breakfast, 605 Richmond Road; (757) 229–0205 or (800) 899–2753; www.williamsburgbandb.com. Four-room Georgian bed-and-breakfast with canopy beds and private baths. Rates: $145–$165.

Colonial Capital Bed and Breakfast, 501 Richmond Road; (757) 229–0233 or (800) 776–0570; www.ccbb.com. Colonial bed-and-breakfast with five guest rooms with private baths. Patio, deck, screened porch, wood-burning stove in guest parlor; full breakfast and afternoon tea. Rates: $145–$175.

Fox and Grape Bed and Breakfast, 701 Monumental Avenue; (757) 229–6914 or (800) 292–3699; www.foxandgrapebb.com. Two-story colonial with pleasant wraparound porch and four rooms with private baths close to the colonial area. Generous breakfasts in the decoy-decorated dining room. Rates: $125–$160.

Williamsburg Inn and Colonial Houses, Francis Street, in colonial area; (757) 229–1000 or (800) 447–8679; www.history.org. There are more than 230 rooms at the inn or in small houses run by the Colonial Williamsburg Foundation. All are well appointed and a nice alternative to standard motel fare. Rooms in the inn are $650 to $820; Colonial Williamsburg also operates the Williamsburg Lodge ($175–$280), the Governor's Inn ($99), and Williamsburg Woodlands ($125–$175); rooms in the colonial houses range from $475 to $540.

Williamsburg has dozens of independent and chain hotels and motels. Nearly all of them, including the Williamsburg Lodge, Inn, and houses run by the Williamsburg Colonial Foundation, belong to the Williamsburg Hotel and Motel Association. You can call the association at (800) 999–4485 (www.williamsburghotel.com), and the staff there will make a reservation for you in your preferred style of accommodation and price range. Summer rates are sometimes expensive, but off-season rates are very reasonable in Williamsburg, with weekend rates often as low as $30 to $50 a night in chain motels.

For More Information

Colonial Williamsburg Foundation, P.O. Box 1776, Williamsburg, VA 23187; (757) 229–1000 or (800) 447–8679; www.history.org.

Williamsburg Area Convention and Visitors Bureau, 421 North Boundary Street, P.O. Box 3585, Williamsburg, VA 23187; (757) 229–6511 or (800) 368–6511; www.visitwilliamsburg.com.

Chincoteague

Family Resort Island / 2 Nights

Residents and visitors who love Chincoteague, the small fishing village on a 7-mile-long, 1.5-mile-wide island off Virginia's Eastern Shore, aren't necessarily happy when people publicize this special little place. Locals and longtime vacationers alike are fiercely protective of the unspoiled, family-friendly town and the quiet and undeveloped shore and wildlife all around it. A Chincoteague fan, when asked what is the best place to eat on the island, gets a dreamy look in the eye and blurts out, "the Island Creamery"—a favorite local ice-cream shop. To say that Chincoteague is a step back in time is a cliché, but it's accurate. With its quiet streets, locally owned stores, restaurants that have been around for decades, and small-town community spirit, it is the kind of place where everyone should have grown up. Those lucky enough to visit Chincoteague before it goes the way of the rest of the Eastern seaboard will understand the traditionalists' concern.

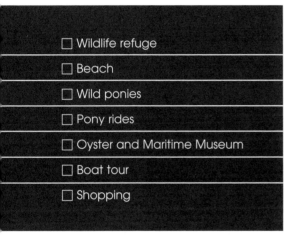

- ☐ Wildlife refuge
- ☐ Beach
- ☐ Wild ponies
- ☐ Pony rides
- ☐ Oyster and Maritime Museum
- ☐ Boat tour
- ☐ Shopping

Day 1 / Morning

The 170-mile drive to Chincoteague from Washington takes a good three hours. On summer weekends, it can take much longer because of traffic. Take U.S. Highway 50 east across the Bay Bridge and down the length of the Eastern Shore to Salisbury. There, pick up U.S. Highway 13 south. In about 40 miles, you'll come to the Virginia state line. Stay on US 13 for 4 more miles, then turn left and head east on Virginia Highway 175. It's about 8 more miles to **Chincoteague.**

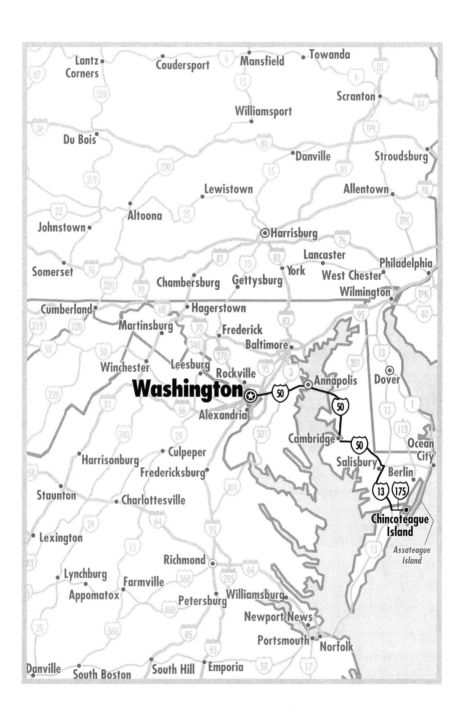

When you cross the bridge over Chincoteague Bay into town (town is really the whole island), turn left on Main Street and drive a couple of blocks to the **Sea Star Cafe,** 4121 Main Street; (757) 336–5442. A husband-and-wife-owned gourmet carryout, the Sea Star has a great sandwich menu, including lots of vegetarian selections, such as the Greek pita, with fresh mixed greens, black olives, red onion, and feta cheese. If you prefer, you can get thick deli-style sandwiches with Black Forest ham, hard salami, or honey turkey. Large salads, chips, and fresh baked goods are also available. It is an obvious choice for picking up a picnic lunch for the beach. Inexpensive.

Although Chincoteague's beaches are actually on Assateague Island, the barrier island across Assateague Channel from Chincoteague Island, they're only about ten minutes' drive from downtown Chincoteague. Take Main Street north to Maddox Boulevard, turn right, and follow Maddox east about 2 miles to **Assateague Island.** Once you cross the Assateague Channel Bridge onto the island, you're in the **Chincoteague National Wildlife Refuge,** Maddox Boulevard (757–336–6122), and you'll have to purchase a park entrance permit. The $10-per-vehicle permit is good for seven days. (A National Parks pass or a Golden Age, Eagle, or Access pass gets you in free.) Pass in hand, follow the signs to **Tom's Cove,** where the National Park Service maintains a visitor center, and where there are portable restrooms and changing rooms as well as outside showers.

L U N C H : Picnic on the beach.

Afternoon

Half of Assateague Island is in the state of Maryland (see Maryland Escape Three), and half is in the state of Virginia. The island has 37 miles of unspoiled beaches that are among the most beautiful on the East Coast. As part of the National Seashore, the area is wholly defended against video arcades, ice-cream vendors, and T-shirt shops. Many of the most beautiful beaches are on the Virginia end of the island, and you can easily while away the afternoon on the beach near Tom's Cove swimming, beachcombing, kite flying, sunbathing, shell collecting, and strolling.

Somewhere during your afternoon on the beach, you're sure to encounter at least one of Assateague Island's wild ponies. The creatures are small because of their poor diet, which consists mostly of salt marsh cord grass and beach grass. Kids love the island's ponies, and it's fun to take photographs of them. But don't get too close; they kick and bite. And obey the numerous signs and refrain from feeding them. It's likely to make them sick, and they'll certainly become dependent on humans for food.

The island's wild ponies (made famous by Marguerite Henry, author of *Misty of Chincoteague*) draw thousands of people to Chincoteague during the last week of July for the annual wild pony swim and penning. The roundup, which local people are very proud of, is like a gigantic family reunion, with relatives and summer visitors returning every year for the festivities. The purpose is to keep the wild ponies healthy and hold the population to a sustainable number (150 adult horses) on the barrier island.

To cull the herd, the Virginia ponies are driven across Assateague Channel at low tide on the last Wednesday of July by "saltwater" cowboys (as thousands watch and cheer), and a certain number are sold at auction the following day. Proceeds from the auction benefit the volunteer fire department. The remainder of the herd is returned to the wild on Assateague Island on Friday.

If you don't visit Chincoteague during pony-penning week, you can learn more about the ponies and the history and traditions behind the pony auction at the **Chincoteague Pony Centre,** 6417 Carriage Drive; (757) 336–2776 or (757) 336–6313; www.chincoteague.com/ponycentre. The Pony Centre has an attractive display of pony information and memorabilia, a film on Chincoteague and the ponies, a gift shop, and several specimens of the real thing in the paddock for you to see up close. Open Monday through Saturday 9:00 A.M. to 10:00 P.M., Sunday 1:00 to 10:00 P.M. during the summer months.

If you have children along, you'll have to let them ride one of the ponies, which—once tamed and trained—are quite docile. Pony rides on a real Chincoteague pony are offered daily from 9:00 A.M. to 1:00 P.M. and from 3:30 to 6:00 P.M. A five-minute ride costs $5.00. You'll also have to bring them back at 8:00 P.M. for the pony show, which also costs $5.00. (There is no pony show on Sunday.) A half-hour riding lesson, available in the morning, costs $35.

DINNER: There are a number of pleasant choices for dinner, but locals pack the **Island Family Restaurant,** 3441 Ridge Road (757–336–1198), a down-home meat, potatoes, and seafood eatery. Two pork chops, mashed potatoes, cooked vegetable, and applesauce will cost you less than $10; substitute two large pan-fried oyster fritters for the chops, and the price goes up a dollar. The seafood selection is predictably large, but you also can choose from liver and onions, hamburger steak, New York strip

Water fowl in Chincoteague National Wildlife Refuge

steak, and fried chicken. And, no matter what time you go, there is certain to be a line.

After dinner, head back to the beach for a twilight stroll or catch the evening pony show at the Chincoteague Pony Centre.

LODGING: The **Refuge Inn,** 7058 Maddox Boulevard (757–336–5511 or 888–257–0039; www.refugeinn.com) sits in the middle of a stand of pines just across the channel from the wildlife refuge. It is convenient both to the beach and to the town and has indoor and outdoor swimming pools, a sauna, a fitness room, picnic tables, hibachis in case you want to grill your own dinner, and phones, TVs, and refrigerators in each of the seventy-two rooms and two suites. Room rates range from $65 to $160 depending on the season; suites (with full kitchens and sleeping accommodations for up to six people) range from $150 to $290.

Day 2 / *Morning*

BREAKFAST: Start the morning with bacon and eggs at **Don's Seafood Restaurant,** a plain, hearty place near the harbor with good coffee and good service. Located at 4113 Main Street; (757) 336–5715. Inexpensive.

After breakfast, make a quick stop at one of the local bike-rental shops unless you've brought your own bike along. (See There's More for details.)

The town of Chincoteague is made for lazy biking, and it is a great way to further explore Chincoteague National Wildlife Refuge. The area is a major resting and feeding area for falcons, eagles, herons, egrets, and nearly 300 other species of birds, as well as elk, deer, and wild ponies. It is also a major resting area for migrating Canada geese, snow geese, tundra swans, and ducks every fall, and birders from all over the United States visit Chincoteague to see them.

Within the refuge, there are two trails (a 3.5-mile wildlife loop and a 1.6-mile woodland trail) for bikers and pedestrians, and a short, quarter-mile walking trail to the old Assateague Lighthouse. The century-old, 142-foot-high, red-and-white-striped brick lighthouse is a beauty; unfortunately, it is open to the public only for one weekend per month from June through August.

As you walk or bike the trails through the refuge, keep your eyes open for large, stately families of ducks or geese as they parade across the trails. During the summer, red-winged blackbirds dive and swoop as great, long-legged fishing birds (including egrets and herons) wade on their spindly legs through the marsh. Keep your ears open as well; the birds of the refuge are seldom quiet, and their calls will help you identify what you are seeing.

LUNCH: Famous Pizza and Sub Shop Family Restaurant, 6689 Maddox Boulevard; (757) 336–3301. Kids will love the thin-crust pepperoni pizza, but you can also get great subs (eggplant Parmesan, hot sausage, many others), salads, soups, and seafood. Inexpensive.

Afternoon

Follow lunch with a stop at the **Island Creamery,** 6243 Maddox Boulevard; (757) 336–6236. With not one but three ice-cream shops to choose from, and all of them very fine, it is pretty clear that daily ice-cream eating on Chincoteague is mandatory. The Island Creamery features homemade ice cream in a dozen or more flavors each day, and you can count on "Marsh Mud" chocolate ice cream and at least one refreshing sorbet being on the list at all times. It has helpful wait staff and plenty of indoor and outdoor seating. Inexpensive. (See Other Recommended Restaurants for ice cream choices on the other days of your visit.)

Next stop is the **Oyster and Maritime Museum,** 7125 Maddox Boulevard; (757) 336–6117; www.chincoteaguechamber.com/oyster/omm.html. This charming community museum is chockablock with information about Chincoteague history and the oystering industry and way of life. Local volunteers are there because they love Chincoteague and are a fount of information about the island. At the museum, there are several dioramas and displays of artifacts; local art and decoys; a small aquarium; special seasonal exhibits; and a pleasant gift shop. The original lens from the Assateague lighthouse was restored at the museum and is on display there. Open Monday through Saturday 10:00 A.M. to 5:00 P.M. and Sunday noon to 4:00 P.M. in the summer; weekends only (Saturday 10:00 A.M. to 5:00 P.M.; Sunday noon to 4:00 P.M.) in the spring and fall; closed in winter. Admission is $3.00 for adults, $2.00 for seniors, and $1.50 for children two to twelve; children under two are admitted free.

After your museum visit, take some time to do a little shopping. On Maddox Boulevard, you'll enjoy The Brant Gifts (6472 Maddox, 757–336–5531), a cheery gift shop with New Age music, a model train running overhead, and scores of Christmas items; White's Copperworks (6373 Maddox, 757–336–1588), where you can get full-size and garden-size weather vanes, wind chimes, garden accessories, and jewelry; Island Gallery and Gifts (6219 Maddox, 757–336–3076) for pony posters and prints; and Island Arts (6196 Maddox, 757–336–5856), where you will find original oil paintings and limited-edition prints of egrets and other shore birds.

Downtown, visit the Main Street Shop and Coffee House (4282 Main Street, 757–336–6782) for coffee—of course—and also designer jewelry, textiles, and pottery; the Osprey Nest Art Gallery (4096 Main Street, 757–336–6042) for a nice selection of Chincoteague artwork, prints, and gifts; and Egret Moon Artworks (4044 Main, 757–336–5775), a tiny art gallery that displays baskets, pottery, glass, jewelry, homemade all-natural doggie biscuits, and lots more.

DINNER: Landmark Crab House, 6172 Main Street; (757) 336–3745 or (757) 336–5552. The Crab House is a great place to unwind and watch the sun set on the water as you relax over dinner. As soon as you're seated, ask for a plate of fresh Chincoteague oysters; if you haven't tasted them before, you'll find them a tad salty. By the time your order is half done, you'll be a convert, and you might even order a second round of appetizers. For your entree there is, of course, crab. There are also other seafood specials, and the steak is quite good. Moderate.

LODGING: The Refuge Inn.

Day 3 / Morning

BREAKFAST: Bill's Seafood Restaurant is a great place to start the day. It serves excellent pancakes, waffles, and muffins for breakfast, starting at 5:00 A.M. Located at 4040 Main Street; (757) 336–5831. Inexpensive.

If you have signed up far enough in advance, you can have a truly grand finale to your Chincoteague weekend by joining **Captain Barry's Back Bay Expedition,** a very special ecotour that both children and adults will love. Dress casually—and apply plenty of insect repellent and sunscreen—because you'll be on the water with Captain Barry for four hours. You'll stop to catch crabs and hunt for jellyfish. You'll stroll through the salt marshes and tidal flats as Captain Barry teaches you all about clams and oysters and how they are caught and grown. Along the way, he'll talk about Chincoteague history, weather forecasting, how to identify birds, and where to find the best seashells on the beach.

He'll also tell you pirate tales and ghost stories and Hollywood gossip. Oh, and you'll swim, sunbathe, take photos, or just hang out depending on your (and Captain Barry's) whims. It's a great way to end your Chincoteague adventure and whet your appetite for a return trip.

Captain Barry's Back Bay Cruises is located at 6248 Ocean Boulevard; (757) 336–6508; www.captainbarry.bigstep.com. Morning and afternoon expedition cruises are offered daily, weather permitting, for a charge of $45 a person. Early morning (7:00 A.M.), ninety-minute birding cruises are $25 a person. Less-active, two-hour twilight cruises cost $35 a person. Reservations are absolutely necessary.

LUNCH: Enjoy a late lunch at **Etta's Channel Side Restaurant,** an upscale, family-friendly restaurant with a great view of Assateague Channel and the lighthouse. The specialty of the house is crab cakes, but you'll be more than satisfied with any of the seafood choices, and you may just have to have one last real Chincoteague oyster before you head home. Located at 7452 East Side Drive; (757) 336–5644. Moderate.

Afternoon

Drive home via VA 175 west, US 13 north, and US 50 west. Allow at least three hours.

There's More

Bike Rentals. Several establishments in Chincoteague rent bikes. Among them are the Bike Depot, 7058 Maddox Boulevard (757–336–5511) and Jus' Bikes, 6527 Maddox Boulevard (757–336–6700). Reservations are strongly recommended; expect to pay about $3.00 an hour or $10.00 a day for a bike rental.

Surfside Amusements. Miniature golf, basketball hoops, batting cages, video games, and snack bar. Open daily 10:00 A.M. to 11:00 P.M. Located at 6557 Maddox Boulevard; (757) 336–4653.

Island Aquarium. Small aquarium with a shark tank, marsh exhibit, eels, terrapins, and a touch tank where kids can handle horseshoe crabs, starfish, whelks, and other marine animals. Located at 8162 Landmark Plaza (on Main Street); (757) 336–2212. Open weekdays 10:00 A.M. to 5:00 P.M., weekends 10:00 A.M. to 9:00 P.M. June through September. Admission is $4.00 for adults and $3.00 for children two through twelve; children under two admitted free.

NASA Visitors Center at Wallops Island. Educational arm of Goddard Space Flight Center, where scientific and commercial satellites are launched; airplane and rocket exhibits; moon rock; astronaut apparel; good exhibit on the history of flight; interactive computer displays; gift shop; picnic tables. Located on VA 175 about 5 miles west of Chincoteague; (757) 824–2298. Open daily 10:00 A.M. to 4:00 P.M. July and August; Thursday through Monday March through June and September through November; and Monday through Friday December through February.

Special Events

March–April. Easter Decoy Art Festival and Auction. Event draws crowds and 150 carvers to Chincoteague for competition and fun. (757) 336–6161.

May. Eastern Shore Annual Seafood Festival. Eastern Shore Chamber of Commerce all-you-can-eat picnic with three decades of tradition draws 3,000 people at $30 a person. (757) 787–2460.

International Migratory Bird Celebration. Annual event at the Wildlife Refuge features workshops, guided walks, crafts, and lectures for birders. (757) 336–6122.

July. Early in the month, the Fireman's Carnival kicks off the pony season with games, rides, food, and entertainment. Later in the month, there's the pony swim, pony penning, and pony auction. (757) 336–6161.

October. Chamber-sponsored Annual Oyster Festival on Columbus Day weekend features all-you-can-eat oysters and sides for $35. (757) 336–6161.

Other Recommended Restaurants

AJ's on the Creek, 6585 Maddox Boulevard; (757) 336–5888. A good choice if you are celebrating. Oysters Rockefeller, seafood pasta, grilled catch of the day, veal, and hand-cut steaks are specialties; for a real treat, try the shellfish bouillabaisse. Moderate to expensive.

Bill's Seafood Restaurant, 4040 Main Street; (757) 336–5831. The locals' "special place" in Chincoteague for dining out for forty-plus years; always-fresh seafood, choice steaks and chops, pasta; nice wine selection; tops for desserts. Moderate.

Don's Seafood Restaurant, 4113 Main Street; (757) 336–5715. Serving fried oysters and seafood platters in Chincoteague for more than thirty years. Moderate.

Village Restaurant and Lounge, 7576 Maddox Boulevard; (757) 336–5120. Waterfront dining on Eel Creek; good choice for Chincoteague oysters; reservations strongly recommended. Moderate.

Steamers, 6251 Maddox Boulevard; (757) 336–5478. Steamed, baked, fried, and broiled fish and shellfish served with corn on the cob, coleslaw, and sweet potato biscuits; all-you-can-eat specials; children's menu also available. Moderate.

Wine, Cheese, and More, 4103 Main Street; (757) 336–2610. A great place to pick up picnic fare. Inexpensive.

Mr. Whippy's, 6201 Maddox Boulevard; (757) 336–5122. Soft-serve ice cream, homemade waffle cones, sundaes, milk shakes, cyclones; casual ambience. Inexpensive.

Muller's Old Fashioned Ice Cream Parlour, 4034 Main Street; (757) 336–5894. Old-fashioned ice cream parlor in a Victorian house; enjoy your warm Belgian waffle topped with ice cream, fresh fruit, and whipped cream while sitting on a candlelit porch. Inexpensive.

Best place for doughnuts: Grubstake Deli, 6194 Landmark Plaza; (757) 336–3166.

Other Recommended Lodgings

Island Motor Inn Resort, 4391 Main Street; (757) 336–3141; www.island motorinn.com. Stately waterfront inn with sixty rooms and mini-suites, each of which has a balcony, cable television, and a refrigerator; two swimming pools, fitness center, hot tub, cafe restaurant on the premises that offers room service. Rates: $68–$175. Open year-round.

Chincoteague Lodge, 4417 Deep Hole Road; (757) 336–6415 or (877) 222–8799; www.chincoteague.com/cml. Clean, pleasant motel with seventy air-conditioned rooms, each complete with refrigerator, telephone, and television; swimming pool, playground, volleyball court, barbecue facilities, screened picnic pavilion. Open April through October. Rates: $69–$152.

The Driftwood Motor Lodge, 7105 Maddox Boulevard; (757) 336–6557 or (800) 553–6117; www.driftwoodmotorlodge.com. Fifty-three large rooms with TVs, refrigerators, balconies; close to the refuge and beach; heated pool. Rates: $51–$225.

The Channel Bass Inn, 6228 Church Street; (757) 336–6148 or (800) 249–0818; www.channelbass-inn.com. Elegant bed-and-breakfast with six spacious, air-conditioned guest rooms, all with private baths and separate sitting areas; children over the age of six are welcome. Rates: $99–$195, including full breakfast. The inn is open to the public for tea and scones (and trifle and sponge cake and fruit tarts) daily except Sunday and Wednesday from 3:30 to 4:30 P.M., and crowds come for this special Chincoteague treat, which costs $17.50 a person.

The Watson House Bed & Breakfast, 4240 Main Street; (757) 336–1564 or (800) 336–6787; www.watsonhouse.com. Charming bed-and-breakfast with five guest rooms and pleasant common areas; complimentary use of bicycles. Rates: $105–$155, including breakfast. The proprietors also rent two large cottages and one town house that are suitable for families (of up to eight people). The cottages rent for $370–$535 for a three-day weekend; $605–$915 for a full week.

Tom's Cove Campground, 8128 Beebe Road; (757) 336–6498; www.toms covepark.com. Huge campground on the water with more than 900 sites, three fishing piers, swimming pool, game room, camp store that also sells groceries. Rates: $27.50–$39.50.

For More Information

Chincoteague Chamber of Commerce, 6733 Maddox Boulevard, P.O. Box 258, Chincoteague, VA 23336; (757) 336–6161; www.chincoteague chamber.com.

See also www.chincoteague.com.

MARYLAND
ESCAPES

Annapolis

City on the Bay / 1 Night

Many Washington area residents don't think of Annapolis, which is a scant 30 miles away, as a weekend escape. But the best way to see Annapolis is to stay over for a night or two and sample a few of its many delights; it could be on another continent for all its differences from Washington.

A beautiful, historic port city on the Chesapeake Bay, Annapolis dates from the seventeenth century. In fact, it was once the governing center of the colonies, where the Continental Congress met in 1783 and 1784. On a weekend visit there, you can see the beautiful capitol building (now the state capitol of Maryland), where the Treaty of Paris, which brought the Revolutionary War to an official close, was ratified.

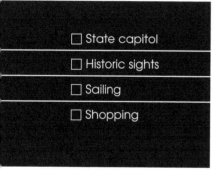

☐ State capitol

☐ Historic sights

☐ Sailing

☐ Shopping

Though no longer a major commercial port, Annapolis is still very much a water town. Hundreds of sails bob and glide in the bay, fresh-seafood restaurants line the narrow streets, and midshipmen from the U.S. Naval Academy stroll about in their crisp white uniforms. Your weekend escape to what some call the sailing capital of the world includes a two-hour sail on the bay, a walking tour of the historic area, great shopping and dining, and an overnight in a centrally located inn just a block from City Dock.

After sampling Annapolis's many attractions, you'll be tempted to make it an annual weekend escape.

Day 1 / Afternoon

Start your weekend right after work, and drive to Annapolis in time for dinner. That way you'll get a jump on the beach crowds, who clog the highway on Saturday morning and can turn the easy forty-five-minute drive into a much longer proposition.

Annapolis is 30 miles east of Washington on U.S. Highway 50. Take exit 24 and follow Maryland Highway 70, Roscoe C. Rowe Boulevard, south into town.

DINNER: Dinner your first night in Annapolis is at **Middleton Tavern Oyster Bar and Restaurant,** located in the heart of the historic district, where Randall Street meets City Dock, at 2 Market Space; (410) 263–3323. Dark, cool, decorated with nautical prints and paraphernalia, the Middleton Tavern serves classic shore fare, fresh pasta, and steaks. Try the smoked bluefish hors d'oeuvre first. Expensive.

After dinner, head to local hotspot **Ram's Head Tavern,** at 33 West Street. Aside from the microbrews made on the premises, the tavern features an eclectic selection of live music and the most extensive beer menu in town. It's a beer joint for those who might be inclined to raise their noses at "beer joints." (410) 268–4545; www.ramsheadtavern.com.

LODGING: **Gibson's Lodgings,** 110 Prince George Street, just a block from City Dock, is actually three separate buildings, two of which are old Annapolis homes. Each building has a clutch of gorgeous period rooms full of antique furniture. There is off-street parking available and a pretty garden courtyard where a continental breakfast is served in the morning. (410) 268–5555 or (877) 330–0057; www.avmcyber.com/gibson/. Rates: $109–$199.

Day 2 / *Morning*

BREAKFAST: After breakfast at Gibson's Lodgings, walk along the City Dock to **Pusser's Landing,** located on the water right in front of the Marriott Hotel. There you'll make reservations for a 4:00 P.M. sail on the schooner *Woodwind,* a beautiful yacht modeled after the century-old fast wooden schooners built to sail on the Chesapeake Bay; (410) 263–7837; www.schoonerwoodwind.com.

Then stroll over to the **Historic Annapolis Foundation Museum Store and Welcome Center** (also known as the Victualling Warehouse Maritime Museum) to pick up brochures and maps. For $5.00 you can rent an audiocassette to guide you on a walking tour of historic Annapolis. None other than Walter Cronkite will talk you through the ninety-minute, 1.5-mile tour. Open daily 10:00 A.M. to 6:00 P.M., later in the summer. Located at 77 Main Street; (410) 268–5576; www.annapolis.org.

Highlights of the walking tour include Maryland's capitol, the **Maryland State House.** This pretty redbrick building has a wooden

The schooner Woodwind

dome (the largest wooden dome in America) with the distinct look of a lighthouse. Inside are a giant sailing ship, the 1788 *Federalist;* a gorgeous rotunda; and beautiful marble House and Senate chambers. Notice the quaint, tiny desks where the legislators sat. Located at State Circle; (410) 974–3400. Open Monday through Friday 8:30 A.M. to 5:00 P.M., Saturday and Sunday 10:00 A.M. to 4:00 P.M. Tours at 11:00 A.M. and 3:00 P.M.

Near the capitol on College Avenue is beautiful **St. John's College,** the third oldest in the nation. St. John's, founded in 1696, is a "great books" school with a rigorous, classical reading regimen. (On a less serious note, the school's official sport is croquet, and you can often see students practicing on the lawns.)

The tour will also take you through the lovely residential neighborhood around the capitol. You'll walk brick streets and sidewalks and see spectacular Georgian architecture, such as the magnificent **William Paca House and Garden,** 186 Prince George Street; (410) 990–4543.

A tour of the garden and inside of the home of three-term governor of Maryland (and signer of the Declaration of Independence) William Paca is an extra $8.00 ($5.00 for children six to seventeen), and it's worth it. You'll see a perfectly restored colonial mansion, with its bright, sky blue walls and ceilings. Period furnishings have been meticulously added, depicting life at the time of the American Revolution. Outside is the stately five-acre garden, with boxwoods lining the paths, a fish-shaped pond, and a little stream. Open Monday through Saturday 10:00 A.M. to 5:00 P.M. and Sunday noon to 4:00 P.M. April through December; open Saturday 10:00 A.M. to 4:00 P.M. and Sunday noon to 4:00 P.M. during January through March. Tours are offered on the half hour.

LUNCH: When you've turned in your audiocassette, walk back to the capitol and around the circle until you get to **Harry Browne's** at 66 State Circle; (410) 263–4332. This quiet, dark, lovely spot has an interesting menu with a variety of sandwiches, salads, and soups, as well as fancy beef, chicken, lamb, and seafood entrees. Moderate to expensive.

Afternoon

After lunch, take advantage of the fact that you are right in the nicest shopping area of Annapolis. A 3-block stroll down the narrow, brick **Maryland Avenue** as it radiates from State Circle yields dozens of attractive shops where you'll find antiques, crafts, jewelry, prints, and gifts. Note particularly the **Aurora Gallery** at 67 Maryland Avenue (410–263–9150), which has beautiful jewelry, glass, prints, and sculpture; and **Maria's Picture Place** at 45 Maryland Avenue, which has an extensive display of Annapolis scenes for sale.

If you're interested in more shopping, head back to **City Dock,** a bustling commercial area right on the water. Here the shopping may be less interesting, with mall chain stores predominating, but there are lots of people and boats to watch. Stop at **Fawcett's Boat Supplies** at 110 Compromise Street (410–267–8681) for all things nautical, including gadgets, clothes, shoes, and maps. Most Annapolis shops are open on Sunday as well as weekdays.

For an afternoon cup of coffee, check out **City Dock Cafe** at 18 Market Space; (410) 269–0969. This small espresso bar also sells gigantic chocolate chip cookies, raspberry bran scones, and doughnuts.

A few minutes before 4:00 P.M., you'll need to be back at Pusser's Landing and ready to board the schooner *Woodwind*. This large yacht can take up to forty-eight passengers. Once you're all settled and comfortable, the *Woodwind*'s friendly crew starts up a small engine and navigates the ship away from the dock. Within a few minutes, the crew members ask for volunteers to run up the sails, and then, magically, the engine is cut, the sails billow, and the *Woodwind* almost silently glides into open water "like swans asleep," as the poet James Elroy Flecker put it.

Your two-hour sail will take you to the bay, and the crew will be glad to give you a turn at the wheel while explaining some sailing basics. They'll also offer free sodas and snacks, and beer and wine for a small fee. The basic cruise costs $31 for adults ($34 on weekends), $29 for seniors ($32 on weekends), and $20 for children under twelve. Special cruises are offered for an additional fee, including a "Race Watch," a microbeer-tasting cruise, and runs with live entertainment aboard.

NOTE: If you want to spend more of the afternoon strolling and shopping, the schooner *Woodwind* also has a "sunset sail" from 6:30 to 8:30 P.M. at $34 for adults, $32 for seniors, and $20 for children under twelve. After the evening cruise, you can even spend the night on board in a tiny, double-berth stateroom complete with hot shower and a big breakfast at a cost of $265 for two people.

After your sail, cross over the short bridge on Compromise Street to **Eastport,** which has a distinctly different personality from the busy commercial activity of Pusser's Landing and City Dock. Here the pace is slower and the tourists fewer, and the area has more the feel of a working port.

D I N N E R : Have dinner at **Carrol's Creek Cafe,** a pleasant, casual restaurant with a selection of excellent American entrees. The cafe offers a full menu but specializes in seafood. Among the most popular offerings are cream of crab soup, roasted herb-encrusted rockfish, and grilled salmon with Parmesan polenta and Mediterranean vegetables. Fabulous desserts such as raspberry tarts and mocha crème brûlée are made on the premises. Carrol's Creek Cafe also provides a great view of the water, historic Annapolis, the sailboats, and the sailors. Located at 410 Severn Avenue in the Eastport section of Annapolis; (410) 263–8102; www.carrolscreek.com. Expensive.

When you're finished for the day, return to Washington via US 50.

There's More

United States Naval Academy. Tours lasting about an hour and a half depart from Ricketts Hall at the naval academy. Brochures are available for self-guided tours as well. You can see the beautiful Beaux Arts Chapel (where Revolutionary War hero John Paul Jones is buried), and lots of naval memorabilia and artifacts at the academy museum on campus. Tours are only by reservation, Monday through Saturday 10:00 A.M. to 2:30 P.M., Sunday 12:30 to 2:30 P.M. Tours include a fifteen-minute introductory film and involve about a mile of walking. The visitor center is located near Gate 1 on King George Street; (410) 263–6933; www.navyonline.com.

Hammond-Harwood House. National Historic Landmark eighteenth-century home, designed by William Buckland. Located at 19 Maryland Avenue; (410) 263–4683; www.hammondharwoodhouse.org. Open daily noon to 5:00 P.M. May through October; daily noon to 4:00 P.M. March, April, November, and December; Saturday and Sunday noon to 4:00 P.M. January and February. Admission is $6.00 for adults, $5.50 for students (through college), and $3.00 for children under six. Buckland also designed the famous **Chase-Lloyd House** at 22 Maryland Avenue, which is now a home for elderly women; (410) 263–2723; www.cr.nps.gov/history/online_books/declaration/site13.htm. The ground floor of the Chase-Lloyd House is open to the public Monday through Saturday 2:00 to 4:00 P.M. March through December. Admission is $2.00. Both the Hammond-Harwood House and the Chase-Lloyd House have exquisite interior and exterior details.

Cruises. Watermark Cruises, located at City Dock in Annapolis (410–268–7600; www.watermarkcruises.com), offers a variety of cruises, including ferry rides on the Severn River, day trips to St. Michaels, and a forty-minute tour of Annapolis Harbor and the area near the naval academy. The forty-minute tour costs $10.00, $4.00 for children three to eleven; children two and under ride free. Call for tour schedule and other rates.

Special Events

August–October. Maryland Renaissance Festival in Crownsville. Gala reenactment of sixteenth-century English festival with food and entertainment draws thousands. Weekends only during fall. (410) 266–7304 or (800) 296–7304; www.rennfest.com.

September. Annapolis Rotary Crab Feast. Maryland Seafood Festival at Sandy Point State Park. Large variety of seafood dishes, with Maryland crab particularly highlighted. Music and entertainment. (410) 841–2841.

December. Eastport Yacht Club Pre-Christmas Lights Parade. Dozens of sailboats and yachts, festooned with lights, parade through Annapolis Harbor and Spa Creek, to the delight of spectators. Much Christmas caroling on deck. (410) 263–0415.

Other Recommended Restaurants

Treaty of Paris Restaurant, 16 Church Circle; (410) 216–6340. Top-of-the-line gourmet American and French dishes in a lovely eighteenth-century inn. If you're splurging, try the four-course dinner. Expensive. The Drummers Lot Pub at the same location serves soups, salads, and sandwiches at moderate prices.

Buddy's Crabs and Ribs, 100 Main Street, second floor; (410) 626–1100. A boisterous eatery with a young crowd and moderately priced menu. Emphasis on seafood and ribs, salads, and sticky desserts like brownie sundaes and caramel apple pie. Sunday brunch buffet is a bargain at $9.95.

Cafe Normandie, 185 Main Street; (410) 263–3382. Small, pretty, country-style French restaurant, offering appetizers like baked Brie and pâté, a wonderful charcuterie, seafood, veal, and crepes, and desserts worth saving room for. Moderate to expensive.

49 West Coffeehouse, 49 West Street; (410) 626-9796. A favorite for light vegetarian dining and lingering over coffee, European-style, with a newspaper. Live entertainment. Moderate.

Ram's Head Tavern, 33 West Street; (410) 268–4545. Popular pub with microbrewery on premises. Sandwiches, specials, and more than two dozen brands of beer on tap. Moderate.

Lewnes' Steakhouse, Severn Avenue at Fourth Street in Eastport area of town; (410) 263–1617. Family-run restaurant serving traditional steak and lobster dinners for more than eighty years. Moderate to expensive.

Other Recommended Lodgings

William Page Inn, 8 Martin Street; (410) 626–1506 or (800) 364–4160; www.williampageinn.com. Five-room bed-and-breakfast furnished with antiques and period reproductions; fireplace in common room. Full breakfast. Rates: $140–$250.

Historic Inns of Annapolis, 58 State Circle; (410) 263–2641 or (800) 847–8882; www.annapolisinns.com. Includes three popular inns in the State Circle area: the Maryland Inn, the Robert Johnson House, and the Governor Calvert House. Together, they have a total of 124 rooms and suites. Rates: $109–$249 for rooms; $249–$329 for suites, which have Jacuzzis, kitchenettes, and living rooms.

Chez Amis Bed and Breakfast, 85 East Street; (410) 263–6631 or (888) 224–6455; www.chezamis.com. Charming bed-and-breakfast that was once a corner grocery store. The four guest rooms all have quilts, brass beds, interesting antiques, and private baths; full breakfast served. Rates: $150–$180.

Annapolis Accommodations is a commercial service that will make reservations at Annapolis hotels and bed-and-breakfasts for individuals, large groups, or conferences. Located at 41 Maryland Avenue; (410) 263–3262; www.stayannapolis.com.

For More Information

Annapolis and Anne Arundel County Conference and Visitors Bureau, 26 West Street, Annapolis, MD 21401; (410) 280–0445; www.visit-annapolis .org.

For more information visit www.hometownannapolis.com.

The Eastern Shore

Water, Water, Everywhere / 1 Night

Water, water, everywhere—in rivers, streams, marshes, and the mighty Chesapeake itself—defines the ecology and the economy of Maryland's

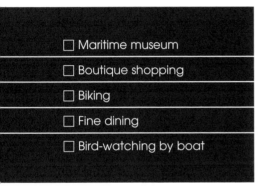

- ☐ Maritime museum
- ☐ Boutique shopping
- ☐ Biking
- ☐ Fine dining
- ☐ Bird-watching by boat

Eastern Shore of the Chesapeake Bay. The level, lush green lowlands of eastern Maryland are home to millions of waterbirds: Canada geese winter here, and other migratory birds stop over on their way south. As for the human inhabitants, almost everybody who lives in the Eastern Shore's quiet little fishing towns seems to be involved with water one way or another. A two-day visit to the Eastern Shore is a delightful opportunity for you to relax in and around the water, too.

With the great Choptank River and the lesser Miles, Tred-Avon, and Wye Rivers, as well as countless creeks and streams flowing into the bay, boats seem to be almost as plentiful as cars in the area. Sturdy fisherfolk still ply their trade, hauling in the oysters, crabs, and fish. Sailboats bob on the bay and in the rivers, and children and old men with fishing poles hunker in solemn lines by the water's edge. Tourist boutiques offer beautiful hand-carved duck decoys, and dozens of restaurants serve up some of the best seafood in America.

This weekend in the bay area includes a popular tourist destination (the Chesapeake Bay Maritime Museum) in St. Michaels, a tiny town of Victorian bed-and-breakfasts, boutique shops, and restaurants. It also gives you the opportunity to spend some time with the great herons, loons, egrets, geese, and wild ducks that frequent the area.

Pick a brilliant spring, summer, or fall weekend for this special quick escape from Washington, because you'll want to spend just about all your time outdoors, and on the water.

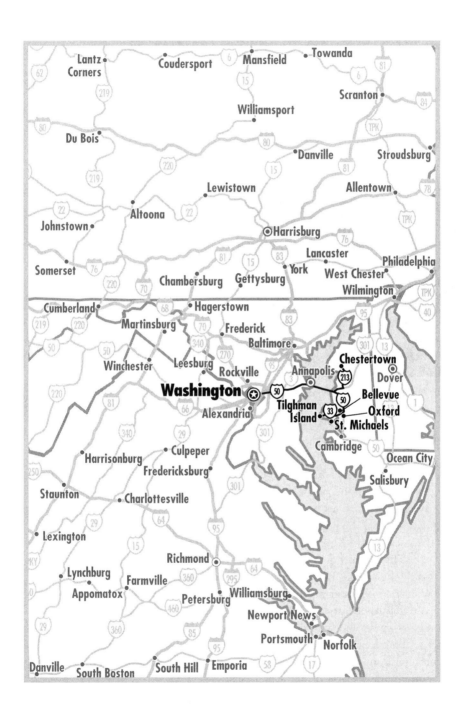

Day 1 / Morning

The Eastern Shore is only about 80 miles from Washington, D.C., but beach traffic in the summer can sometimes turn the trip into an hours-long nightmare. If you can, get an early start to beat the rush. The route there is simple: Follow U.S. Highway 50 east from Washington over the Bay Bridge, and you're on the northern tip of the Eastern Shore.

After you cross the Bay Bridge, continue east on US 50 a little more than 25 miles, then take the Easton Parkway (Maryland Highway 322) 2 or 3 miles to Maryland Highway 33 west. Within fifteen minutes, you'll be in the quaint and beautiful town of **St. Michaels.**

Your first destination in St. Michaels is the **Chesapeake Bay Maritime Museum,** an eighteen-acre "museum campus" with several displays of Maryland maritime history. It's located on the main road (Talbot Street) right on the bay in St. Michaels; (410) 745–2916; www .cbmm.org. Open daily 10:00 A.M. to 6:00 P.M. during the summer; closes at 5:00 P.M. in spring and fall and 4:00 P.M. in winter. Admission is $10.00 for adults, $9.00 for seniors, and $5.00 for children six through seventeen. Children under six are admitted free.

Nearly everyone's favorite stop at the museum is the beautiful, restored nineteenth-century "screwpile" lighthouse, one of the last three cottage-type lighthouses in existence. The lighthouse's winding staircases, tiny and neat rooms, cunning housekeeping arrangements, and 360-degree view of the harbor and the Chesapeake Bay from 40 feet off the ground will make you yearn to live in it yourself. (In fact, the museum sometimes offers an evening and overnight program about life in the lighthouse— think children's birthday parties—on a handful of summer evenings.) Other displays at the museum are devoted to decoys, ancient fishing craft, bay history, and ship repair.

L U N C H : Amble next door for lunch at **The Crab Claw,** a tourist-friendly, casual restaurant specializing in seafood and burgers. If you get there before noon, you might snare an outdoor table along the water. The Crab Claw's prices are reasonable: Burgers are $5.00 to $8.00, and seafood platters are in the $12.00 to $18.00 range. Located at 304 Mill Street (Navy Point); (410) 745–2900; www.thecrabclaw.com. Open March through mid-December.

Afternoon

After lunch, take an hour to stroll through St. Michaels, which has more than a mile of tempting shops and boutiques lining **Talbot Street.** This is

Hooper Strait Lighthouse and Chesapeake Bay Maritime Museum

the place to pick up an ice-cream cone or an espresso and cruise the strip for antiques, jewelry, gifts, crafts, nautical prints, and decoys. If you're a real shopper, an hour won't be long enough!

When you're finished shopping, rent a bicycle or a tandem at **St. Michaels Marina,** 305 Mulberry Street, just a block off Talbot Street; (410) 745–2400. Bikes rent for $4.00 an hour, $11.00 half day, or $16.00 for the whole day. (Bike rentals are also available on Tilghman Island from Island Treasures, Wharf Road, 410–886–2058, for approximately the same rates.)

The Eastern Shore's flat terrain is ideal for biking, and most of the roads in the area have wide shoulders set aside for bikers. You can bike west on MD 33, and if you go to the end of Tilghman Island, you'll have made a 30-mile round-trip. Or you can bike east on MD 33 to Easton and back, a 20-mile round-trip. Both are pleasant jaunts.

But the best bike ride in the area is a 20-mile round-trip that takes you from St. Michaels to Oxford and back, with stops in Bellevue and Oxford and a ferry ride across the Tred-Avon River. Take MD 33 east from St. Michaels about 4 miles to Bellevue Road. Then head south another 5 miles until you reach Bellevue. The hills are gentle, and there's very little traffic to distract you from the beauty of the countryside.

In **Bellevue** you can grab a soda before boarding the **Oxford-Bellevue Ferry,** the nation's oldest continuously operating ferry service. Although it can take only six cars at a time, plenty of pedestrians and bikers can be accommodated. The ferry is in operation daily 9:00 A.M. to 9:00 P.M., June 1 through Labor Day. The rest of the year, except for the winter months when it is closed, the ferry runs weekdays from 7:00 A.M. to sunset, weekends from 9:00 A.M. to sunset. The ferry ride takes about twenty minutes and costs $5.00 round-trip for cyclists and $12.00 for a driver and car; additional car passengers pay $1.00; pedestrians pay $2.00. (410) 745–9023.

When you disembark, spend some time biking around the tiny town of **Oxford,** one of the oldest and prettiest towns in the state. Oxford's tree-lined streets, stately old homes, churches, and lovely riverside park make it a perfect place for a picnic, or a lazy afternoon watching the sailboats on the river. There are also a number of quaint shops with antiques, gifts, tourist trinkets, baked goods, and bike supplies available.

After touring Oxford, retrace your bike route back through Bellevue to St. Michaels. If biking is not for you, consider a one- to two-hour walking tour through St. Michaels. **St. Mary's Square Museum,** near the corner of Talbot and Mulberry Streets (410–745–9561), publishes a brochure outlining a thirty-stop historical walking tour of St. Michaels, which likes to call itself "the town that fooled the British" because, during the War of 1812, its residents hoisted lanterns to the masts of ships and the tops of trees, forcing the British ships' cannons to overshoot the town. The museum itself is only open Saturday and Sunday from 10:00 A.M. to 4:00 P.M. from May through October, but you can pick up the brochure at most tourist attractions.

After your bike ride or walking tour, retrieve your car and head for **Tilghman Island,** 15 miles west of St. Michaels on MD 33, where you'll dine and spend the night. Tilghman Island is still very much a working fishing village on an island surrounded by the Chesapeake Bay, the Choptank River, and Harris Creek. You'll enjoy the drive down the island and the less-touristy atmosphere there.

DINNER: Join locals and visitors for dinner at **Harrison's Chesapeake House,** in operation since the 1890s and renowned for its seafood. The service at Harrison's is friendly, the seafood tantalizingly fresh, the coffee strong, and the side dishes (including mashed potatoes, excellent coleslaw, potato salad, and warm rolls) are served "family style" on large platters set in the center of the table. Entrees include crab cakes, of course, as well as fried clams, the fresh catch (which might be sea trout, flounder, or blue-fish), and oysters. For dessert, the lemon chess pie is a standout. There is also an outdoor crab bar if you're in the mood for fresh steamed crabs. Located at Wharf Road, Tilghman Island; (410) 886–2121; www.chesapeake house.com. Moderate.

LODGING: The Tilghman Island Inn is located at 21384 Cooper-town Road, just 2 blocks west of Knapps Narrows Bridge; (410) 886–2141 or (800) 866–2141; www.tilghmanislandinn.com. This twenty-room resort has a tennis court, pool, croquet court, fishing, biking, docking facilities, and a gourmet dining room overlooking the water at Knapps Narrows. Rooms are modern and lovely and are filled with local original art, which is for sale. Rates: $125–$300.

Day 2 / Morning

BREAKFAST: The Tilghman Island Inn provides a continental breakfast of fruit, cereal, muffins, and wonderful coffee.

After breakfast, head for **Harris Creek Kayak** and another outdoor adventure. If you've made an advance arrangement, you will be taken kayaking or rowing to see waterfowl along the shore. An early-morning jaunt provides an opportunity to see—besides ducks and loons—great blue herons, egrets, and ospreys wading, fishing, and diving. Bald eagles are also frequently sighted in the area. The best time to see the waterbirds is spring and summer, but September and October, when the birds begin to migrate, offer other pleasures—wild geese fly overhead, and the foliage is glorious.

You don't have to be an experienced kayaker or rower to join in exploring the Tilghman Island shore area for waterfowl; Harris Creek Kayak offers courses in both activities. A two- to three-hour nature outing costs $65 a person for a party of six. Located at 7857 Tilghman Island Road; (410) 886–2083; www.harriscreekkayak.com.

If you want a less strenuous water jaunt, drive back to St. Michaels and snare a seat on the 180-passenger *Patriot,* which is berthed at the Chesapeake Bay Maritime Museum. The *Patriot* cruises the Miles River, a beautiful tributary of the bay. On your one-hour outing, you'll see plenty of local and migratory birds and watermen at work harvesting crabs or tonging for oysters. (410) 745–3100; www.patriotcruises.com. Cruises depart St. Michaels at 11:00 A.M., 12:30, 2:30, and 4:00 P.M. March through October. Cost is $11.50 to $19.50 for adults, $10.00 to $15.00 for children under twelve.

After your water adventure, head back east on MD 33 and MD 322 (the Easton Parkway) to US 50 west. Follow it northwest and begin your exploration of the northern tip of the Eastern Shore.

About 8 miles north of Easton on US 50, you'll see a sign for **Wye Oak State Park,** which until recently was the home of a 400-year-old white oak tree thought to be the oldest white oak in the nation. Although the tree was felled by a storm in 2002, there are still two good reasons for taking the short detour to visit Wye Oak. Just before you reach the site of the park on Maryland Highway 662 is **Orrell's Maryland Beaten Biscuits,** which bakes and ships more than a half million of these Eastern Shore delicacies a year. Orrell's bakes fresh biscuits only on Tuesday and Wednesday, but it's open daily for retail sales to the public from the home/business where the biscuits are baked; it's a good idea to call ahead (410–827–6244) to see if the proprietors are at home and have any biscuits left.

Down the road from Orrell's is the **Wye Gristmill and Museum.** From mid-April through mid-November, it's open to the public Friday through Sunday from 10:00 A.M. to 4:00 P.M. and Monday through Thursday from 10:00 A.M. to 1:00 P.M. On the first and third Saturday of the month, you can watch workers grind the grain. But you can purchase freshly ground wheat, rye, buckwheat, and corn meal every day, and your taste buds will thank you. (410) 827–3850; $2.00 donation requested.

As you leave Wye, take Maryland Highway 404 west (you'll actually be traveling north) 1 mile to Maryland Highway 213 north and follow it about 25 miles to **Chestertown,** the county seat of Kent County and one of the most delightful towns on the Eastern Shore.

L U N C H : It's worth a visit to the **Imperial Hotel and Restaurant,** 208 High Street (410–778–5000), just to see the beautiful, dark green plaid dining room. But don't be daunted by the elegant surroundings: Dinner may be elegant and expensive, but lunchers (lunch is available only on Sunday) are likely to be wearing boating shorts, and prices are an affordable $8.00 to $12.00 for crab-melt sandwiches or grilled-steak salads.

Afternoon

After lunch, take a walking tour of old Chestertown. Walking tour brochures are available at most hotels and shops or at the Kent County

Office of Tourism at 400 South High Street; (410) 778–0416. Many of Chestertown's gorgeous old homes and buildings date from the eighteenth century. The walking tour will take you about two hours. Among the top attractions are the circa 1747 **Customs House** on Water Street, with its Flemish Bond brickwork, and the **Geddes–Piper House,** a beautifully restored and beautifully furnished mansion that serves as the headquarters of the Historical Society of Kent County. Both are open to the public. Most of the houses on the tour are privately owned and are open for viewing only once a year during Chestertown's annual Candlelight Walking Tour. You can, however, enjoy gazing at the architecture of the 200-year-old gems that housed the wealthy local merchants and get a peek at many of the splendid gardens.

The restored **White Swan Tavern** at 231 High Street (410–778–2300) dates from 1733. This old jewel has been lovingly polished and filled with period furniture and furnishings to museum-like perfection. You can tour the building and refresh yourself with afternoon tea, which is served from 3:00 to 5:00 P.M. George Washington himself had tea there. Indeed, Chestertown is justly proud of its "tea party" history. Five months after the Boston Tea Party, in May 1774, the citizens of Chestertown boarded a British ship and threw both tea and crew members into the Chester River.

If you decide to stay over an extra day on the Eastern Shore, you can take a 110-mile driving tour of Kent County the next morning. Tour instruction brochures are available from the Kent County Office of Tourism. On the driving tour, you'll see wildlife refuges, picturesque villages, two or three small museums, and Washington College, one of the ten oldest colleges in America.

To return to Washington from Chestertown, take MD 213 south about 20 miles, U.S. Highway 301 south about 5 miles, and US 50 west about 50 miles. It will take you more than ninety minutes.

There's More

Boat Rentals. St. Michaels Marina, Mulberry Street; (410) 745–2400; www.stmichaelsmarina.com. Full range of services for boaters, including overnight dockage, motel rooms, showers, swimming pool, marine store, and ice, as well as powerboat rentals.

Cruises. A two-hour sail on the **Rebecca T. Ruark,** the oldest skipjack on the Chesapeake Bay (built in 1886), is available for $30 adults, $15 children twelve and under. (410) 829–3976; www.skipjack.org.

Easton. You can while away a couple of hours with a walking tour of some of the sights of downtown Easton. Make sure to stop at the **Historical Society Museum** at 25 South Washington Street; (410) 822–0773; www.hstc.org. Open Monday through Saturday 10:00 A.M. to 4:00 P.M.; admission is free. A guided tour of its three galleries is available at 11:30 A.M. and 1:30 P.M. for $5.00. Also worth seeing in Easton are the two-century-old Talbot County Courthouse at the corner of Washington and Dover Streets, the Academy of the Arts at 106 South Street, and the Third Haven Friends Meeting House at 405 South Washington Street.

Fishing. Harrison's Chesapeake House and Sports Fishing Center on Tilghman Island has the largest privately owned fishing fleet on the Chesapeake. Harrison's will take you out for striper, bluefish, Spanish mackerel, and sea trout at a rate of $109 a person for eight hours of fishing. (410) 886–2121; www.chesapeakehouse.com.

Special Events

May. Chestertown Tea Party Festival. Reenactment of the boarding of the Brigantine *Geddes* and the dumping of its stores of tea into the Chester River. (410) 778–2262; www.chestertownteaparty.com.

June. Antique and Classic Boat Show, Chesapeake Bay Maritime Museum. (410) 745–2916.

September. Annual Candlelight Walking Tour of the historic district of Chestertown to benefit the Historical Society of Kent County. (410) 778–3499.

October. Tilghman Island Day. Skipjack races, boat docking contests, auction, music, and seafood, of course. (410) 745–2882.

Mid-Atlantic Small Craft Festival, St. Michaels. Kayaks, canoes, rowing shells, and sailing skiffs show their stuff. Workshops, races, and kids' activities. (410) 745–2916.

November. Waterfowl Festival, Easton. Exhibition of more than 400 wildlife artists. Includes retriever demonstrations and seminars. Proceeds go toward waterfowl conservation efforts. (410) 822–4567; www.waterfowlfestival.org.

Other Recommended Restaurants

Oxford

Robert Morris Inn, 312 Morris Street; (410) 226–5111; www.robertmorris inn.com. Excellent seafood and classic American dishes. Dining room overlooks the Tred-Avon River. Moderate to expensive.

St. Michaels

208 Talbot, 208 North Talbot Street; (410) 745–3838. Contemporary menu, daily specials, delightful ambience, tops in town. Open for dinner Wednesday through Sunday. Expensive.

Bistro St. Michaels, 403 South Talbot Street; (410) 745–9111. Charming, well-received restaurant that offers a blend of casual French and elegant New American cuisine. The crispy soft-shell crabs come with pesto couscous and grilled vegetable ratatouille. Expensive.

Town Dock Restaurant, 125 Mulberry Street; (410) 745–5577 or (800) 884–0103. Casual, crowded eatery with outside bar and grill; good choice for seafood. Moderate.

Poppi's, 207 North Talbot Street; (410) 745–3158. Breakfast, lunch, hand-dipped ice cream. Inexpensive.

Tilghman Island

Best place for doughnuts: So-Neat Cafe and Bakery, 5772 Tilghman Island Road, Tilghman Island; (410) 886–2143.

Easton

Washington Street Pub, 20 North Washington Street; (410) 822–9011. Good choice for deli sandwiches, burgers, pizza, chili, and drinks. Inexpensive to moderate.

Tidewater Inn, 101 East Dover Street; (410) 822–1300. Gracious dining room serving Eastern Shore specialties. Moderate to expensive.

Other Recommended Lodgings

Tilghman Island

Chesapeake Wood Duck Inn, Gibsontown Road at Dogwood Harbor; (410) 886–2070 or (800) 956–2070; www.wooduckinn.com. Formerly a boardinghouse and bordello, now a lovely six-room Victorian bed-and-breakfast, furnished with antiques, which serves a full gourmet breakfast. Rates: $149–$229 in season.

Harrison's Chesapeake House Country Inn, Wharf Road; (410) 886–2121; www.chesapeakehouse.com. Pleasant waterfront inn catering to families and sports anglers; large country breakfast served. Rates: $115–$130.

Chestertown

White Swan Tavern Bed and Breakfast, 231 High Street; (410) 778–2300; www.whiteswantavern.com. Lovely, completely renovated 200-year-old tavern with four guest rooms and two suites, all with private baths. All guests get continental breakfast, afternoon tea, and a complimentary fruit basket. Rates: $140–$240.

Imperial Hotel, 208 High Street; (410) 778–5000 or (800) 295–0014; www.imperialchestertown.com. Restored Victorian hotel with eleven luxurious rooms and suites, all with private bath, air-conditioning, and cable TV. Rates: $95–$250.

Oxford

Robert Morris Inn, 312 Morris Street; (410) 226–5111 or (888) 823–4012; www.robertmorrisinn.com. Romantic eighteenth-century inn with thirty-five rooms. Most have porches and water views. Rates: $110–$290.

St. Michaels

The Inn at Perry Cabin, 308 Watkins Lane; (410) 745–2200 or (866) 278–9601; www.perrycabin.com. Luxurious eighty-room inn on the water; topflight restaurant; you won't want to leave. Rates $310–$725, including full breakfast and afternoon tea.

Barrett's Bed and Breakfast Inn, 204 North Talbot Street; (410) 745–3322; www.barrettbb.com. Seven-room bed-and-breakfast in an 1860s home that also houses a tearoom and quilt shop. The $200 to $260 tariff includes a full breakfast.

The Parsonage Inn, 210 North Talbot Street; (410) 745–5519 or (800) 394–5519; www.parsonage-inn.com. An 1880s brick Victorian with eight guest rooms, all with air-conditioning and private baths. Full breakfast; free use of bikes. Rates: $100–$195.

Harbour Inn and Marina, 101 North Harbor Road; (410) 745–9001 or (800) 955–9001; www.harbourinn.com. A forty-six-room luxury hotel along the water; includes harborside pool and bar, and the Harbour Lights Restaurant. Bicycle rentals and workout room available. Rates: $189–$459.

Easton

Historic Tidewater Inn, 101 East Dover Street; (410) 822–1300 or (800) 237–8775; www.tidewaterinn.com. Elegant inn with old world charm; 114 beautifully appointed rooms. Air-conditioning, fireplaces, pool, restaurant on premises. Rates: $99–$329.

For More Information

The Talbot County Visitors Center, 11 South Harrison Street, Easton, MD 21601; (410) 770–8000; www.tourtalbot.org.

Chesapeake Bay Maritime Museum, P.O. Box 636, St. Michaels, MD 21663; (410) 745–2916; www.cbmm.org.

Kent County Office of Tourism, 400 South High Street, Chestertown, MD 21620; (410) 778–0416; www.kentcounty.com/visitor.

St. Michaels Business Association, P.O. Box 1221, St. Michaels, MD 21663; (800) 808–7622; www.stmichaelsmd.org.

For more information visit www.tilghmanisland.com.

MARYLAND ESCAPE THREE

Berlin, Assateague Island, and Ocean City

Crowds and Solitude / 2 Nights

The Maryland shore of the Atlantic Ocean is full of delights and contrasts. In this weekend escape you browse the elegant little town of Berlin (where the 1940s-era theater now houses a coffee bar, bookshop, and gallery of top-quality art for sale) and stay in a luxurious restored mansion, with Victorian furniture in every room and a full-course gourmet breakfast in

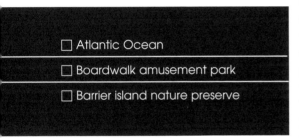

☐ Atlantic Ocean

☐ Boardwalk amusement park

☐ Barrier island nature preserve

the morning. You also get to spend a day at Ocean City—where you'll ride the water slides and roller coasters, eat greasy funnel cakes and cotton candy, and toss balls to win a stuffed bear at a gaudy, joyous carnival on the boardwalk. Combine that with dinner at one of the region's finest restaurants and a day at a peaceful and unspoiled oasis of natural beauty at the Assateague Island National Seashore, where there's just you, the white-sand beach, the wild ponies, and the Atlantic Ocean, and you'll have a truly memorable minivacation.

Day 1 / Morning

Get an early-morning start from Washington, D.C., for a three-hour drive to Berlin, Maryland. Follow U.S. Highway 50 east from Washington for about 140 miles. Eight miles short of the ocean, turn south on U.S. Highway 113, and you'll be in Berlin (accent on the first syllable) within five minutes.

Your immediate destination is the **Merry Sherwood Plantation,** a recently restored mansion that is now a bed-and-breakfast a couple of miles south of Berlin on US 113 at 8909 Worcester Highway; (410) 641–2112 or (800) 660–0358; www.merrysherwood.com. The owners

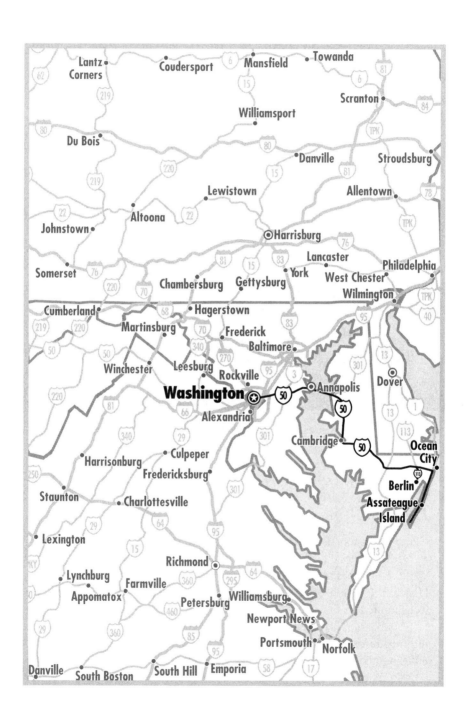

spent two years restoring this old prize, and their love for Victorian furnishings is apparent the minute you step into the foyer and the grand ballroom, where you'll see 14-foot ceilings, chandeliers, velvet furniture, paintings, carved-plaster molding, and bronze statuary.

Each of the eight guest rooms at the Merry Sherwood is different, and all are lovely. Some have their own marble bathrooms, and those on the second floor have working fireplaces. The architectural details and the decorations throughout the mansion delight you with every door you open. Rates: $100–$175 a night during the summer and $75–$150 a night from October through May.

Once you've left your bags and strolled the plantation grounds, head back to **Berlin** for a look around. Be sure to visit the **Globe Theatre,** a beautifully restored theater that has been turned into an upscale community center. Located at 12 Broad Street; (410) 641–0784; www.globe theater.com. Open Monday through Thursday 7:30 A.M. to 10:00 P.M., Friday 7:30 A.M. to midnight, Saturday and Sunday 9:00 A.M. to midnight.

The little theater—its old-fashioned iron seats painted lipstick pink—is still in use, and local artists, including folksingers, jazz musicians, and storytellers, appear regularly.

What's more, the Globe's management has opened up the space around the theater for selected shops and stores, including a charming bistro, a wine bar, a bookstore, and gift shop and an upstairs gallery selling exquisite handmade jewelry, sculpture, oil and watercolor paintings, and polished wooden bowls.

Ocean City is a 10-mile drive east from Berlin via US 113 and 50. Ignore the strip and head south for the public parking lots near the **boardwalk.** Begin your walk up through the amusement parks and arcades at the south end of the boardwalk, and prepare to enjoy every bit of it. Where else can you buy five tasteless T-shirts for $10; have a funnel cake, candy apple, and bag of caramel corn for lunch; and win an appalling stuffed animal by throwing baseballs just right? And then you can lose it all on a gut-flinging "carny" ride like the Viking Ship, which rocks you back and forth until you're nearly upside down and shrieking for mercy. You'll love it.

L U N C H : Have lunch on the Ocean City boardwalk. The possibilities here are legion.

Afternoon

There are two main amusement parks at Ocean City: **Trimper's Rides of Ocean City** at Boardwalk and South First Street (410–289–8617; www.beach-net.com/trimpers) and the **Jolly Roger Amusement Park** at Thirtieth Street and Coastal Highway (410–289–3477; www.jollyroger park.com). Trimper's is open from 1:00 P.M. to midnight weekdays and noon to midnight weekends. A "wristband special" permitting unlimited rides between noon and 6:00 P.M. costs $20. The Jolly Roger is open 2:00 P.M. to midnight March through October. Its afternoon special costs about $16.

The Jolly Roger also operates **Splash Mountain Water Park,** which has ten water slides. There, kids can spend happy hours shooting down the labyrinth of curves, bumps, and incredibly long descents on their inner tubes, propelled by streams of water until they go flying into a pool of water. Then they climb to the top and do it again. And again. Open 10:00 A.M. to 9:00 P.M. A four-hour pass costs $31 for adults, $11 for children shorter than 42 inches. Located at 2901 Philadelphia Avenue; (410) 289–6962.

Teenagers seem to be drawn to the arcades full of video games on the boardwalk. If you dare to venture in, you'll feel like you're in Dante's *Inferno* or, at a minimum, a Mad Max movie. The noise is incredible, the games assault your eyeballs, and the kids have a ball.

Don't think that Ocean City is just for big kids and lunatics. There is a section of rides for little children set aside within the arcade building, near the south end of the amusement park. Here, tiny kids can enjoy gentle carousel rides and slow-moving cars, protected from the hubbub of the carnival going on outdoors.

Ocean City is a scene. It's a little like a county fair on fast-forward, set right on the ocean. One of the things you must do is buy a big bucket of **Thrashers** french fries, douse them with vinegar and salt, stick a straw into a long glass of lemonade, and park yourself on a bench and just watch the people go by. There are halter-topped and muscle-shirted couples with arms around each other and tattoos rippling. There are older couples holding hands and remembering the carnivals of their youth. There are proud parents snapping pictures of their three-year-olds on the carousel ponies. And there are the shrieks of older kids as they go flying by on the Tilt-a-Whirl or roller coaster.

But not all of Ocean City is boardwalk. When you've had your fill, take a stroll out to the beach—about a hundred yards away—and get your feet wet in the Atlantic Ocean.

DINNER: Another Ocean City trademark is its large selection of restaurants, most specializing in seafood. Try one of the fresh fish specials at the **Angler Restaurant,** a sixty-plus-year-old mainstay at the beach, and you'll receive a complimentary hour-long scenic cruise. Located at 312 Talbot Street; (410) 289–7424. Moderate.

LODGING: Merry Sherwood Plantation.

Day 2 / Morning

BREAKFAST: Have some piping-hot coffee, fruit, homemade bread and rolls, and an omelette or quiche at the Merry Sherwood to start you on your way.

After breakfast, drive into Berlin and pick up a picnic-lunch-to-go at the **Raynes Reef** lunch counter, at the corner of South Main and Broad Streets; (410) 641–2131. This old-time classic diner, complete with stools along the counter and ice-cream sodas, will pack you some submarine sandwiches and bags of chips for a picnic lunch at the beach. Stop at the drugstore across the street and pick up lots of bottled water, sunblock, and, above all, insect repellent.

Your destination today is **Assateague Island National Seashore,** which you reach by driving 3 miles east of Berlin on Maryland Highway 376 and about 5 miles south on Maryland Highway 611 to the Verrazano Bridge, which crosses over to Assateague Island. This lovely spot is only 10 miles from Ocean City, but it could be on another planet. When you reach Assateague, be sure to stop at the **Barrier Island Visitor Center,** which has exhibits, an aquarium, maps, and publications. It is located just north of the Verrazano Bridge; (410) 641–1441; www.nps.gov/asis.

Assateague is a barrier island, with clean Atlantic surf, rolling dunes, and scrubby forests of loblolly pines, bayberry trees, tall grasses, and wildflowers. Because it is owned by the National Park Service, it has absolutely none of the urban sprawl, concessions, and billboards that have marred so many of the East Coast beaches. Assateague is a national treasure, kept safe and pristine for you and the wild ponies who share the island.

At the visitor center you can learn more about the ponies, which are said to be descended from a herd left on the island in the 1700s by Eastern Shore planters. Beware: The ponies bite and kick, and feeding them is prohibited.

Assateague offers primitive camping but little else, so once you've parked your car and lugged your picnic provisions out to the sand, you can find yourself virtually isolated within a few hundred yards of the parking area. Lay out your blanket, and settle in for the day.

LUNCH: Picnic at the beach.

Afternoon

More fun at the beach, but a word to the wise—bring lots of ultrastrong sunblock and rub it everywhere. Also, the mosquitos and flies on the island, once you've left the water's edge, are legendary. They'll carry you off if you haven't slathered on repellent.

Assateague is as idyllic a spot as you'll ever find. Plan to spend the full day here. When you're ready to get out of the water, take one or all of three short nature walks that explore the unusual foliage on the island, including wind-stunted trees and bushes. Don't forget your camera. The ponies, as well as small sika deer, are liable to pop up anywhere!

Back at the Merry Sherwood, treat yourself to a long soak or shower, then drive into Berlin for a fine gourmet meal.

DINNER: The **Atlantic Hotel,** 2 North Main Street (410–641–3589), has an award-winning kitchen that serves up tasty seafood, poultry, and meat dishes with style. The dining room is exquisite, set with crystal, china, and crisp linen, and the service is attentive. In addition to the staples you'd expect at a very good seafood restaurant, the chef here prepares daily specials such as grilled tuna steak topped with corn and saki relish accompanied by a coriander purple sticky rice cake and bok choy. Follow that with any of the excellent desserts, and you have the perfect meal. Expensive. Should the dining room at the Atlantic be booked, or if you are in search of a more casual meal, you'll eat very well indeed at the Atlantic Hotel's **Drummer's Cafe,** which serves sandwiches as well as full-course meals both inside and out on the garden patio.

LODGING: The Merry Sherwood.

Day 3 / Morning

BREAKFAST: On your last day in the area, sleep in at the Merry Sherwood, grab breakfast there, then drive to the beach one last time for a walk along the waves or a quick dip. If you swim or sunbathe at Ocean City, there are public bathhouses on the boardwalk at North First Street and at Wicomico Street, so you can shower and change. On Assateague

Island, you can rinse off and change at the restrooms at the camp-grounds.

Your return trip home via US 50 will take about three hours.

There's More

Parasailing. O.C. Parasail, located at the Talbot Street Pier in Ocean City (410–723–1464; www.ocean-city.com/parasail), offers short 400- to 800-foot-high rides for $45–$70.

Sailing. You can rent a sailboat for $45–$50 an hour or $120–$150 a day at Sailing, Etc., 4605 Coastal Highway, Ocean City; (410) 723–1144. Lessons are an extra $30 an hour. You can also rent kayaks, sailboards, and in-line skates.

The **Sea Rocket.** The *Sea Rocket,* an enormous speedboat (150 passengers), offers a fifty-minute ride on the ocean and along Assateague Island for pony watching. Wear casual clothes. Rates: $16 for adults, $12 for seniors, free for children twelve and under; each adult can bring an additional child under twelve for $5.00. Located at Talbot Street Pier; (410) 289–5887; www.searocket.com.

Planet Maze. Rainy-day fun for kids of all ages at indoor high-tech arcade. Located at 3305 Coastal Highway, Ocean City; (410) 524–4386; www.planetmaze.com. Open year-round from 9:00 A.M. to midnight.

Special Events

April. Ward World Championship Wildlife Carving Competition. Decoy carving in Ocean City. (410) 742–4988; www.wardmuseum.org.

June. Village Fair in Berlin. Arts and crafts, live entertainment, museum tours, bathtub races, a lawn mower parade, food, games. (410) 641–4775.

August. White Marlin Open. Hundreds of anglers and thousands of spectators flock to the white marlin capital of the world to watch contestants compete for more than $2 million in prize money. (410) 289–9229 or (800) 626–2326; www.whitemarlinopen.com.

September. Sunfest. Ocean City celebrates the end of summer in late September with food, games, arts and crafts, kite flying, and music. (410) 289–2800 or (800) 626–2326; www.ococean.com.

Other Recommended Restaurants

Berlin

Blue Water Cafe, 9913 Old Ocean City Boulevard; (410) 641–3250. A pleasant and comfortable restaurant with traditional offerings: steak, chicken, pasta, sandwiches, salads, and—of course—seafood. Inexpensive to moderate.

Best place for doughnuts: DelVecchio's Bakery, 120 North Main Street; (410) 641–2300. Open Wednesday through Sunday.

Ocean City

Phillips Crab House, Twenty-first Street and Coastal Highway; (410) 289–6821; www.phillipsseafood.com/phillipscrabhouse. Crown jewel of the local chain that may serve the best crab in Maryland. Seats 1,200 people, so arrive early. Moderate.

Bayside Lunch Box, Eighty-first Street and Coastal Highway; (410) 524–6700. First-rate Philly cheesesteaks, vegetarian sandwiches, salads, baked goods. Inexpensive.

Reflections Restaurant and Wine Bar, Sixty-seventh Street and Oceanside; (410) 524–5252. Dress for dinner. Nicely prepared and presented continental and local cuisine. Try one of the specialties cooked tableside. Moderate to expensive.

Hobbit, Eighty-first Street and the bay; (410) 524–8100. Casual year-round dining with pub atmosphere; fresh seafood, beef, veal. Moderate.

English's Family Restaurant, Fifteenth Street and Philadelphia Avenue; (410) 289–7333. Local chain featuring bargain breakfast and dinner buffets; good choice for families, especially if you like fried chicken and sweet potato biscuits. Inexpensive to moderate.

For additional restaurants in the area, see Delaware Escape Two.

Other Recommended Lodgings

Berlin

Atlantic Hotel, 2 North Main Street; (410) 641–3589 or (800) 814–7672; www.atlantichotel.com. Hundred-year-old Victorian luxury hotel known up and down the coast for its charm, hospitality, and kitchen. Sixteen rooms with private baths; complimentary continental breakfast. Rates: $65–$215.

Ocean City

An Inn on the Ocean, 1001 Atlantic Avenue; (410) 289–8894 or (888) 226–6223; www.innontheocean.com. Year-round bed-and-breakfast on the ocean with six guest rooms; all have private baths, televisions, VCRs, and air-conditioning. Free use of bicycles and beach equipment; continental breakfast. Rates: $130–$350.

Atlantic House, 501 North Baltimore Avenue; (410) 289–2333; www.atlantichouse.com. Seventy-plus-year-old Victorian house with eleven guest accommodations, ranging from an apartment to bedrooms with shared baths. Air-conditioning and cable TV; full breakfast. Rates: $50–$225.

Talbot Inn, located at the Talbot Street Pier; (410) 289–9125 or (800) 659–7703; www.talbotstreetpier.com. Year-round bayside motel with forty-five efficiency units; cable and microwaves. Rates: $35–$139, depending on the season.

Inlet Lodge Motel, 804 South Boardwalk; (410) 289–7552 or (800) 294–6538; www.inletlodge.com. Family-friendly motel with thirty-six rooms, all with cable TV, air-conditioning, telephone, and private bath. Convenient to the boardwalk; coffee shop on the premises. Open April through October. Rates: $80–$100.

Dunes Motel, on the beach at Twenty-seventh Street; (410) 289–4414 or (800) 523–2888; www.ocdunes.com. Oceanfront motel with 103 rooms and suites; most have a view of the ocean. Rooms are $29–$224; suites, $59–$299.

Assateague Island

Assateague National Seashore Campgrounds, National Seashore Lane; (410) 641–3030 or (800) 365–2267; www.nps.gov/asis. Call the 800 number for reservations. Forty-nine bayside sites and 104 oceanside sites; restrooms but no hookups. Camping costs $16–$20 a night.

Assateague State Park, MD 611; (410) 641–2120. The campground has 350 sites with restrooms and hookups. Rates: $30–$40.

For additional lodgings in the area, see Delaware Escape Two.

For More Information

Ocean City Convention and Visitors Bureau, 4001 Coastal Highway, Ocean City, MD 21842; (410) 289–2800 or (800) 626–2326; www.ococean.com.

Worcester County Tourism Bureau, 104 West Market Street, Snow Hill, MD 21863; (410) 632–3110 or (800) 852-0335; www.visitworcester.org.

Antietam National Battlefield, Gettysburg, and Catoctin Mountain

A Look at the Past / 2 Nights

> Fourscore and seven years ago our fathers brought forth upon this continent a new nation, conceived in liberty, and dedicated to the proposition that all men are created equal. Now we are engaged in a great civil war, testing whether that nation, or any nation so conceived and so dedicated, can long endure. We are met on a great battlefield of that war. . . .

Thus began one of the greatest speeches in American history: Abraham Lincoln's address at Gettysburg, Pennsylvania, on November 19, 1863. As the National Park Service brochure notes, Lincoln's eloquence four and a half months after the battle "transformed Gettysburg from a scene of carnage into a symbol, giving meaning to the sacrifice of the dead and inspiration to the living."

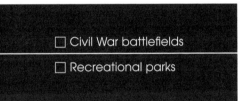

☐ Civil War battlefields

☐ Recreational parks

Gettysburg National Military Park is the centerpiece of a weekend escape to north-central Maryland and south-central Pennsylvania. The battle of Gettysburg holds a particular fascination for many, not only because it is considered to be the decisive battle of the Civil War, but also because the carnage there was so extensive. In the first three days of July 1863, some 51,000 soldiers were killed, wounded, or captured. Gettysburg was the war's costliest battle for both sides, and the bloodiest event on American soil in history.

On your way to Gettysburg, you really should take a short detour to Sharpsburg, Maryland, and the less-crowded Antietam National Battlefield. There, the National Park Service brings the past to life with lectures, tours, war relics, and an excellent film reenacting the epic September 17, 1862, battle between Union and Confederate troops. In that daylong battle, nearly 23,100 people were killed and wounded—more than on any other single day of the Civil War. One historian describes the

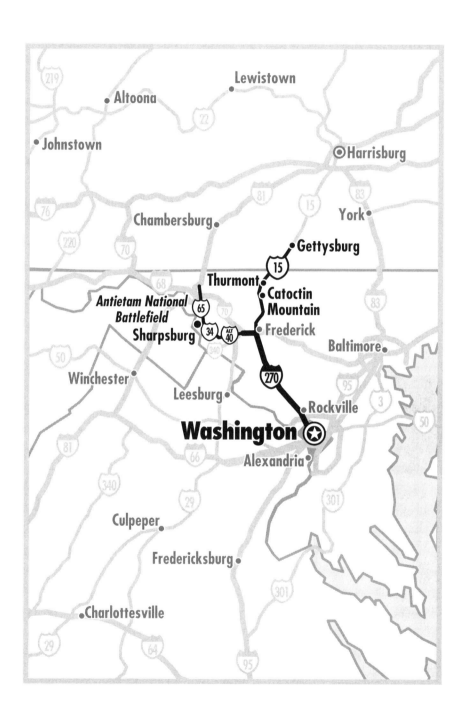

guns of Antietam "slashing at rows of men and corn," and as you walk through the battlefield, you can imagine what it must have been like.

On the way home from Gettysburg, you'll enjoy a stop at Catoctin Mountain, where a national park and a Maryland state park combine to offer hiking, swimming, canoeing, and some of the prettiest scenery Maryland has to offer.

Day 1 / Morning

Antietam National Battlefield is 70 miles from Washington, and if you leave by 10:00 A.M., you can have an early lunch en route before touring the battlefield. To reach Antietam, take Interstate 270 north to Frederick, Interstate 70 west a few miles to exit 49, and Alternate U.S. Highway 40 west about 12 miles over South Mountain to Boonsboro. There, turn left onto Maryland Highway 34 and follow it 6 miles to Sharpsburg. The battlefield is located 1 mile north of Sharpsburg on Maryland Highway 65.

LUNCH: About 7 miles before you reach Antietam, there is a great place for a weekend lunch: **Old South Mountain Inn,** 6132 Old National Pike, Boonsboro; (301) 432–6155. This beautiful and capacious restaurant, located in a 250-year-old building, was once regularly frequented by the likes of Henry Clay and Daniel Webster as they traveled to and from Washington. Today, it offers a contemporary menu in a colonial setting. For lunch you can get country ham, beef tenderloin tips with wild mushrooms, chicken, or pasta. The garden room has an excellent view of the surrounding countryside. Moderate to expensive.

Afternoon

The afternoon is devoted to an exploration of **Antietam National Battlefield,** which is one of the National Park Service's many great historic treasures. The battlefield is located just north of Sharpsburg on MD 65; (301) 432–5124; www.nps.gov/anti. Open daily 8:30 A.M. to 6:00 P.M., until 5:00 P.M. in winter. Admission is $4.00 per adult; children under sixteen accompanied by an adult are admitted free.

Here, on just a few acres of hills and cornfields, 12,410 Confederates and 10,700 Federal troops were killed or wounded in a single day, September 17, 1862. While the battle itself was not a definitive victory for either side—both sides might be said to have lost, given the massive casualties—Antietam was significant in that the North's failure to convincingly defeat General Lee's army prolonged the war by many months.

At the same time, the failure of the Confederates to hold the area was important because it caused Great Britain to postpone recognition of the Confederacy, a move that was under consideration at the time.

Begin your tour at the visitor center. There you can pick up a map of the battlefield and watch an excellent orientation film. With a background of Civil War songs and quotes from actual soldiers' letters, the film reenacts the battle of Antietam (or the battle of Sharpsburg, as the Confederates called it).

Be sure to visit the small museum at the lower level of the visitor center. It features a collection of artifacts from the battle, including weapons, uniforms, letters, photographs, and medical equipment. It also has an interesting display of quotations from those who participated in the battle. Consider this from one of the soldiers: "The consuming passion in the breast of the average man is to get out of the way . . ." Union major Joseph Hooker wrote, "It has never been my fortune to witness a more bloody, dismal battlefield."

But the highlight of the park is the battlefield itself. You can take a self-guided 8- or 9-mile tour by bike, foot, or car. Each site is carefully labeled with signs describing the battle in detail, and you can rent a tape recorder and cassette that walks you through every phase of the battle. Better, go on an hour-and-a-half tour with a Park Service guide. These Interior Department employees are exceptionally knowledgeable, friendly, and eager to share their love of Civil War history.

When you have completed your visit to Antietam, retrace your 20-mile drive to the western edge of Frederick, where you will connect with U.S. Highway 15 north, which you follow 40 miles to Gettysburg. Once you cross the state line into Pennsylvania, look for signs to Business Route 15 and follow them.

DINNER: **Dobbin House,** 89 Steinwehr Avenue in Gettysburg; (717) 334–2100; www.dobbinhouse.com. Built in 1776, this inn is the oldest building in Gettysburg and has a long and honorable history. During the Civil War it was used as a hospital for wounded soldiers from both sides and, in the 1850s, was a way station on the Underground Railroad for runaway slaves. As part of the house's meticulous restoration, life-size models have been placed in the ceiling crawl space where the real slaves hid.

These days, Dobbin House is a fine restaurant with colonial-era food served by wait staff in period dress. Casual fare is served in the Springhouse Tavern, located in the basement of the house. Huge deli-style sandwiches, grilled chicken, ribs, steak, fish, salads, and soups are available, as well as such homey desserts as hot apple pie and warm gingerbread. For a fancier dinner, head for the Alexander Dobbin Dining Rooms, a set of six different candlelit dining rooms, and enjoy your choice of roast duck, lamb chops, imperial crab, or any of a number of examples of traditional American cuisine. Dinner at the Springhouse Tavern is moderate in price; at the Alexander Dobbin Dining Rooms, expensive.

LODGING: Gettystown Inn, the bed-and-breakfast side of the Dobbin House, has eight comfortable guest rooms and suites decorated with period furniture and Oriental rugs. All rooms have private baths and air-conditioning. Rates: $95–$185.

Day 2 / Morning

BREAKFAST: Enjoy a full breakfast of pancakes and eggs in the parlor of the Dobbin House.

Then, make the visitor center at the **Gettysburg National Military Park** your first stop of the day. It's located on Taneytown Road (Pennsylvania Highway 134, just off Business Route 15); (717) 334–1124; www.nps.gov/gett. Gettysburg National Military Park is open daily 6:00 A.M. to 10:00 P.M. April through October and daily 6:00 A.M. to 7:00 P.M. November through March. The park's visitor center is open 8:00 A.M. to 6:00 P.M., later in the summer. Admission to the park itself is free, but a fee is charged for some of the attractions.

The visitor center has orientation displays; Civil War exhibits; a free film about the battle, *Gettysburg 1863;* and a **Museum of the Civil War.** It also has a fascinating "Electric Map," which uses different-colored lights to show the troop movements and tactics during the course of the three-day battle. Admission to the half-hour electric map show is $4.00 for adults, $3.00 for seniors and children six to sixteen; children under six are admitted free.

Adjacent to the Gettysburg Battlefield is the **Eisenhower National Historic Site,** which was the presidential retreat of Dwight D. Eisenhower. A fifteen-minute orientation tour of the gardens and farm machinery begins the visit. Next is the house tour, which gives a good view of what the President's and Mamie's lives were like at this retreat.

Visitors must take the shuttle bus from the Gettysburg park visitor center and can purchase tickets there as well. Open daily 9:00 A.M. to 4:00 P.M. Admission is $6.00 for adults, $4.50 for ages thirteen through sixteen,

Historic Gettysburg Battlefield

and $3.50 for ages six to twelve; children under six are admitted free. (717) 338–9114; www.nps.gov/eise/index.htm.

LUNCH: After your orientation to the battle of Gettysburg at the visitor center and the Eisenhower site, take a break for lunch at **Dunlap's Restaurant and Bakery,** 90 Buford Avenue; (717) 334–4816. Dunlap's has meat loaf, fresh-roasted turkey sandwiches (hot or cold), dozens of other sandwiches, and a nice salad bar. It also has fresh doughnuts. Inexpensive to moderate.

Afternoon

After lunch, return to the park for a walking or driving tour of the battle-field sights. Rangers conduct free tours at regular intervals or can provide you with the names of Civil War experts who will give you a private tour for a fee—about $40 for one to six people. The Park Service also arranges numerous walking tours with a special emphasis on particular military maneuvers and offers special programs for children.

The driving loop through Gettysburg National Military Park is 18 miles long and is well marked with informative signs about the intricate military maneuvers of the three-day campaign. You'll see such landmarks as the High Water Mark, where—on the second day of battle—the Confederates were said to have reached their highest military achievement of the Civil War with the capture of much of the land near General Meade's headquarters on Cemetery Ridge. Hours later, the Union forces repulsed Pickett's Charge, turning the war to the North's advantage and eventually forcing the Confederates to fall back.

Don't leave the park without walking through the National Cemetery, where thousands of Union and Confederate soldiers who died during the battle of Gettysburg are buried. It was here that Lincoln delivered his two-minute speech four and a half months later, dedicating the cemetery to the proposition that "government of the people, by the people, for the people, shall not perish from the earth." A walk through the cemetery at dusk is a fitting way to end your day at Gettysburg.

DINNER: The Gingerbread Man is a casual publike eatery where you can get decent steaks, broiled or fried seafood, gyros, burgers, and Mexican fare. Located at 217 Steinwehr Avenue; (717) 334–1100. Moderate.

LODGING: Gettystown Inn.

Day 3 / Morning

BREAKFAST: After breakfast at the Gettystown Inn, head for Catoctin Mountain, which you reach by driving 40 miles south on US 15 back toward Frederick and Washington.

There are two adjoining parks located on Catoctin Mountain: **Catoctin Mountain Park,** administered by the National Park Service, and **Cunningham Falls State Park.** The parks, which are in a 6,000-acre forest preserve, offer wilderness hiking, camping, horseback riding, and swimming. Start at the visitor center at Catoctin Mountain Park and pick up a map. There are more than 25 miles of marked trails, so there is a hike for everybody, from thirty minutes of easy walking to a six-hour round-trip of strenuous scrambling.

In spring and fall, Catoctin offers orienteering courses, but the classes fill up quickly, so reserve early if you're interested. Other activities you can enjoy at the parks are scenic drives, snowshoeing, cross-country skiing, canoeing, sailing, and swimming. So pick your pleasure and relax for the day at the "park of presidents." (Camp David is located within Catoctin Mountain Park but is not available for touring.)

Afternoon

LUNCH: There are two snack bars at Cunningham Falls State Park. One is located at the swimming area at Hunting Creek Lake, the other near the falls. Both have sandwiches and ice cream.

While you're there, be sure to see the spectacular waterfall, the largest in Maryland. You can take a long hike and end up at the falls or go there directly from your car on a wheelchair-accessible, 200-yard trail.

The parks are open dawn to dusk, except for campers. Call (301) 663–9388; www.nps.gov/cato. For Cunningham Falls State Park, call (301) 271–7574.

If you're traveling with children, leave time at the end of the afternoon for one final activity. Just 3 miles south of the parks is **Catoctin Wildlife Preserve and Zoo,** US 15, Thurmont; (301) 271–3180; www.cwpzoo .com. Open 9:00 A.M. to 6:00 P.M. from May through September, 10:00 A.M. to 5:00 P.M. in April and October; closed November through March except for occasional weekends. Admission is $13.95 for adults, $11.95 for seniors, and $8.95 for kids two to twelve; children under two admitted free.

Here, many of the animals are outdoors and have plenty of space to roam. There are also a few cages of wild animals, including a tiger and a grizzly bear. For the most part, though, animals and visitors alike seem to be pleased. A peacock struts about on the same paths as the people, and emus, deer, and other creatures graze happily in a large enclosure. There is an aviary full of bright parrots, a baboon cage, and a large collection of reptiles.

The best thing about the zoo park, though, is the petting area, where you can enter a large pasture and pet and snuggle the animals to your heart's content. There is a 575-pound tortoise, a potbellied pig, goats, and sheep. But the most affectionate of all are the pygmy goats from Africa. These darling creatures (the young stand no more than 18 inches high) will come thundering toward you the minute you enter their pen and frisk about joyfully when you scratch their ears. Even the tiniest child (or the oldest adult) will want to pat them.

DINNER: After an afternoon of outdoor activity, an all-you-can-eat dinner seems just right. Go where everybody who visits the area eventually ends up: the **Cozy Restaurant,** 103 Frederick Road (Maryland Highway 806) about 5 blocks from US 15, Thurmont; (301) 271–7373.

You sort of have to see the Cozy to believe it. In the first place, it's anything but cozy. With room after adjoining room, the Cozy can feed more than 700 people in a pinch. And when is the last time you ate at a restaurant that had its own newspaper? You might call it "the diner that ate Thurmont."

Consider the food: For starters, there's always fried chicken, meat loaf, fried fish, ham, mashed potatoes, macaroni salads, and dozens of other home-style dishes at reasonable prices. (Kids under twelve can get a chicken drumstick dinner with unlimited trips to the salad and dessert bars for $4.99.) The dessert bar is enormous; there are eighteen different kinds of pie alone. Also there's a separate ice-cream parlor, a darkly lit bar, and a bakery. Pinball machines line the hallways, and there are lots of trinkets for sale. The trinkets have expanded to the Cozy's cluster of stores across the street. Needless to say, kids and tourists of every description adore the place, and they come here by the busload.

The 60-mile drive back to Washington via US 15 and I–270 will take you just over an hour.

There's More

Miniature Golf. Gettysburg Family Fun Center has a miniature golf course, baseball and softball batting cages, an arcade, and ice cream. Located 1 mile east of the square on U.S. Highway 30 east; (717) 334–4653. There is a similar park near Antietam: Family Recreation Park, 21036 National Pike, Boonsboro; (301) 733–2333.

Antiques. New Oxford, Pennsylvania—about 8 miles east of Gettysburg on US 30—is one of the best antiques-shopping spots within easy driving distance of Washington. Also worth a visit are the shops in Emmitsburg, Maryland (on US 15 just before you cross the state line into Pennsylvania); the shops in Middletown, Maryland (on U.S. Highway 40 about 8 miles west of Frederick); and the shops on Main Street in New Market, Maryland (about 10 miles east of Frederick on Maryland Highway 144).

Used Books. Wonder Book and Video, the largest used bookstore in the Washington-Baltimore area (with more than a million books and thousands of used comic books), is located at 1306 West Patrick Street (US 40 west) in Frederick; (301) 694–5955. Open daily 10:00 A.M. to 10:00 P.M.

Special Events

May. Memorial Day Parade and Ceremony. Oldest Memorial Day parade in the nation. Antietam National Battlefield. (301) 432–8410.

June–July. Civil War Heritage Days. During the last weekend in June and the first week of July, there are parades, concerts, and lectures in Gettysburg, and a reenactment of the 1863 battle at Gettysburg National Military Park, complete with artillery fire and thousands of marching "soldiers." (717) 334–6274.

September. Battle Anniversary Weekend at Antietam National Battlefield Park. Annual event features battlefield encampments, special walking tours, and a Saturday-night torchlight tour. Reservations are necessary. (301) 432–5124.

October. Catoctin Colorfest. Arts and crafts fair in Thurmont. (301) 271–4432; www.colorfest.org.

November. Remembrance Day. Parade and wreath-laying ceremony held in observance of anniversary of Lincoln's Gettysburg Address. (717) 334–6274.

Other Recommended Restaurants

Frederick

Di Francesco's Ristorante, 26 North Market Street; (301) 695–5499. Fresh pasta; casual setting. Moderate.

The Province Restaurant, 129 North Market Street; (301) 663–1441. Elegant but casual restaurant with New American menu in downtown Frederick. Moderate.

Gettysburg

Farnsworth House Inn, 401 Baltimore Street; (717) 334–8838. Civil War–era menu features peanut soup, game pie, spoonbread; candlelight and garden dining. Located in a historic house converted to a bed-and-breakfast inn; not open for lunch. Moderate.

The Herr Tavern and Publick House, 900 Chambersburg Road (US 30 west); (717) 334–4332 or (800) 362–9849. American and continental cuisine in a charming old inn. Moderate to expensive.

General Pickett's Buffet Restaurant, 571 Steinwehr Avenue; (717) 334–7580; www.generalpickettsbuffets.com. All-you-can-eat beef, chicken, ham, salad, dessert; a family favorite. Moderate.

Centuries on the Square (at the Gettysburg Hotel), 1 Lincoln Square; (717) 337–2000; www.gettysburghotel.com. Large, hotel-based restaurant in the heart of downtown. Continental cuisine; dining room and outdoor cafe. Moderate to expensive.

Thurmont

Shamrock Restaurant, 7701 Fitzgerald Road (on US 15); (301) 271–2912; www.shamrockrestaurant.com. Forty-year-old restaurant serving fantastic corned beef and fresh-daily seafood. Also steak, prime ribs, and chicken; everything comes with a potato and vegetable. Moderate.

Mountain Gate Family Restaurant, 133 Frederick Road; (301) 271–4373. Breakfast, lunch, and dinner buffets. Also full menu with dinner specials and sandwiches. Moderate.

More doughnuts: Busy Bee Bakery, 410 Frederick Road; (301) 271–4100. Open at 4:00 A.M. for early birds.

Other Recommended Lodgings

Sharpsburg

Inn at Antietam, 220 East Main Street, Sharpsburg; (301) 432–6601 or (877) 835–6011; www.innatantietam.com. Restored country Victorian nicely furnished with antiques; four guest suites with private baths. The wraparound porch with swings and rockers is a great place to relax. Full breakfast served. Rates: $120–$155. A fifth, extra-large suite (1,000 square feet) rents for $150–$185 a night.

Antietam Overlook Farm, Keedysville; (301) 432–4200 or (800) 878–4241; www.antietamoverlook.com. Mountaintop country inn with a four-state view. All of the inn's six rooms have antiques, fireplaces, and garden baths; full country breakfast. Rates: $165–$240.

Gettysburg

The Brickhouse Inn Bed and Breakfast, 452 Baltimore Street; (717) 338–9337 or (800) 864–3464; www.brickhouseinn.com. Eight guest rooms and two suites in century-old, in-town mansion; queen-size beds, private baths, and air-conditioning; cookies with lemonade or cider in the afternoon; full breakfast always includes shoofly pie. Rates: $99–$169.

Gaslight Inn, 33 East Middle Street; (717) 337–9100 or (800) 914–5698; www.thegaslightinn.com. Downtown bed-and-breakfast with eight guest rooms, all with private baths; fireplaces, gardens; friendly and helpful proprietors. Rates: $119–$195.

Baladerry Inn, 40 Hospital Road; (717) 337–1342 or (800) 220–0025; www.baladerryinn.com. Quiet eight-bedroom bed-and-breakfast in the country just outside Gettysburg; served as a field hospital during the Civil War. Tennis courts and gardens; large rooms with queen-size or twin beds and private baths; full country breakfast. Rates: $135–$235.

Brafferton Inn, 44 York Street; (717) 337–3423 or (866) 337–3423; www.brafferton.com. Restored 1780s home in historic district with twelve guest rooms, all with private bath. Spacious common areas include atrium, deck, garden, and sitting rooms; full breakfast. Rates: $80–$195.

James Gettys Hotel, 27 Chambersburg Street; (888) 900–5275; www.jamesgettyshotel.com. Renovated two-century-old historic hotel with eleven guest suites; each has a bedroom, sitting room, kitchenette, and private bath. Rates: $130–$250.

Thurmont

Cozy Country Inn, MD 806 just off US 15; (301) 271–4301; www.cozyvillage.com. Standard motel with twenty-one remodeled rooms, some with Jacuzzis. Fine for families; presidential aides and the national press corps staking out Camp David often stay here. Rates: $60–$165.

Catoctin Mountain National Park (301–663–5895) has a fifty-one-site, wooded, no-reservation campground. Sites rent for $20; cabins rent for $40 and up. Cunningham Falls State Park (301–271–7574) has 180 campsites that rent for $25–$30.

For More Information

Tourism Council of Frederick County and Frederick Visitors Center, 19 East Church Street, Frederick, MD 21701; (301) 228–2888 or (800) 999–3613; www.fredericktourism.org.

Antietam National Battlefield and Cemetery, P.O. Box 158, Sharpsburg, MD 21782; (301) 432–5124; www.nps.gov/anti.

Gettysburg Visitors Information Center, 89 Steinwehr Avenue, Gettysburg, PA 17325; (717) 334–2100; www.gettysburg.com.

Western Maryland

Heading West on the National Pike / 2 Nights

This weekend escape is a driving trip in western Maryland that lets you travel in time as well as space. You'll take the interstate to Frederick, then pick up the National Pike and follow it as far as Grantsville, Maryland, and beyond to southern Pennsylvania. You'll exchange the chain hotels, the fast-food franchises, and the four lanes of whizzing cars on the interstate for a back-roads route that is nearly deserted in places.

☐ Back-roads drive

☐ Mountain crafts community

☐ Shopping

☐ Country stores

☐ Old inns and hotels

☐ C&O Canal

Your drive will take you by ancient stone fences and emerald green forests and fields, and through quaint little towns that time seems to have passed by. Best of all, you'll get to experience a bit of American history while you're at it.

The National Pike is really four roads in one place, built over one another as the country's needs grew and changed. Starting out as an Indian trail winding up and down hills and through the Allegheny Mountains, it grew to be a gravel post road for travelers in colonial times, and the section between Cumberland, Maryland, and Wheeling, West Virginia, was the first road financed by the federal government. The advent of the automobile brought paved roads, three lanes in places, but still narrow and winding as they snaked their way through the mountains of western Maryland.

The most recent chapter in the story of the National Pike was the development of the interstate highway system in the 1950s and 1960s. Now it almost seems that the small communities that grew up and thrived along the National Pike in its heyday have been forgotten in the noisy race to progress on the nearby interstate. But there is still lots to explore, from the distinctive

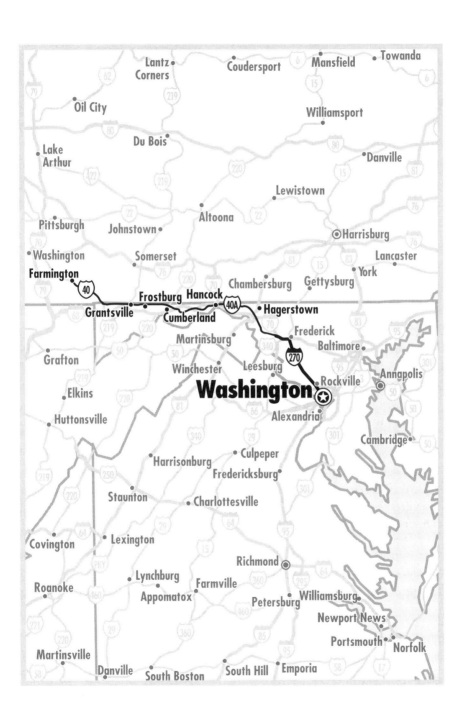

National Pike mile markers that you can still see here and there, to the crafts and music of Appalachia, which are much in evidence in this area.

So take a spin on the National Pike—variously called Route 40, Alternate Route 40, Scenic Route 40, and Maryland Highway 144. In addition to the pure pleasure of the drive, you'll have a chance to visit an artisans' community where mountain crafts such as quilting, ironwork, and wood carving are demonstrated in a small settlement of restored eighteenth-century cabins. There's a century-old country store to explore, majestic old inns and hotels to stay in, and the C&O Canal path to tempt you to slow down and take a stroll.

In short, driving the National Pike lets you explore and enjoy 200 years of American history. All this, and some of the prettiest countryside the state of Maryland has to offer. Ladies and gentlemen, start your engines!

Day 1 / *Morning*

Leave Washington by early morning on a Friday, if you can, to get a jump-start on a terrific weekend. Take Interstate 270 to the outskirts of Frederick, then follow U.S. Highway 15 north a couple of miles to U.S. Highway 40 west. Follow US 40 west a half mile or so and turn left to get onto the National Pike (Alternate Route 40). You'll notice the difference almost immediately. The strip-mall commercialism of the western side of Frederick gives way to rolling countryside, and there's not a fast-food joint in sight!

About 2 miles up the Pike, there is a pullover at **Braddock Heights** with a beautiful view of the verdant valley below. A few miles farther is the little town of **Middletown**—which you would never even know about if you confined your driving to the expressway. Notice how the houses, with their low front porches, are built right up against the road. It's as if their owners didn't want to miss one minute of the traffic passing to and fro in front of them on the National Pike.

Six or 7 miles past Middletown, you'll come to **Washington Monument State Park** about a mile or so north of the Pike on Monument Road; watch for signs on the right-hand side of the road. Take a quarter of an hour to walk up to the monument, which the citizens of Boonsboro erected in two days in 1827 in honor of George Washington. It is said to be the first-ever monument to Washington's memory. After falling into disrepair, the monument was restored in 1882 by the citizens of Boonsboro and again in 1933 by the Civilian Conservation Corps. The oddly shaped building (rather like a great, stone milk bottle) commands a panoramic view of the valley below and the Blue Ridge Mountains beyond, which you can see even better by climbing up the interior stairway to the top. (301) 791–4767.

After another 4 or 5 miles, you'll drive through **Boonsboro,** and there you'll see your first franchise: a '50s-era Tastee-Freez. As you continue your drive, notice the bright red farmhouses and barns and stone fences in the area.

When you reach **Hagerstown,** about 35 miles from where you started on the Pike, abandon the Alternate Route 40 signs and take a driving tour through town in the square mile bounded by Potomac Street on the south, East Avenue on the east, Prospect Street on the north, and Memorial Boulevard on the west. It's a great way to see the European architecture, with Dutch- and German-influenced trimmings and roofs.

Don't miss the small, pretty **City Park** at 110 Key Street (at the intersection of Prospect Street and Memorial Boulevard), where you can visit the 1739 **Jonathan Hager House and Museum,** authentically restored with furnishings of the period, and the **Mansion House Art Center,** where local artists have studios. The Hager House (301–739–8393; www .hager house.org) is open Tuesday through Saturday 10:00 A.M. to 4:00 P.M., Sunday 2:00 to 5:00 P.M., April through December; closed Thanksgiving, Christmas, and the last week in November through the first Tuesday in December. Admission is $3.00 for adults, $2.00 for seniors, and $1.00 for kids six to twelve; children under six are admitted free. The Mansion House Art Center (301–797–6813) is open Thursday, Friday, and Saturday 11:00 A.M. to 4:00 P.M., Sunday 1:00 to 5:00 P.M. April through December; Friday and Saturday 11:00 A.M. to 4:00 P.M., Sunday 1:00 to 5:00 P.M. January through March.

LUNCH: Take advantage of the city's German heritage with a Bavarian feast at **Schmankerl Stube,** 58 South Potomac Street (301–797–3354), thought by some to be the best German fare within a hundred miles of Washington. The Schmankerl Stube is fragrant and homey, with wood beams and red-and-white-checked tablecloths, and a Munich beer on tap. Lunch offerings include Bavarian meat loaf with cabbage and potatoes, lots of sausage choices, goulash, and potato soup. Moderate.

Afternoon

After lunch, find US 40 west and drive 6 or 7 miles until, at the top of a hill, you'll come to Wilson Village, the heart of which is **Wilson's General**

Store, an absolutely terrific old emporium that has been in operation since 1852. Unlike kitschy country-store wannabes everywhere, Wilson's is a real treasure, without a false note in the place. All the beautiful old antique counters, shelves, cracker boxes, and containers are there, and ancient pots, pans, baskets, bridles, and farm equipment dangle from the ceiling.

It's not always clear what's for sale and what's not, because it seems more like a museum than a store. There are huge chunks of cheese in the antique cheese safe, crackers in the Sears Cracker box, dog collars, colored thread, bolts of cloth, seed packets, dozens of jars of penny candy on the counter, an antique tricycle on the ceiling, and lots of pretty blue and white reproduction crockery, and, yes, they're all for sale. There's even an old checkerboard set up, inviting you to sit down and play. Located just off US 40 at 14921 Rufus Wilson Road; (301) 582–4718. Open Monday through Saturday 7:30 A.M. to 6:00 P.M., Sunday 9:00 A.M. to 5:00 P.M.

Be sure your wanderings take you upstairs for an entirely different shopping experience, though it is owned by the same store. The **Upstairs Emporium** sells beautiful women's clothing, with everything from hand-woven jackets to silk scarves. There are lots of unusual imports and original designs. Open Monday through Saturday 10:00 A.M. to 5:00 P.M., Sunday 1:00 to 5:00 P.M.

When you can pull yourself away from the country store, follow Alternate 40 west for 12 miles until it ends just past Indian Springs. Then you'll have to take Interstate 70 west for 9 miles along the upper Potomac River and MD 144 west for 2 miles to your next destination, **Hancock.**

There, take a half hour to study a little local history (and stretch your legs) with a walk along the **C&O Canal,** which runs right by Hancock. Pick up a map at the visitor information center and museum at 326 East Main Street, Hancock; (301) 678–5463; www.nps.gov/choh. This National Park Service facility also has a slide show, and artifacts and photos of canal life. Open Friday through Tuesday 9:00 A.M. to 4:30 P.M.

For Washingtonians familiar with the pedestrian, bike, and dog congestion of the canal towpath north of Georgetown, this quiet section of the very same towpath will be a welcome contrast. You can walk for miles without running into anybody, with the Potomac by your side the whole way.

While you are in Hancock, make a beeline for **Weaver's Restaurant and Bakery,** which is right along the Pike at 77 West Main Street; (301) 678–6346. There you can get a restorative cup of coffee.

Weaver's is clearly a beloved institution. The booths are full of locals, and lines form at the bakery counter for fancy decorated cakes, or baked specialties like "garlic pull–apart" rolls and potato fudge. (Go ahead, try the potato fudge. It's like soft, smooth fondant swirled with peanut butter. Delicious!)

And, yes, Weaver's has doughnuts. In fact, the National Pike may be a doughnut fancier's version of heaven. For example, besides Weaver's, there's also Lorenzo's in Frostburg (301–689–6570) and Krumpe's in Hagerstown (301–733–6103). The latter is open only from 7:30 P.M. to 2:30 A.M.

Heading west from Hancock, the National Pike is MD 144, and it parallels Interstate 68. If you are interested in some of the geological history of the area, you might consider getting on I–68 at exit 77 and getting off at exit 74 in order to visit the **Sideling Hill Exhibit Center** located on the interstate. It shows some of the rock formations of the mountains in this area, as well as local flora and fauna; (301) 842–2155; www.dnr.state.md.us/public lands/western/sidelinghill.html. Open daily 9:00 A.M. to 5:00 P.M.; free.

Get back on the Pike for the approximately 40-mile drive from Hancock to Cumberland. Here the National Pike is variously labeled MD 144, Scenic Route 40, and Alternate Route 40. For the last 2 miles into Cumberland, you'll have to get on I–68 at exit 46. Get off again at exit 44 and take Alternate US 40 into **Cumberland,** where you'll spend the evening.

DINNER: If you lived in Cumberland and you wanted steak, seafood, or pasta, you'd likely head for **Geatz's Restaurant,** 202 Paca Street (301–724–2223), which has been pleasing locals for more than a century and a quarter at moderate prices. On the other hand, if you overdid lunch or had more than potato fudge at the bakery, you might gravitate toward **Curtis' Coney Island Famous Weiners,** where the hot dogs have been served with mustard, onions, and meat sauce for almost a century. Located at 35 North Liberty Street; (301) 759–9707. Inexpensive.

LODGING: **The Inn at Walnut Bottom** consists of two adjacent town houses, one built in 1820, the other in 1890. Both houses are beautifully furnished with antiques and period reproductions. There are twelve air-conditioned guest rooms and suites; most have private baths, and all have phones and televisions. Located at 120 Greene Street; (301) 777–0003 or (800) 286–9718; www.iwbinfo.com. Rates: $107–$162.

Day 2 / Morning

BREAKFAST: The Inn at Walnut Bottom serves a large country breakfast that includes fruit, an entree, and something (like pecan sour cream coffee cake) from the oven.

After breakfast, resume your trek west. A highlight of your road trip this morning will be winding through the **Cumberland Narrows.** The threadlike passage runs through a valley with mountains on both sides of you. The layered rock is massively exposed and towers above you. Locals call the cliff on the left "Lovers Leap," although there are no known cases of leaping lovers.

Be sure to stop at the **LaVale Toll Gate House,** about 5 miles west of Cumberland. This beautifully proportioned, seven-sided brick structure, with a tower, bright yellow door, and dark green shutters, was built in 1836 and was one of the first toll-collecting facilities in America. You can see the posts on each side of the road, from which a chain was stretched to stop the horses, buggies, and carriages. Tours of the inside are available on summer weekend afternoons. (310) 777–5132.

From LaVale, continue driving west on Alternate US 40 about 5 miles to the picturesque town of **Frostburg.** There, pick up a map of the town at one of the local businesses and spend an hour or so exploring Main Street and the adjoining cross streets, which are lined with historic buildings and homes. Notice the **Nelson Beall House,** built in 1876, at 49 West Main Street; **St. Michael's Church,** dating from 1870, at 28 East Main Street; and the **Frost Mansion** at 56 Frost Avenue, which was a renowned hotel retreat for Washington and Baltimore residents a hundred years ago.

Also stop at **Shops by the Depot,** where you can buy (or look at) antiques, pottery, Amish furniture, mountain crafts, and quilts. For kids, there is a handful of toy stores, including one that sells toy trains. Located on Depot Street; (301) 689–3676. Open daily except Monday (hours vary).

Heading west from Frostburg, your final morning destination is Grantsville, about 15 miles away. As you continue your trip, keep your eyes peeled for the distinctive obelisk-shaped National Pike mile markers (looking like miniature Washington Monuments) that once marked every single mile on the Pike. Most are gone now, but every now and then you'll see one, standing about 3.5 feet tall. Also notice the roadside parks, built by the Civilian Conservation Corps in the 1930s, which still serve as handy picnic stops for travelers.

When you arrive in **Grantsville,** look first for the **Casselman Hotel.** It started out as a hostelry, serving Pike travelers in 1824. It is now showing its age, but it's still full of National Pike character. Its dining room serves Amish food, and downstairs is a bakery where Mennonite and Amish women whip up fresh rolls, pies, and bread, both to serve in the restaurant and to sell. Located on Main Street in Grantsville; (301) 895–5266; www .thecasselman.com.

Western Maryland Scenic Railroad

LUNCH: It's best to be hungry when you go to lunch at the **Penn Alps Restaurant,** located on Alternate US 40 in Grantsville; (301) 895–5985; www.pennalps.com. The Penn Alps features a fairly standard middle-America menu, but it has Mennonite and Pennsylvania Dutch dishes as well. Prices are inexpensive to moderate—a sausage, potato, coleslaw, and dried-corn special costs about $10. There are also chicken, fish, and beef dishes on the menu, and on weekend evenings, there's an all-you-can-eat smorgasbord.

Afternoon

After lunch, peek in at the **Penn Alps Craft Shop** in the same building. There are hundreds of crafts from Appalachia on display, including beautiful handmade baskets, textiles, carved birds, and dulcimers. Open daily 9:00 A.M. to 8:00 P.M. Memorial Day through October; Monday, Tuesday, Thursday 10:00 A.M. to 7:00 P.M., Wednesday and Friday through Sunday 10:00 A.M. to 8:00 P.M. in winter.

The Penn Alps building itself is worth an extended look; three of the six dining rooms were once part of the log cabin hospitality house and stagecoach stop called Little Crossings Inn.

Take a moment to cross the grounds to the beautiful **Casselman River Bridge** just next door. It was the longest single-span stone bridge when it was built nearly two centuries ago. Also nearby is Stanton's Mill, a restored 1797 grain mill operated by waterpower.

Adjacent to Penn Alps and affiliated with it is the fascinating **Spruce Forest Artisans Village,** a small cluster of original eighteenth- and nineteenth-century log cabins that were moved to this secluded spot under tall pine trees. Open Monday through Saturday 10:00 A.M. to 5:00 P.M. (301) 895–3332; www.spruceforest.org.

The Artisans Village was the creation of an elderly Mennonite scholar, Dr. Alta Schrock. She started the nonprofit enterprise (which also includes the gift shop, the flourishing restaurant, and a museum) as a way to honor and save the ancient crafts of Appalachia.

Here, talented artisans in period dress work at their looms, forges, quilt frames, and potter's wheels just as they might have a hundred years ago. Each of the cabins is a working studio as well as a gift shop, and the artists are glad to answer questions about their work.

At the end of the afternoon, follow the National Pike (now US 40) west from Grantsville 9 miles to the Pennsylvania state line and then another 15 miles or so to your resting spot for the day—the **Stone House Restaurant and Country Inn,** 3023 National Pike, Farmington, Pennsylvania; (724) 329–8876 or (800) 274–7138; www.stonehouseinn .com. The Stone House was one of the first inns on the National Pike and has been welcoming visitors since 1822. It has ten small but very comfortable Victorian guest rooms and six larger rooms in the new wing. It also has a lounge, a tavern, two dining rooms, and a first-rate restaurant. Rates at the Stone House are $89 to $149 a night.

DINNER: The cheery Stone House Restaurant offers a traditional menu with a wide selection of seafood, beef, and Italian entrees. Prices are moderate.

LODGING: The Stone House Inn.

Day 3 / *Morning*

BREAKFAST: The Stone House serves a continental breakfast of breads and muffins.

Within a few miles of the Stone House are four historic sites maintained by the National Park Service that are worth a morning's study. There's **Fort Necessity National Battlefield,** where the French and Indian War began in 1754 and where the young George Washington fought his first battle (on behalf of the British, who lost); **Mt. Washington Tavern,** a restored 1820s tavern commemorating the early days of the trek west on the Old National Pike; British general **Braddock's Grave,** located 1 mile west of Fort Necessity; and **Jumonville Glen,** where British forces surprised a French troop in a prelude to the battle of Fort Necessity. The attractions are open from 8:00 A.M. to sunset year-round; the visitor center at the fort is open daily from 9:00 A.M. to 5:00 P.M. Admission to all the sites is $5.00 for everyone age sixteen and older; children fifteen and younger are admitted free. (724) 329–5512; www.nps.gov/fone.

LUNCH: After your morning of historical touring, retrace your steps to Grantsville for lunch at the **Hilltop Inn Restaurant,** US 40; (301) 895–5168. There you can get no-frills, home-style cooking, or you can make your own lunch at the salad bar.

Afternoon

From Grantsville, you can make the 180-mile return trip to Washington in just over three hours via I–68 east, I–70 east, and I–270 south.

There's More

Washington County Museum of Fine Arts. Hagerstown museum with a permanent art collection of old masters, portraits, and landscapes, as well as changing exhibits; also home to chamber music series. Located at City Park; (301) 739–5727; www.washcomuseum.org. Open Tuesday through Friday 9:00 A.M. to 5:00 P.M., Saturday 9:00 A.M. to 4:00 P.M., Sunday 1:00 to 5:00 P.M. Admission is free.

Western Maryland Scenic Railroad. Three-hour 1916 Baldwin steam locomotive ride along scenic railroad passes in the Allegheny Mountains; includes lunch stop in Frostburg. Located at 13 Canal Street, Cumberland; (301) 759–4400 or (800) 872–4650; www.wmsr.com. Open Friday through

Sunday May through September, daily in October, and weekends in November and early December. Reservations are necessary; call for hours of departure. Summer ticket prices: $23 for adults, $21 for seniors, and $12 for children two to twelve. Children under two travel free.

Thrasher Carriage Museum. Collection of nineteenth- and twentieth-century horse-drawn conveyances, including sleighs, carriages, and dog carts. Located at the old railway depot in Frostburg; (301) 689–3380; www.thrashercarriage.com. Open Wednesday through Saturday 10:00 A.M. to 4:00 P.M., Sunday 10:00 A.M. to 3:00 P.M. March through December; closed January and February. Admission is $4.00 for adults, $2.00 for children six to eighteen; children under six are admitted free.

Deep Creek Lake. Maryland's largest freshwater lake, located south of the National Pike near Oakland; (301) 387–4386 or (888) 387–5237; www.deepcreeklake.org. Numerous attractions, including swimming, boating, fishing, hiking, and skiing in winter. Dozens of places to stay and eat.

Special Events

June. Annual Heritage Days Festival. Food, music, crafts, children's rides in Cumberland. (301) 722–0037; www.heritagedaysfestival.com.

July. Summerfest and Quilt Show. Dozens of craft workers and quilters gather at Penn Alps in Grantsville; music and storytelling. (301) 895–5985.

August. Augustoberfest. Hagerstown celebrates its German heritage with food, music (Bavarian and rock 'n' roll), and crafts. (301) 739–8577, ext. 116.

Other Recommended Restaurants

Boonsboro

Old Pike Inn Grill and Draft Pub, 7704 Old National Pike; (301) 416–2444. Friendly pub in a very old cattle auction hall; good choice for fried catfish, chicken, steaks. Inexpensive to moderate.

Cumberland

Oxford House Restaurant, 129 Baltimore Street; (301) 777–7101. Upscale restaurant with contemporary continental menu. Moderate to expensive.

When Pigs Fly, corner of Valley and Mechanic Streets; (301) 722–7447. Delicious barbecue and more. Inexpensive to moderate.

Hagerstown

Junction 808, 808 Noland Drive at Virginia Avenue; (301) 791–3639. Family-run and family-oriented railroad theme restaurant serving '50s-style main dishes and sandwiches kids will love. Inexpensive.

Frostburg

Giuseppe's Italian Restaurant, 11 Bowery Street; (301) 689–2220. Pasta, veal, seafood, and vegetarian entrees in a casual setting. Moderate.

Au Petit Paris, 86 East Main Street; (301) 689–8946 or (800) 207–0956. French cuisine, good wine list, pleasant ambience. Moderate.

Gandalf's, 20 East Main Street; (301) 689–2010. Eclectic selection of offerings, including organic and vegetarian meals as well as Mexican, African, Middle Eastern, and Thai dishes. Inexpensive.

For additional listings see Maryland Escape Four and Pennsylvania Escape Three.

Other Recommended Lodgings

Cumberland

The Holiday Inn in Cumberland, 100 South George Street; (301) 724–8800; www.cumberland-dtn.holiday-inn.com. If you enjoy train watching and partying, this is the place to be. Request a trackside room, and join the crowds who stay up to watch the freight trains that pass within yards of the motel. Rates: $89–$179.

Grantsville

Stonebow Inn, 146 Casselman Road; (301) 895–4250 or (800) 272–4090; www.stonebowinn.com. Elegant Victorian bed-and-breakfast on seven riverfront acres. Seven guest rooms, all with private baths, air-conditioning, cable TV and VCR, private telephones, antiques and quilts, hair dryers, complimentary coffee and soft drinks. The $130–$185 tariff includes a three-course gourmet breakfast for two at the adjacent Penn Alps Restaurant. Two-day minimum on weekends. Children must be twelve or older.

Walnut Ridge Bed and Breakfast, 92 Main Street; (301) 895–4496 or (888) 419–2568; www.walnutridge.net. Two guest rooms and one suite in a farmhouse on the edge of town. Large porches, hot tubs, separate entrance, country breakfast. Rates: $80–$150.

Frostburg

Failingers Hotel Gunter, 11 West Main Street; (301) 689–6511, www
.failingershotelgunter.com. This once-grand seventeen-room hotel was
partially restored in the 1960s, and the magnificent central staircase is
Failingers' pride. Although the lobby and dining room are far from fancy,
the hotel captures the feel of what it was like to travel the National Pike
in luxury a century ago. Rooms are $64 to $66 a night; a single suite rents
for $89.

Farmington

Historic Summit Inn, 101 Skyline Drive; (724) 438–8594 or (800)
433–8594; www.summitinnresort.com. Delightful, turn-of-the-twentieth-
century resort inn at the top of a mountain on the National Pike. Henry
Ford, Thomas Edison, and presidents Harding and Truman stayed here, and
the Summit hasn't changed all that much since then. Delightful restaurant;
also pool, golf course, shuffleboard. Open April through November. Rates:
$110–$207.

The Lodge at Chalk Hill, US 40; (724) 438–8880 or (800) 833–4283;
www.qcol.net/~thelodge/. Modern lakeside lodge with sixty-four units,
some of them efficiencies. Cable TV, continental breakfast. Rates:
$49–$179.

For additional listings see Maryland Escape Four and Pennsylvania Escape
Three.

For More Information

Hagerstown/Washington County Convention and Visitors Bureau, 16
Public Square, Hagerstown, MD 21740; (301) 791–3246 or (800) 257–
2600; www.marylandmemories.org.

Allegany County Visitors Bureau, Western Maryland Station, 13 Canal
Street, Cumberland, MD 21502; (301) 777–5132 or (800) 425–2067;
www.mdmountainside.com.

Garrett County Chamber of Commerce, 15 Visitors Center Drive,
McHenry, MD 21541; (301) 387–4386 or (888) 387–5237; www.garrett
chamber.com.

WEST VIRGINIA
ESCAPES

Berkeley Springs and Harpers Ferry

Spas, Massages, Clean Water, and History / 2 Nights

If you totaled all the places in the country where the local tourist board made the claim, "George Washington slept here," you'd figure the man lived 150 years. But the claim is true for Berkeley Springs. Also true: Our first president took a bath in Berkeley Springs—and they've got the stone vessel to prove it.

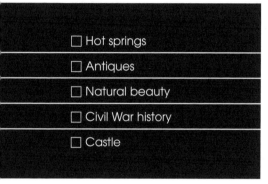

- ☐ Hot springs
- ☐ Antiques
- ☐ Natural beauty
- ☐ Civil War history
- ☐ Castle

What brought Washington here in 1748 was work: He did surveying for Lord Fairfax. But he fell in love with the place, mostly because of its beautiful natural setting and its luxuriant natural springs. Guess what? The same attractions still beckon two centuries later.

Berkeley Springs has carved out a niche as an arts and spa town. If you're a bit stressed out, this is the place to come. But make sure you've got energy to spare: relaxation and pampering is serious work. On the way home, sober up a bit at Harpers Ferry, site of John Brown's unsuccessful slave revolt.

Day 1 / Morning

Take Interstate 270 to Interstate 70 west at Frederick. Follow I–70 to U.S Highway 522 south; cross over the Potomac and head straight into **Berkeley Springs.** The whole trip from D.C. should take less than two hours.

Head to the center of town; you won't have any problem finding it. Look for **Berkeley Springs State Park.** Warm Springs Run meanders through mature shade trees and past a gazebo. It's a pleasant scene, but the park's chief attraction is the nine-room **Roman Bath House,** 2 South Washington Street; (304) 258–2711; www.berkeleyspringssp.com/spa.html.

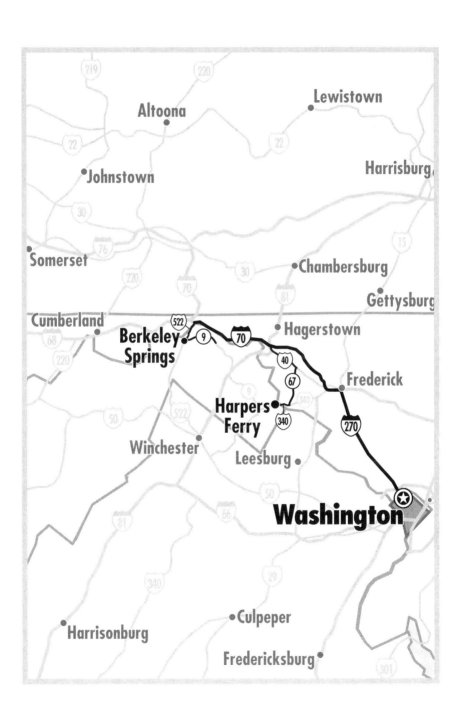

Built in 1815, the bathhouse sits on the same spot where George Washington and others "took the waters." In fact, the stone vessel outside once served as the old man's tub. Inside the bathhouse, take a dip in the relaxing waters. The springs that feed the baths remain a steady 74 degrees.

Of course, if it's a warm day, that's a chilly bath. No worries: Among the wide range of spa options is the Roman Bath, heated to 102 degrees. There are also massages and heat treatments. Baths, with thirty- to sixty-minute massage, range from $40 to $80 ($36 to $72 for seniors). Half-hour baths in the mineral waters are $20. Shower, bath, and heat treatment combinations range from $10 to $45. Open daily 10:00 A.M. to 6:00 P.M. (last appointment at 4:30). Friday hours extended to 9:00 P.M. April through October.

LUNCH: All that relaxing builds up a hunger. Head north just down the block to **Tari's,** 33 North Washington Street; (304) 258–1196; www .tariscafe.com/. The food is consistently solid, with enough choices to satisfy anyone. Specialty sandwiches, pastas, and a range of starters make this a perfect lunch spot (I generally don't bother with crab cakes outside of Baltimore, but the crab cakes at Tari's are quite good). While the food is good, the atmosphere doesn't disappoint either. The decor is a hodgepodge of work by local artisans; the art ranges from paintings and prints to jewelry, pottery, and stained glass. Most of it is for sale. Moderate.

Afternoon

No doubt on your little stroll to Tari's you noticed the collection of unique shops that line Fairfax and Washington Streets. Take a couple of hours to browse—among the many choices are shops featuring antiques, coffee, homeopathy products, Himalayan handicrafts, and even quilting supplies. Plus, there are art galleries and a bunch of eclectic shops offering impossibly cute and clever pieces for home and garden. The **Berkeley Springs Antique Mall** houses more than thirty dealers under one roof. It's located at 7 Fairfax Street (304–258–5676) and is open 10:00 A.M. to 5:00 P.M. every day but Wednesday.

While walking around, you're sure to notice many historical buildings— just off the main drag, in the residential area of town, there are many more. Compact and very walkable, a historical tour is easy to do by going to www.berkeleysprings.com/walkingtour/map.html and printing out the interactive walking-tour map.

DINNER: Lot 12, 117 Warren Street, offers Berkeley Springs's most imaginative and succulent meals. There's an emphasis on local foods, so the menu changes with the seasons. The chef is a master at combining sometimes disparate ingredients to create some wonderful dinners. His main influence is Northern Italian cuisine; that, mixed with local ingredients, means the results will most likely have you raving. Service matches the food: excellent! Open Wednesday through Saturday 5:00 to 9:00 P.M., Sunday 5:00 to 8:00 P.M. (304) 258–6264; www.lot12.com/. Expensive.

Before you turn in, see what's playing at the **Star Theatre,** Congress and North Washington Streets, a Depression-era movie house showing first-runs a few weeks past their openings. You can't beat the prices at $3.00 for kids and $3.50 for adults. For an extra 50 cents, grab a couch and eat your popcorn (with real butter) in comfort. Don't be surprised when the owner comes out before the show and admonishes any noisemakers. All shows start at 8:00 P.M. (304) 258–1404; www.starwv.com/star/. Or check out what's going on at the **Ice House,** headquarters of the Morgan Arts Council. Art shows, concerts, and theater productions run continuously; the theater shows are stocked with a local ensemble that never fails to put on a good show. Showtimes are Friday and Saturday at 7:30 P.M., Sunday at 3:00 P.M., and a special "Pay-What-You-Can Performance" on Thursday at 7:00 P.M. Independence and Mercer Streets (1 block off US 522); (304) 258–2300; www.macicehouse.org/.

LODGING: The **Inn & Spa at Berkeley Springs,** 1 Market Street; (304) 258–2210 or (800) 822–6630; www.theinnandspa.com/. Located adjacent to Berkeley Springs State Park, this Berkeley Springs institution used to be known as the Country Inn. The name has changed, but the pleasure of staying there hasn't. The inn's historic building offers sixty-two rooms and five suites, and, of course, spas and massages (sensing a theme?). There's also a pub and 1 Market Street Grill. Rooms, comfortable and roomy, continue the "home-away-from-home" theme the outside gardens and porch fronts exude. Rates: $69–$160.

Day 2 / Morning

BREAKFAST: Stock up on the complimentary breakfast at the Inn & Spa, and then get an early start; some physical activity awaits you.

A big part of the area's attraction, for eighteenth-century colonialists as well as today's visitor, is the natural beauty. Berkeley Springs sits in a valley, so today head for the hills at **Cacapon State Park.** From Berkeley Springs, drive 9 miles south on US 522. It's located at 818 Cacapon Lodge Drive; (304) 258–1022 or (800) CALL–WVA; www.cacaponresort.com/.

The opportunities are endless: There are more than 6,000 acres and 20 miles of trails for hiking or horseback riding, swimming and boating at Cacapon Resort State Park Lake, and a Robert Trent Jones–designed golf course, rated one of the 130 best in the United States. Greens fees range from $18 to $32.

LUNCH: Grab lunch at the restaurant in the main lodge. It's standard American fare, reasonably priced. Moderate.

Afternoon

After a tough day on the trail or the green, it's time for some more relaxation—this is why you came, remember. Head back into Berkeley Springs and go west on West Virginia Highway 9 toward **Coolfont Resort,** your afternoon destination. Just after turning onto WV 9, look for the unmistakable **Berkeley Castle** on your right. Begun in 1885, it's West Virginia's Taj Mahal, but it looks better suited for Scotland. It was built by Maryland businessman Samuel Taylor Suit for the daughter of an Alabama businessman, but he never saw its full construction as he died in 1888. The castle was completed four years later, and the young widow spent the next decade burning through her late husband's fortune by hosting parties for society's upper crust.

Continuing on WV 9, once you come to the top of the hill, head left onto Cold Run Valley Road at the Coolfont signs and follow the road to Coolfont Resort, 3621 Cold Run Valley Road. It's time for an invigorating massage given by an experienced masseuse. Full-body massages, facials, stone massages, Chinese, Reiki, Shiatsu—you name it; this place performs it. Procedures range from $49 to $119. There's a salon on the premises, too, where you can get mud treatments, facials, manicures, and pedicures, among other services. Prices range from $30 to $119. There's also yoga, Tai Chi, Pilates, meditation, and other wellness exercises. (304) 258–4500 or (800) 888–8768; www.coolfont.com.

DINNER: Go back to WV 9 and take it west for a few miles until you come to **Panorama at the Peak,** WV 9 West, Panorama Overlook; (304) 258–9847; www.panoramaatthepeak.com/. The restaurant overlooks an astounding view. A diner could be forgiven for swearing that the sweeping vista encompasses twenty states (it's only three, in actuality). The danger in a place like this is that with the view it has, the food need not be special. Fortunately, the food's good, too. The traditional is here: chicken,

Berkeley Castle

steaks, fish. But vegetarians and vegans can find dishes as well. For a special treat, watch the sun set while you eat. Expensive.

LODGING: The Highlawn Inn, 171 Market Street; (304) 258–5700 or (888) 290–4163; www.highlawninn.com/index.htm. An intimate and immaculate Victorian overlooking town with ten rooms in two buildings, plus a carriage house and bathkeeper's quarters. Rates from $95 to $155 for the main house and Aunt Pearl's Building, $199 for the carriage house, and $210 for the bathkeeper's quarters. Includes a scrumptious breakfast.

Day 3 / Morning

BREAKFAST: The Highlawn Inn.

After breakfast, head back out to I–70 and pick up U.S. Highway 40 east at Hagerstown. Past Boonsboro, take Maryland Highway 67 south to U.S. Highway 340 west to **Harpers Ferry.**

Harpers Ferry is most famous as the site of John Brown's unsuccessful slave revolt. The plan was relatively straightforward: storm the armory, grab the guns, arm the slaves, and massacre the enemy. In the end, it didn't quite work out that way, with John Brown being hanged and cementing his place as perhaps the single most controversial figure in the history of the Civil War. Loved and despised to this day, Brown's legacy is still debated with fervor.

But Harpers Ferry is much more than John Brown. It enjoys an important place in American history not only in the Civil War, but in manufacturing, railroading, and integration. When you arrive, park your car at the visitor center (signs pointing the way are prominent) and take the free shuttle bus into town. While many visitors seem frustrated by having to abandon their vehicle, the subsequent lack of traffic along pedestrian byways in town makes visiting Harpers Ferry all the more pleasant. The historical park is open daily from 8:00 A.M. to 5:00 P.M. and costs $6.00 per vehicle. (304) 535–6029; www.nps.gov/hafe/.

The bus drivers are courteous and knowledgeable, and they can answer any questions you have. While lacking the overwhelmingly reconstructionist feel of Williamsburg, Harpers Ferry manages to stay true to its historical past. Museums line the streets of the lower area of town where the shuttle bus drops you off; more historical attractions mingle on the upper part of town with shops and eateries.

In addition to all the history, Harpers Ferry sits in a beautiful spot overlooking the confluence of the Potomac and Shenandoah Rivers. The view from above town has been inspiring visitors for centuries. Thomas Jefferson, an early visitor to Harpers Ferry, noted that "The passage of the Patowmac through the Blue Ridge is perhaps one of the most stupendous scenes in Nature." The "Jefferson Rock," where our country's second president made that observation, is an easy walk from town. Again, prominent signs make finding it a breeze.

There are plenty of places to eat in town (the business district is very compact and easy to find), but if you want a special treat, head up the hills to the **Hilltop House Hotel,** located at 400 East Ridge Street. The century-old stone inn sits overlooking town and offers good views and good food. The menu consists of food typical of that served in area restaurants: chicken, steaks, pastas, veal, pork, and crab cakes. The fried chicken is a local favorite. Moderate to expensive. (304) 535–2132 or (800) 338–8319; www.hill tophousehotel.net/.

To get back to D.C. from Harpers Ferry, take US 340 east toward Frederick, I–70 east, and then I–270 toward Washington.

There's More

Paw Paw Tunnel. From Berkeley Springs take WV 9 past the Berkeley Castle, the turnoff for Coolfont, and the Panorama Steak House, and follow the road—a beautiful thoroughfare all the way—through the small towns of Great Cacapon and Paw Paw. After about half an hour, you'll cross the Potomac; take the first right into the lot for the C&O Canal Paw Paw Campground. From the lot, it's a short walk (less than a mile) along the canal towpath to the Paw Paw Tunnel. Begun in 1836, the tunnel bores through more than 3,100 feet of cliff and rock. It remains an extremely impressive engineering marvel today, and it's not hyperbole to pronounce it among the great engineering feats anywhere in North America when it was built.

Special Events

February. Berkeley Springs International Water Tasting, Berkeley Springs. Competition for the title of best-tasting water draws entrants from around the country and the globe. Featured on NPR, BBC, and CNN, among other outlets. (304) 258–9147 or (800) 447–8797; www.berkeleysprings .com/water/about.

March. George Washington's Bathtub Celebration, Berkeley Springs. Does have a commercial tinge to it, but there's still much love for the country's first president, who so loved this town. (304) 258–9147 or (800) 447– 8797; www.berkeleysprings.com/.

April. Uniquely West Virginia, held in the Berkeley Springs Antique Mall, Berkeley Springs. All things West Virginia: crafts, food, even wine. (304) 258–9147 or (800) 447–8797; www.berkeleysprings.com/.

October. Apple Butter Festival, Berkeley Springs. Celebrates all things apple—includes live music, parades, and craft making. (304) 258–9147 or (800) 447–8797; www.berkeleysprings.com/.

December. Olde Tyme Christmas, Harpers Ferry. Takes place during the first two weekends of the month. The town of Harpers Ferry and the National Historical Park hold seasonal musical celebrations jointly. Shops in town are decked out with the season's finery. (800) 848–TOUR; www .harpersferrywv.net/.

Other Recommended Restaurants

Berkeley Springs

Creekside Creamery, 123 Congress Street; (304) 258–4271. Treats of all kinds—the ice cream is especially good. Inexpensive.

Donna's Coffee Stop, 758 South Washington Street; (304) 258–0020; www .donnascoffeestop.com/. What a coffee bar should be—offering baked goods, organic and fair trade coffees and teas, wireless Internet, and crafts for sale. Inexpensive.

Fairfax Coffee House, 23 Fairfax Street; (304) 258–8019; www.mtn-laurel .com/fairfax. Coffee drinks, baked goods, and filling sandwiches. Inexpensive.

Mi Ranchito Mexican Restaurant, 87 North Washington Street; (304) 258–4800. If you want ethnic in Berkeley Springs, for now, this is the only place to go. Typical Mexican fare—tacos, burritos, enchiladas, and other filling and flavorful dishes. Inexpensive to moderate.

Other Recommended Lodgings

Berkeley Springs Cottage Rentals, Berkeley Springs; (304) 258–5300, (304) 258–2685, or (866) 682–2246. Choose from a variety of lodging options, both in town and in the surrounding countryside. Rates start at $95 per night for one-bedroom cabins and chalets.

Cacapon Resort State Park, 818 Cacapon Lodge Drive, Berkeley Springs; (304) 258–1022 or (800) CALL–WVA; www.cacaponresort.com/. Choose from the lodge, Cacapon Inn, bungalows, and cabins. Lodge rates: $64–$86; inn: $51–$60; bungalows: $65; cabins: $68–$183.

Coolfont Resort, Berkeley Springs, offers campsites from $20 to $35 dollars (weekend; electric sites); comfortable, woodsy chalets from $119 to $179; and two-night vacation home rentals ranging from $600 to $950. 3621 Cold Run Valley Road; (304) 258–4500 or (800) 888–8768; www.coolfont.com.

The Inn on Fairfax, 151 Fairfax Street, Berkeley Springs; (304) 258–4502; www.innonfairfax.com/. Victorian home in town, features five rooms with elegant settings. Rates range from $100 to $200 and include breakfast. There is a two-night minimum, but if there are rooms available, a one-night stay can be arranged.

The Manor Inn, 234 Fairfax Street, Berkeley Springs; (304) 258–1552 or (800) 974–5770; www.bathmanorinn.com/. Listed on the National Register of Historic Places, this century-old Second Empire Victorian once served as the home of the town mayor. Four comfortable rooms with a big front porch perfect for relaxing evenings. Rooms start at $85.

Sleepy Creek Mountain Inn, 877 Winstead Road, Berkeley Springs; (304) 258–0234 or (877) 258–0234; www.sleepycreekmountaininn.com/. Manages to be rustic and comfortable at the same time. The reason for this is simple: While the most recent addition to the inn was added in 1975, the oldest portion of the inn dates from 1800. For those looking for the "wild" (yet comfortable) side of West Virginia. The inn is about 5 miles outside of town. Rates: $92–$172.

For More Information

Travel Berkeley Springs, 127 Fairfax Street, Berkeley Springs, WV 25411; (304) 258–9147 or (800) 447–8797; www.berkeleysprings.com/.

Harpers Ferry National Historic Park, P.O. Box 65, Harpers Ferry, WV 25425; (304) 535–6029; www.nps.gov/hafe/.

Travel Harpers Ferry, (304) 535–9909; www.harpersferrywv.net/.

WEST VIRGINIA ESCAPE TWO

Elkins and Canaan Valley

A Four-Season Paradise / 2 Nights

The Monongahela National Forest, a gigantic wilderness area in West Virginia's Allegheny Mountains, is home to some of the most magnificent

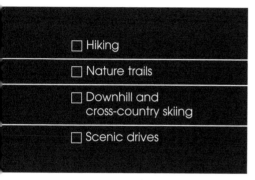

parks in the United States. West Virginia is for people who love to hike, ski, take pictures, fish, and raft on white water. It's also for people who want to get away from cities and crowds and lose themselves in a place where the scenery is ravishing, the air is clean, and the surroundings remarkably unspoiled.

☐ Hiking

☐ Nature trails

☐ Downhill and cross-country skiing

☐ Scenic drives

Among the best of West Virginia's many parks are Canaan Valley Resort Park and nearby Blackwater Falls State Park. They are your destination for this weekend escape, which also includes visits to Elkins, the home of an acclaimed monthlong summer folk-life festival, and a stop at Seneca Rocks to watch the rock climbers.

Day 1 / Morning

Your day begins with a leisurely drive into West Virginia. Take Interstate 66 west from Washington about 75 miles to Interstate 81 just past Front Royal, Virginia. Follow I–81 south for 4 miles to the second exit, marked Strasburg. There you'll be able to pick up West Virginia Highway 55 heading west into and through the Potomac Highlands section of West Virginia. Prepare to enjoy every minute of your drive on WV 55, which winds up and down mountain roads with 9 percent grades. As you go deeper into West Virginia, the sights along the way get more and more beautiful.

As you approach **Seneca Rocks** (about 80 miles and two hours after you pick up WV 55), the mountains become increasingly rugged until you can see the extraordinary thousand-foot-high outcropping of bare, sheer

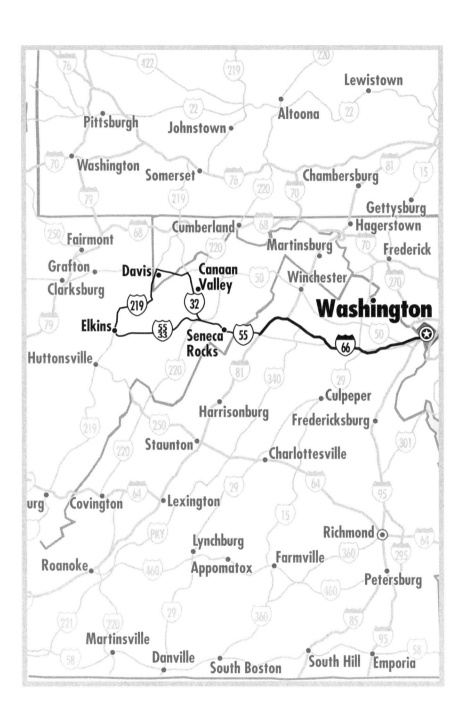

rock face that makes Seneca a destination of most serious local rock climbers. Phone (304) 567–2827 for the Seneca Rocks Discovery Center.

LUNCH: A great place to watch these athletes climb is from **The Front Porch,** located at the junction of WV 55 and U.S. Highway 33; (304) 567–2555. This funky restaurant is the upstairs of Harper's Old Country Store, a mellow, old-time store that still sells groceries, hardware, hunting and fishing equipment, sheepskins, pottery, tourist stuff, and snacks. The Front Porch restaurant has a low-priced menu of whole-wheat pita sandwiches, salads, and spaghetti, with "fresh dough" pizza a specialty. Grab a table on the porch itself (there are also tables indoors) and get out your binoculars. There's sure to be something interesting going on across the highway on the face of Seneca Rocks.

Afternoon

From Seneca Rocks take WV 55 west about 12 miles, then head north on West Virginia Highway 32 about 10 miles to **Canaan Valley Resort State Park.** The park offers weeks' worth of things to do in gorgeous surroundings. Like all of West Virginia's state parks, it is immaculate, moderately priced, and unspoiled by commercial development. Check in at the Lodge, where you'll be staying the weekend; grab your skis, golf clubs, running shoes, hiking boots, swimsuit, tennis racket, or basketball; and get going!

Canaan Valley is popular year-round, and with good reason. If you visit in July or August to escape Washington's heat and humidity, it's likely to be a breezy 80 degrees at the park's 4,000-foot altitude, and, at night, the temperature may even drop into the 60s. Summer visitors enjoy both an indoor and outdoor pool, tennis courts, golf links, and many miles of hiking trails. The scenery is truly lovely, as Canaan is in a valley surrounded by some of the highest peaks in West Virginia.

The best time to visit Canaan Valley, however, just might be the dead of winter. This "snow bowl" gets more snow than Vermont—averaging more than 150 inches per year—and, just in case the sky doesn't cooperate, the park has equipment to cover most of its slopes with machine-made snow. It is also a perfect ski resort for families; it offers babysitting as well as classes for kids.

Canaan Valley has thirty-four slopes, with 30 percent of the ski terrain designated for beginners, 40 percent intermediate, and the remainder for experienced skiers. All-day adult lift tickets are $32 on weekdays and $54 on weekends. You can also buy cheaper half-day tickets or two- or three-day package plans. Fringe-season rates are significantly lower. Ski rental is $24 for adults, $22 for kids. Group and private lessons are also available.

In addition to the state park at Canaan Valley, there are numerous commercial resorts nearby. **Timberline Four Seasons Resort,** for example, offers competitively priced ski packages, and, when the snow is gone, it's a good place to rent mountain bikes and explore miles of rough trails. (304) 866–4801 or (800) 766–9464; www.timberlineresort.com.

For cross-country skiers, trails at Canaan Valley connect with nearby Dolly Sods Wilderness Area and White Grass Touring Center, making a 78-mile cross-country network. If you don't know yet if you're up to cross-country skiing and want to give it a try, rental equipment and lessons are available at Canaan Valley at the nature center.

DINNER: A good choice is the **Blackwater Brewing Company,** located a few miles north of the park on WV 32 (Williams Avenue) in Davis; (304) 259–4221; www.blackwater-brewing.com. This brewpub and restaurant has a very good selection of German dishes, such as beer-batter fish, paprika chicken, and rouladen (rolled beef) with potato dumplings, an equally good selection of Italian entrees—including three or four vegetarian offerings—plus the usual sandwiches you'd expect in a brewpub. Microbrews include a porter and a stout, which nicely complement the German food. Moderate.

LODGING: **Canaan Valley Resort Park Lodge** has 250 modern rooms and suites with remote-control TV, cable, and complimentary in-room coffee. Rates are $87–$188 for a room, $149–$199 for a suite. Twenty-three deluxe cabins start at $168 for a two-bedroom unit ($739 per week). There are also thirty-four campsites available in summer for a $25-per-day fee. On most weekends, a two-night minimum stay is required at the lodge. Midweek ski, golf, and family vacation packages are available. (304) 866–4121 or (800) 622–4121; www.canaanresort.com.

Day 2 / *Morning*

BREAKFAST: At least one of your days in the area should be devoted to sightseeing in the area around Canaan Valley State Park. Begin by driving about 15 miles north on WV 32 to **Blackwater Falls State Park.** There, at the **Lodge Restaurant,** you can get a hearty and inexpensive breakfast with a fantastic view of Blackwater Canyon. (304) 259–5216; www.black waterfalls.com.

The falls are the pride of the park. The park system has built a quarter-mile boardwalk so that it's an easy fifteen-minute walk to get down close to the falls; there's also a ramp to an overlook for visitors in wheelchairs. Bring lots of film, because you'll want to capture the breathtaking view of the lake and gorge, the 50-foot falls, and the rim of tall pines all around.

There's lots more to see and do at Blackwater Falls State Park. If you visit in summer, there's swimming and boating at Pendleton Lake, tennis courts, a volleyball court, and picnic facilities. Spring and summer are perfect for hiking or horseback riding; the park has horses and ponies for children, and usage fees are reasonable. Mountain biking is permitted on two of the eighteen trails.

In winter, Blackwater Falls offers sledding, and the extensive trail system is ideal for cross-country skiing. The trails are rated from beginner to advanced, and you can pick up a map at the lodge or recreation building that will show you how to combine trails to devise a loop at a distance and difficulty level to suit your tastes. A favorite trail in any season is the Balsam Fir Trail, a 1.5-mile loop (beginning at the recreation building) that winds through beech and maple groves and then passes through a stand of balsam fir.

Just outside the park is **Davis,** a pleasant little town offering food, lodging, and services to the downhill and cross-country skiers, sledders, mountain bikers, climbers, kayakers, and, yes, plain old tourists who have discovered the beauties of Canaan Valley.

LUNCH: You can catch an early lunch at **Sirianni's Pizza Cafe** on Main Street in Davis; (304) 259–5454. Sirianni's offers pasta, hot and cold meat and vegetarian subs, and, of course, pizza in a friendly, generally crowded storefront restaurant. Inexpensive to moderate.

Afternoon

Two miles north of the park entrance on WV 32, you'll connect with U.S. Highway 219. Follow it south for 34 miles and you'll be in **Elkins.**

Take some time to explore the town. You can pick up maps and brochures at the **Randolph County Convention and Visitors Bureau,** 315 Railroad Avenue; (304) 636–2780 or (800) 422–3304; www.randolph countywv.com. Elkins offers the opportunity to explore early Native American settlements in the area, take a historical tour of buildings erected by early European settlers, walk or drive through nearby Civil War battlefields, or enjoy the splendid Victorian architecture of **Davis and Elkins College** (304–637–1900).

The college, in particular, is worth a look. You'll see the Gate House, Albert Hall, the Boiler House Theatre, Graceland Mansion, and the fifty-six-room **Halliehurst Mansion.** College tour information is available from the visitors bureau, which can also supply a historic Elkins walking tour brochure with a map and information about twenty-six houses of particular interest. The walking tour will take you a little more than an hour to complete.

For shoppers, there are lots of gift and craft shops in Elkins. Two particularly nice ones are the **Artists at Work Gallery,** 329 Davis Avenue (304–637–6309), where local artists work and sell their creations, and **Expressions,** 303 Davis Avenue (304–636–5087), a shop with hand-crafted pottery, baskets, and toys, as well as local honey, syrup, and jams.

Plan your sightseeing and shopping itinerary so that you'll have time for a doughnut break. Where US 33 meets US 219 north, you'll see **Ye Olde Doughnut Shop,** 400 South Randolph Avenue; (304) 636–0223. Open 4:00 A.M. to 3:30 P.M. It's where locals come to drink coffee, talk politics, and wrap themselves around blueberry turnovers and maple doughnuts. The shop doesn't appear to have changed in fifty years; grilled cheese sandwiches are only a buck and a quarter. Fast-food franchises are putting places like "Ye Olde" out of business, and it's a shame. Be a contrarian and buy an extra sack of fresh-made doughnuts for the road.

Elkins is also the site of the **Augusta Heritage Arts Workshops** at Davis and Elkins College. Here, for five weeks in July and August, musicians, folk dancers, artisans, and storytellers gather to share techniques, swap stories, and make music late into the night. There are dances, workshops for beginners, and jam sessions where teenagers and octogenarians play side by side.

The historic music and crafts of the Appalachian Mountains are the focus of the activities, so there's lots of country fiddling, zither playing, basket weaving, bread baking, quilting, and more. And for two weekends in August, the **Augusta Festival** spills out into the town itself, with a crafts fair and clogging, fiddling, and storytelling open to everybody. It's a wonderful occasion, and it draws a good-size crowd, so make your reservations early if you plan to attend. (304) 637–1209 or (800) 624–3157; www.augustaheritage.com.

To find your final stop of the day, drive 3 miles east of Elkins on US 33. Just after US 33 becomes a limited-access, four-lane road, you'll see a left turn exit for Stuarts Recreation Area. Take that exit and proceed just over a mile to a blue bridge that spans the Cheat River. Don't cross; the inn where you'll dine is located just short of the bridge.

DINNER: The Cheat River Inn, which looks from the outside like a private home, was operated as a tavern until 1988. Inside it still has the casual feel of a tavern, but this is one of the best restaurants in the state. The emphasis here is on fresh vegetables and fish, and many of the dishes have a hint of the Caribbean about them, a reflection of the owner's years of living in Key West. You can, for example, get your steak with Jamaican jerk seasoning or your crab cake with Key lime mustard sauce. Everything is delicious here, including the desserts, like chocolate amaretto brownies with ice cream, and Key lime pie with raspberry sauce and whipped cream. (304) 636–6265; www.cheatriverlodge.com/inn. Moderate.

After dinner, it's a half-hour drive back to Canaan Valley Resort Park via US 33 east (15 miles) and WV 32 north (10 miles).

LODGING: Canaan Valley Resort Park Lodge.

Day 3 / Morning

BREAKFAST: Enjoy a hearty pancake or waffle breakfast in the lodge's **Aspen Dining Room.** Inexpensive.

After breakfast, spend the rest of the day playing. If you want a break from skiing, rent a snowboard all day for $34, hone your ice skating skills at the outdoor lighted rink for $6.50 ($5.25 for children), or relax in the lodge's health club, with its indoor pool, hot tub, sauna, and fitness center.

If you're visiting Canaan Valley in spring, summer, or fall, you can rent bikes at the recreation center, sign up for a guided tour at the nature center, or get in a couple of sets of tennis before lunch.

Golfers will enjoy the eighteen-hole, par 72, 6,984-yard championship course. Greens fees are $28 to $40 for eighteen holes. You can rent clubs, carts, and even balls at the golf shop. For the kids, miniature golf is $3.00.

LUNCH: Aspen Dining Room at Canaan Valley Resort Park Lodge.

Afternoon

It's more than four hours back to Washington via WV 32 south and 55 east, linking up with I–81 north and then I–66 east, so plan your departure based on when you want to get home, and drive safely—especially if the roads are packed with snow.

There's More

Dolly Sods Scenic Area and Wilderness Area. Sitting high atop the Allegheny plateau is the largest inland wetlands area in the United States. You can spend hours exploring the scenic area by car on narrow gravel roads or discover the wilderness area on foot or horseback. The bogs, blueberries, and wildflowers will excite both photographers and painters. Located just east of Canaan Valley State Park; (304) 257–4488.

Climbing. Beginning, intermediate, and advanced lessons are available from Seneca Rocks Climbing School (304–567–2600 or 800–548–0108) or from Seneca Rocks Mountain Guides (304–567–2115 or 800–451–5108; www.senecarocks.com). Expect to pay about $80 to $120 a day for a three-day lesson. Climbing shoes and technical equipment are provided. Both schools are located at the junction of WV 55 and US 33.

Boating and White-Water Rafting. You can canoe, fish, float in rubber canoes ("duckies"), or get shuttled to the white-water rafting section of the Cheat River (Class I to Class V rapids) from Blackwater Outdoor Adventures on WV 32 in Davis; (304) 478–3775; www.blackwateroutdoors.com. It's around $50 for the 5-mile Cheat Narrows.

Smoke Hole Caverns. A guided tour of the 200-plus-million-year-old cavern used by Seneca Indians to smoke game—and Union and Confederate soldiers to store ammunition—lasts forty-five minutes. Commercialized and sometimes crowded, but interesting. Open daily year-round from 9:00 A.M. to 5:00 P.M., later in summer months. The temperature is a constant 56 degrees in the caverns, so dress accordingly. Located on WV 55 about 13 miles north of Seneca Rocks; (304) 257–4442, (304) 257–1705, or (800) 828–8478; www.smokehole.com. Admission is $9.00 for adults, $5.00 for children five to twelve; children under five are admitted free.

Special Events

March. March Madness, a monthlong series of ski events, including the Governor's Cup ski race always held at or near Canaan Valley Resort Park. (800) 622–4121.

April. Annual Ramp Cookoff and Festival, Elkins. Ramps are wild leeks (members of the lily family) that grow in the forests of the Potomac

Highland region of West Virginia in early spring. Ramps taste like green onions (times ten!), and, once you've eaten one, you'll remember what it tastes and smells like for days. So will your family and friends. The Elkins Festival gives a prize for the most potent concoction. A good introduction for the uninitiated is ramp jam, which makes for a pretty mean substitute topping for garlic bread. (304) 846–6790 or (800) 422–3304.

July–August. Augusta Heritage Arts Workshops culminating in the Augusta Festival, Davis and Elkins College, Elkins. (304) 637–1209; www.augustaheritage.com.

September–October. The Mountain State Forest Festival, celebrated in Elkins and throughout the region, is the state's oldest and largest festival. It features exhibits and entertainment, arts and crafts, athletic contests, and spectator sports. (304) 636–1824; www.forestfestival.com.

Other Recommended Restaurants

Canaan Valley

Golden Anchor and Portside Pub, WV 32 about 2 miles south of Canaan Valley State Park; (304) 866–2722; www.goldenanchorcabins.com/restaurant.htm. Fresh fish, crab, and other seafood specials near the slopes. Moderate.

Deerfield Restaurant, Deerfield Village Resort, WV 32 near the parks; (304) 866–4559. Steak, pasta, chicken in resort setting. Moderate.

Big John's Family Fixins, WV 32 between Canaan Valley and Blackwater Falls Parks; (304) 866–4418. Sandwiches, pizza, and video and board games. Inexpensive.

White Grass Cafe, Cross-Country Ski Resort, Freeland Road, Canaan Valley; (304) 866–4114. Ski hangout with gravel floor and potbellied stove. Good soup; vegetarian and fish dishes. Open daily in winter for lunch and, on weekends, for dinner as well. Inexpensive.

Elkins

The Mingo Room, Graceland Inn and Conference Center, Davis and Elkins College; (304) 637–1600 or (800) 624–3157. Continental and regional cuisine served in an elegant red-oak dining room; pleasant for Sunday brunch; reservations necessary. Moderate.

1863 Tavern, Elkins Motor Lodge, just west of town on US 33 (Harrison Avenue); (304) 636–1400. Everyone goes for the prime rib special; open only for dinner. Moderate.

Other Recommended Lodgings

Canaan Valley

Blackwater Falls State Park Lodge has fifty-four air-conditioned rooms with private baths, color TV, and phones, and a common game room and sitting room. The park also has twenty-six deluxe year-round vacation cabins with stone fireplaces, and a sixty-five-unit tent and trailer campground that is open from May through October. For reservations call (304) 259–5216 or (800) 225–5982; www.blackwaterfalls.com. Rates: lodge, $70–$109 for a double; cabins, $652–$998 a week in summer and winter, $96–$164 a day in other seasons; campground, $17–$20 per site.

Black Bear Resort, Northside Cortland Road; (304) 866–4391 or (800) 553–2327; www.blackbearwv.com. Forty-four pedestal homes and twelve inn suites with refrigerators, Jacuzzi tubs, and fireplaces; access to swimming pool and tennis courts. Rates: $90–$110 at the inn. Cottages are $500–$1,050 a week.

Bright Morning Inn, William Avenue, Davis; (304) 259–5119 or (866) 537–5731; www.brightmorninginn.com. Former boardinghouse restored as a bed-and-breakfast with seven rooms and one suite, all with private baths. Rates: $65–$109, which includes full breakfast.

Meyer House Bed and Breakfast, Thomas Avenue, Davis; (304) 259–5451; www.meyerhousebandb.com. An 1880s Victorian with three bedrooms, some with private baths; full breakfast. Rates: $89–$99.

Elkins

Cheat River Lodge, 3 miles east of Elkins on US 33; (304) 636–2301; www.cheatriverlodge.com. Charming lodge with six guest rooms, all with two double beds, private baths, and a picture-window view of the Cheat River. Rates: $68–$83. Also available are six three- and four-bedroom cottages in the woods along the water. The cottages also have kitchens and outdoor hot tubs. Rates: $171–$196 a night; weekly rental is $1,076.

Graceland Inn and Conference Center, Davis and Elkins College; (304) 637–6244 or (800) 624–3157; www.gracelandinn.com. The inn has eleven rooms furnished with antiques and Victorian reproductions; all have private baths, many of which are marble-lined; many other amenities. Rates: $89–$166 for a double. The twenty-six rooms in the Conference Center have queen-size beds, private baths, TV, and private phones. Rates: $73–$79. Rooms must be rented by the week during the Augusta Festival.

Tunnel Mountain Inn, located east of Elkins near Stuarts Recreation Park, old Route 33; (304) 636–1684 or (888) 211–9123. Three guest rooms, all with private baths; large health-conscious country breakfasts. Rates: $70–$80.

For More Information

West Virginia Division of Tourism & Parks, 90 MacCorkle Avenue Southwest, South Charleston, WV 25303; (304) 558–2200 or (800) 225–5982; www.wvtourism.com.

Canaan Valley Resort State Park, HC 70, Box 330, Davis, WV 26260; (304) 866–4121 or (800) 622–4121; www.canaanresort.com.

Tucker County Convention and Visitors Bureau, P.O. Box 565, Davis, WV 26260; (304) 259–5315 or (800) 782–2775; www.canaanvalley.org.

Randolph County Convention and Visitors Bureau, 315 Railroad Avenue, Elkins, WV 26241; (304) 636–2780 or (800) 422–3304; www.randolphcountywv.com.

Lewisburg

West Virginia Highlights / 2 Nights

One of the best weekend escapes imaginable is a visit to the historic town of Lewisburg, which is about a five-hour drive from Washington, D.C. Lewisburg has all the advantages of other West Virginia destinations—clean air, cool temperatures, nearby mountains and forests, and abundant recreational facilities—but this little town is worth a visit in its own right because of its beauty and charm.

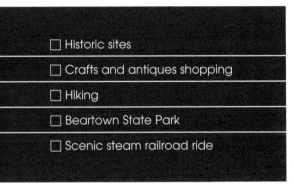

- ☐ Historic sites
- ☐ Crafts and antiques shopping
- ☐ Hiking
- ☐ Beartown State Park
- ☐ Scenic steam railroad ride

Your weekend escape to the area takes advantage of both town and country by including a ride up the mountainside on an ancient steam engine, a hike through a magical forest of tumbling cliffs and ferny glades, a stay at an antique-packed inn, and a walking tour through town that takes in historic buildings and interesting little shops. There's also time for a long hike and picnic lunch along the Greenbrier River, and a visit to a fancy resort near Lewisburg that once hid a secret bomb shelter for high government officials.

The Lewisburg area is a perfect weekend destination all four seasons of the year. Summer offers hiking, canoeing, fishing, swimming, and evenings of repertory theater and chamber music, or simply sitting in a rocking chair on the front porch of an inn and watching the fireflies come out. Spring brings out the wildflowers and swells the streams. Lewisburg is also a wonderful winter getaway: Cross-country skiing is readily available in the area, and local inns tend to have log fires blazing and hot cider handy for guests who breeze in from an afternoon trek.

But Lewisburg is best in the fall, when the trees turn red, yellow, brown, and orange and blanket the mountains like a patchwork quilt. It's

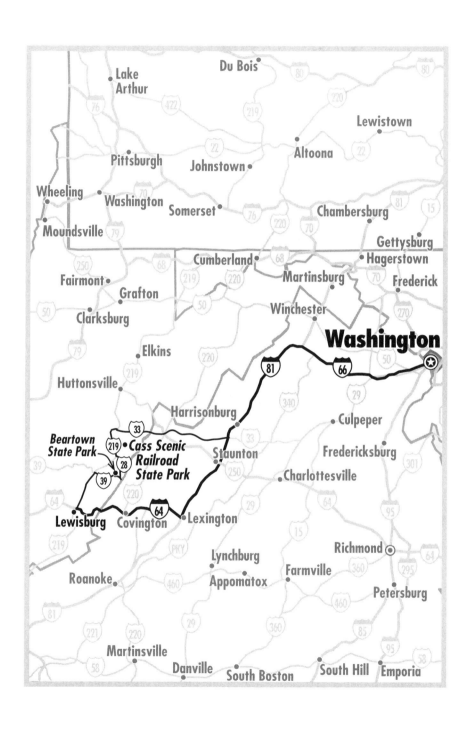

a perfect time to visit roadside fruit stands for apples and take long walks through the woods or along the Greenbrier River. Make early lodging reservations for autumn visits—and don't forget your camera!

Day 1 / Morning

Start early in the day for the drive to Lewisburg. It's a smooth drive on the expressway, and you can make the trip in less than five hours by taking Interstate 66 west, Interstate 81 south, and Interstate 64 west. Take exit 169 (U.S. Highway 219 south), and Lewisburg is only a few miles from I–64.

However, if you save the easy driving for the return home and take the scenic route a portion of the way, the trip will be one of the best parts of the weekend. After taking I–66 west for 75 miles and I–81 south for about 50 miles, exit the freeway near Harrisonburg, Virginia, and take U.S. Highway 33 west. From the exit, it's 26 miles to West Virginia. There, the backcountry roads up, over, and down the Appalachian Mountains are like a roller coaster through paradise. The modest towns and farms are few and far between, and mostly it's just you and the mountains.

Once you reach West Virginia, continue west on US 33 for 33 miles to Judy Gap. As you turn south on West Virginia Highway 28, you will see **Spruce Knob,** the highest point in West Virginia—elevation 4,861 feet— just on your right. Follow WV 28 about 35 miles to a point just beyond Green Bank, then begin looking for the sign for Cass Scenic Railroad State Park, your first stopping point of the day.

LUNCH: Just before you reach the railroad, you come to **Meck's Home Bakery,** located in Cass on West Virginia Highway 66 just off WV 28; (304) 456–4042. Make it your lunch stop. The German-style bakery serves great pastrami, home-roasted beef, and cheese sandwiches on fresh-from-the-oven bread. You can get chowchow, pickled beets, and fresh vegetables on the side. And, of course, you'll want a slice of pie or a sweet roll—and a box of doughnuts to get you through the weekend. Inexpensive.

Afternoon

Cass Scenic Railroad State Park is one of the few places in the United States where an authentic steam engine locomotive still operates. Once a logging line that operated until 1911, the Cass Railroad uses old Shay locomotives that have been authentically restored. The logging cars have been converted into open-air passenger coaches. A train ride will take you up the mountain at an astonishingly steep incline of 11 percent, with several switchbacks and reverses along the way.

The ride takes about ninety minutes round-trip, including a short stop at Whittaker Station in a pretty meadow halfway up the mountain. There are, of course, wonderful vistas as the train climbs the mountain. If you're really an enthusiast, you can take the four-and-a-half-hour ride all the way to the top of Bald Knob (elevation 4,842 feet) for a stunning view of the surrounding mountains and valleys.

Reservations in advance are strongly recommended; (304) 456–4300 or (800) 225–5982; www.cassrailroad.com. The train to Whittaker Station departs Cass at noon and 2:30 P.M. daily from just before Memorial Day through Labor Day and for two weeks at the peak of the fall color season. For the rest of September and part of October, it runs Friday through Sunday. Closed November through May. Adults are $14 on weekdays, $17 on weekends. Children five through twelve ride for $9.00 on weekdays and $12.00 weekends; children under five ride free. The longer train ride to Bald Knob departs at 10:30 A.M. and is $3.00 to $5.00 more than the short ride. During peak leaf season, ticket prices are $3.00 higher.

Your next stop en route to Lewisburg is tiny **Beartown State Park,** a forest wonderland on Droop Mountain, approximately an hour-and-a-half drive from Cass. To get there, follow WV 28 south for 22 miles to Huntersville, West Virginia Highway 39 west for 6 miles to Marlinton, and US 219 south about 15 miles. Watch for the small sign on your left after you pass through the town of Droop.

Beartown State Park is an area of gigantic rock outcroppings that have been exposed, eroded, and forested over the eons. So named because bears found natural homes in the caves, Beartown has an eerie, fantastic beauty that surpasses description and is an absolute must-see when you are in the area. There is a half-mile boardwalk that goes up, under, and around the geological formations. If you're lucky, you'll be the only one on the walkway, so that you can hear the wind sighing in the stratospherically tall pines overhead and the water dripping from the rocks. Beartown, like all the West Virginia state parks, is free of charge. Open 8:00 A.M. to 6:00 P.M. daily except in winter. (304) 653–4254; www.beartownstatepark.com.

By late afternoon or early evening, you'll arrive at the town of **Lewisburg,** about 23 miles south of Beartown State Park on US 219. There are several places to stay in the area, but the best is the **General Lewis Inn,** 301 East Washington Street; (304) 645–2600 or (800) 628–4454; www.generallewisinn.com. The General Lewis Inn started out as a home, built in 1834. It has had numerous additions since then and now has twenty-six guest rooms. It's as inviting a place to stay as you'll ever find.

Although it is packed with antiques, there's nothing "ye olde," fussy, or precious about the General Lewis. Rooms are eccentrically furnished with a jumble of old stuff, including century-old prints on the walls and high four-poster beds, all of which are more than a hundred years old. The dining room has cheerfully mismatched cotton tablecloths and napkins, and an old quilt is flung over the hall railing.

The downstairs lobby area is as warm and cozy as your grandmother's house; there's likely to be a fire in the grate on chilly days (with rockers surrounding it), and board games and jigsaw puzzles are set on tables. Be sure to take a look at the side hallway on the ground floor. The walls are covered, higgledy-piggledy, with antiques, from ancient horse bridles to kitchen tools to helmets and guns. Outside, huge rocking chairs line the front porch.

Rates for this jewel of an inn are quite affordable. Rooms with double beds, private baths, air-conditioning, telephones, and cable television are $100–$145. A suite with two large rooms (and three separate beds) is $145.

DINNER: For your first night in Lewisburg, stay for dinner at the General Lewis Inn. Service is friendly and leisurely, and the menu is traditional. The buttermilk biscuits are perfect, and you will get a good steak or chop in pleasant surroundings. Moderate.

LODGING: The General Lewis Inn.

Day 2 / Morning

After you scramble into your clothes, grab a wake-up cup of coffee in the living room of the inn, then take an early-morning walk through town.

BREAKFAST: The General Lewis Inn serves full country breakfasts, including wonderful biscuits with sausage gravy, as well as cereal and muffins. Moderate.

Spend the rest of the morning exploring Lewisburg. You can pick up a free pamphlet and a map to Lewisburg at the General Lewis Inn or at the **Greenbrier County Convention and Visitors Bureau,** 540 North Jefferson Street; (304) 645–1000 or (800) 833–2068; www.greenbrierwv .com. The pamphlet also includes a listing of most of the antiques and specialty stores in Lewisburg, as well as the restaurants and lodging establishments. At the visitor center, you can also get materials for a one-hour, thirty-nine-site, self-guided walking tour or a two-and-a-half-hour, seventy-two-site tour.

Of particular historic interest in one of the state's oldest cities are the following: Carnegie Hall (see There's More), built in 1902 as an auditorium for Lewisburg Female Institute, later Greenbrier College; the Old Stone Church, across the street from Carnegie Hall, which is the oldest church in continuous use west of the Allegheny Mountains; North House Museum, just north of Carnegie Hall, where the attractions are the woodwork, period furniture, and china; and the Greenbrier County Library, across the street from the museum, which served as a hospital during the Civil War. If you're a Civil War buff, the visitor center has literature, maps, and a self-guided tour of the major sites of the May 1862 battle.

But save some time for shopping. Among Lewisburg's attractions are several pleasant little stores. There are a number of nice gift shops, including **High Country Gallery,** 122 West Washington Street (304–645–5222; www.highcountrylewisburg.com), which has art, jewelry, clothing, and other handcrafted items; and the **Old Hardware Gallery,** 118 West Washington Street (304–645–2236), a huge old hardware store that now sells decorative glass, Christmas items, wooden crafts, pottery, and more. At 204 North Lee Street, just 2 blocks from downtown, is **Clayworks,** a pottery studio and showroom open to the public; (304) 647–5800. There are also bookstores, clothing stores, and three very nice antiques stores in the 100 block of East Washington Street. Most of the stores are open Monday through Saturday from 9:00 A.M. to 5:00 P.M.

LUNCH: For lunch stop at the **Greenbrier Valley Baking Company,** 110 South Jefferson Street (304–645–6159), which specializes in hearty breads and European-style pastries. Have them pack some sandwiches, dessert, and drinks for a picnic, then head off for a lengthy hike along the beautiful Greenbrier River Trail. Inexpensive.

Afternoon

To get to the base of a very scenic trail near Lewisburg, drive about 2 miles east of Lewisburg on U.S. Highway 60, turning left immediately before you get to the bridge over the Greenbrier River. Drive 1.5 miles north to a parking lot (on the left-hand side of the road) where there is a small sign announcing parking for the **Greenbrier River Trail** (800–336–7009 or 800–833–2068; www.greenbrierrivertrail.com).

The Greenbrier River Trail is one of those walks that draw you farther and farther, because each bend in the river brings some freshly beautiful sight. The trail has hills on each side and the river sparkles down the middle, broken up with large boulders that create eddies and tiny rapids. In the fall (when the leaves are absolutely gorgeous), the river is often low enough to hop across on the rocks.

The river trail extends 76 miles north from the outskirts of Lewisburg nearly all the way to Cass, crossing thirty-five bridges and passing through two tunnels. You might consider renting mountain bikes and seeing some of it that way. The path is gravel and relatively flat, making it an easy ride. (See There's More for information on renting bicycles in the Lewisburg area.)

After a shower and a rest back at the General Lewis Inn, dinner is a short ten-minute walk away.

DINNER: Food and Friends, 213 West Washington Street (304–645–4548), is a casual, friendly place with a nice selection of steaks, chicken dishes, seafood, and Italian and Southwestern offerings. The crab dip served with bruschetta bread is a popular starter, and the sautéed chicken breast is quite tasty. Moderate.

On summer evenings, you might scope out the **Greenbrier Valley Theatre,** a local repertory group that gives regular performances of plays and musicals on Thursday, Friday, and Saturday evenings in the summer, beginning at 8:00 P.M., at the Greenbrier Valley Airport, north of town on US 219. During the nonsummer months, there are occasional performances at the theater quarters at 113 East Washington Street. For information and tickets call (304) 645–3838 or (800) 833–2068; www.gvtheatre.org.

LODGING: The General Lewis Inn.

Day 3 / Morning

BREAKFAST: Before you leave the General Lewis Inn, eat breakfast, then be sure to stroll through the backyard. There are several quiet areas where you can catch up on your reading. There is also a croquet set freely available to guests; you might want to set it up and knock around a few balls.

Your final destination in the area is the famous **Greenbrier** resort, located in White Sulphur Springs just 7 miles east of Lewisburg on US 60; (304) 536–1110 or (800) 453–4858; www.greenbrier.com. This lavish edifice is thought by some to be the finest resort east of the Mississippi. It has some 700 rooms and is set on 6,500 beautiful acres. But one of the most interesting things about the Greenbrier was, until recently, one of the best-kept secrets in America.

In the 1950s, during the height of the Cold War "bomb scare," the U.S. government built an enormous bomb shelter underneath the resort. This wasn't a shelter for local West Virginia residents; rather it was intended to be a postnuclear hideaway for the U.S. Congress. According to the *Washington Post,* the three-story, 150-room bunker included meeting rooms for Congress and could provide food, shelter, and filtered air for up to 1,000 government leaders for a month or two. The lawmakers were to enter through elaborate decontamination chambers and were to be issued "survival bags" containing toothpaste, hair tonic, and deodorant. The accommodations consisted of bunk beds, and the provisions included such delicacies as freeze-dried chicken a la king. Once the secret of the bunker got out, the Greenbrier began offering ninety-minute public tours of the underground facility (adults $30, children ten to eighteen $15). Call (304) 536–7810 or (800) 453–4858, ext. 7810 for more information.

There are plenty of other ways to amuse yourself, and you'll note that the Greenbrier folks take pretty good care of their guests aboveground. There's shopping at Ralph Lauren, Land Rover, the lovely Carleton Varney Gift Gallery, and the Christmas Shop, which features handmade ornaments. The resort also has velvet-turfed golf courses, a spa, horseback riding, beautiful indoor and outdoor swimming pools, tennis courts, a private bowling alley, and gorgeous rooms. The upper lobby is so fancy that there's a sign on the stairs leading to it that warns guests that men must wear jackets "or attractive golf sweaters" to even walk through it. After 6:00 P.M., golf sweaters are out and jackets are required.

The price for staying at the resort is predictably high (roughly $400 to $1,000 a night for a party of two), although the tariff includes dinner and breakfast. But you can stroll through the beautiful grounds for free. On a ridge across from the lodge, there is a line of small, upscale gift shops that are particularly fun to prowl.

LUNCH: Draper's Cafe at the Greenbrier has Reuben sandwiches and chili with scallions and blue corn chips that are fantastic. Forget about your diet and heap on the sour cream, but leave room for one of the cafe's famous desserts.

Afternoon

After lunch—and more shopping if you're up for it—begin your four- to five-hour drive home via I–64 east, I–81 north, and I–66 east.

There's More

Carnegie Hall. Carnegie Hall, 105 Church Street, has a museum and gift shop, a foreign- and art-film series, the free Ivy Terrace Concert Series on the lawn, a children's film series, a classical-music series, and numerous changing art exhibits. To find out what's happening during your visit to Lewisburg, call (304) 645–7917; www.carnegiehallwv.com.

Biking. At Free Spirit Adventures, located on US 60 just east of the Greenbrier River Trail (and about 5 miles east of Lewisburg), you can rent a mountain bike for $35 for the whole day and a tandem bike for $75. For a fee, you can get a shuttle up the trail and you can bike back, or it can pick you and your bike up at a predetermined time and place. Reservations necessary. Call (304) 536–0333 or (800) 877–4749; www.free spiritadventures.com.

Canoeing. The folks at Greenbrier River Campgrounds rent canoes for $30 to $60 for an afternoon. They also rent inner tubes, fishing gear, and mountain bikes. Located on West Virginia Highway 63 south of Lewisburg near Ronceverte; (304) 645–2760 or (800) 775–2203; www.greenbrier river.com. Open April through October.

Golf. The Greenbrier, where for years Sam Snead was the club pro, has three championship eighteen-hole golf courses. Greens fees and cart rental cost $185 for guests staying at the resort and $350 for guests of guests, April through October; off-season rates are about half those prices. (304) 536–1110 or (800) 624–6070.

Pearl S. Buck Museum. If you're not a train fan and want a stopping point midway to Lewisburg, consider a visit to this small museum in Hillsboro on US 219 just north of Beartown State Park; (304) 653–4430; www.pearlsbuckbirthplace.com. Buck is the only American woman to win both the Nobel Prize for Literature and the Pulitzer Prize. The tour of the museum emphasizes the house rather than her writings, and it's kid-friendly. Open Monday through Saturday 9:00 A.M. to 4:30 P.M. Closed November through April. Admission is $6.00 for adults, $5.00 for seniors, and $1.00 for students; children under six are admitted free.

Special Events

January. Shanghai Parade. For more than 150 years, the citizens of Lewisburg have held a community parade on New Year's Day afternoon.

If you're there, you might see fire trucks, horses, scout troops, the high school band, a toddler dance class, and a bunch of people in costumes banging on pots and pans; all are having fun. There are no rules and no committee to screen entrants. (304) 645–1000 or (800) 833–2068.

June. Lewisburg Antique Show and Sale, West Virginia State Fairgrounds, on the southern edge of Lewisburg. (304) 645–1000 or (800) 833–2068.

August. West Virginia State Fair. Nine-day event featuring agricultural exhibits, livestock and horse shows, a midway, a circus, and nationally known entertainers. (304) 645–1090; www.wvstatefair.com.

October. Taste of Our Towns. A festival of food and entertainment to benefit Carnegie Hall. (304) 645–7917.

Other Recommended Restaurants

Tavern 1785, 208 West Washington Street; (304) 645–1744. Upscale restaurant in an old (c. 1785) log building in downtown Lewisburg. Contemporary American menu, patio dining; also nice for Saturday or Sunday brunch. Moderate.

Julian's Restaurant, 102 South Lafayette; (304) 645–4145. New American and Northern Italian cuisine; its fans call it one of the best restaurants in the state. Open for dinner only, Wednesday through Sunday. Moderate.

Lewis Theatre Cafe, 113 North Court Street; (304) 645–6038. Enjoy soup, sandwiches, and desserts on the balcony while you watch first-run movies on the big screen; $4.00 for adults, $3.00 for children; plus food, of course. Call for current feature and showtimes. Inexpensive.

The Market, 215 West Washington; (304) 645–4084. Sandwiches, salads, and ice cream. Outdoor seating available. Inexpensive.

Other Recommended Lodgings

Lynn's Inn B&B, 3 miles north of Lewisburg, just off US 219; (304) 645–2003 or (800) 304–2003. Pleasant three-bedroom bed-and-breakfast with private baths, antiques, and local craft items. Farm setting with a large front porch and rockers; continental breakfast. Rate: $85.

Brier Inn Motel, 540 North Jefferson, on US 219 just north of downtown Lewisburg; (304) 645–7722; www.brierinn.com. More than 160 rooms and suites; in-room phone and TV; game room; swimming pool; restaurant on premises. Rates: $64–$119.

White Oaks Bed and Breakfast, Big Draft Road, White Sulphur Springs; (304) 536–3444 or (800) 536–3402. Pleasant four-bedroom bed-and-breakfast in the country. Shared baths; full breakfast. Rates: $90–$200. There's also a small garden cottage that rents for $225.

Lillian's Bed and Breakfast, 204 North Main Street, White Sulphur Springs; (304) 536–1048 or (877) 536–1048. Century-old Victorian with three guest rooms, all with private baths. Full country breakfast; antiques for sale on the premises. Rates: $85–$125.

The James Wylie House, 7 miles east of Lewisburg at 208 East Main Street, White Sulphur Springs; (304) 536–9444 or (800) 870–1613; www.james wylie.com. Bed-and-breakfast with Flemish-bond brickwork. Four nicely furnished rooms and one suite, all with private bath, TV, full breakfast. Behind the bed-and-breakfast is an eighteenth-century log cabin guest house with the original stone fireplace. Rates: $115–$160 for a double, $160 for the log cabin.

For More Information

Greenbrier County Convention and Visitors Bureau, 540 North Jefferson Street, Lewisburg, WV 24901; (304) 645–1000 or (800) 833–2068; www.greenbrierwv.com.

WEST VIRGINIA ESCAPE FOUR

Pipestem Resort State Park and the New River Gorge

West Virginia Jewels / 3 Nights

Once synonymous with coal mining, steel manufacturing, and gaping ecological destruction, West Virginia today is deservedly famous for the beauty of the Appalachian Mountains chain that runs its length and the great variety of outdoor activities in its magnificent state park system.

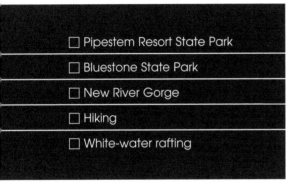

☐ Pipestem Resort State Park

☐ Bluestone State Park

☐ New River Gorge

☐ Hiking

☐ White-water rafting

The transformation is nothing short of astonishing. The New River Gorge, the canyon that cuts through the lushly forested Appalachian Mountains, is called by some the Grand Canyon of the East. Once it was the site of intensive coal mining, logging, and railroad operations; at the New River Gorge Canyon Rim Visitors Center, you can see photographs and films of that era. Today, it's hard to believe that the stripped, gouged, ruined hills in the photographs are the same ones you see before your very eyes.

During this four-day escape, you will have a chance to explore both old and new West Virginia. Your itinerary starts with a long drive from the city to Pipestem Resort State Park, a mountainous park that is sometimes called the jewel of the West Virginia park system. Minutes away from Pipestem is Bluestone State Park, for those more interested in water sports. About an hour's drive from Pipestem is the New River Gorge, one of the premier recreational areas in the eastern United States. You can't leave West Virginia without getting into a raft to ride the white water, and rafting outfitters in the area offer trips varying from the gentle to the wild and woolly.

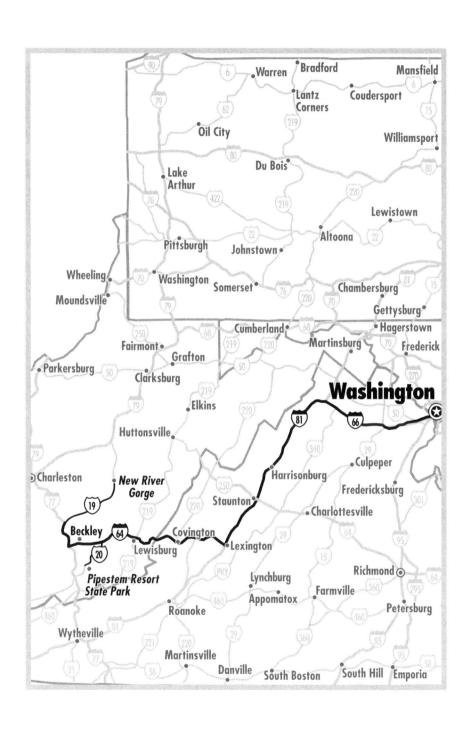

Day 1 / *Morning*

The quickest route to Pipestem is via the interstate system. Take Interstate 66 west about 78 miles to Interstate 81, I–81 south 107 miles to Lexington, Virginia, Interstate 64 west 105 miles to exit 139, and West Virginia Highway 20 south about 30 miles to the park. Allow five to six hours for the 330-mile drive.

LUNCH: A good place to stop for lunch on the way is the **Southern Inn,** 37 South Main Street, in Lexington, Virginia, about three hours into your trip; (540) 463–3612. You can get great sandwiches, large salads, or regional dishes there at reasonable prices. The restaurant is located a mile or so south of exit 55, the first exit on I–64 once you begin heading west from I–81 toward West Virginia.

Afternoon

When you arrive at **Pipestem Resort State Park,** take a few moments to drive through the huge park to acclimate yourself; then make **McKeever Lodge** (also called the Main Lodge) your first stop.

There, park guides will spend as much time as you'd like helping you plan your stay. Make sure you pick up a trail guide as well as a general map of the park.

No matter how tired you might be when you arrive, stretch your legs and refresh your spirits with a two-hour hike, which may be the most beautiful walk you've ever taken. Begin by walking from the Main Lodge down the mountain on the River Trail. It is approximately 2.5 miles to the bottom, with just the right amount of scrambling over rocks to make it interesting. After a mile or so, the River Trail intersects with the Canyon Rim Trail. Take a 1-mile detour on the Canyon Rim Trail, and you'll have a breathtaking view of the canyon and Bluestone River a thousand feet below you.

The Canyon Rim Trail rejoins the River Trail close to where it left it. One of the best parts of the hike is when you reach the bottom of the canyon on the River Trail. There you'll ford the Bluestone River (there is no bridge), where the water probably won't be higher than your knees unless there has been flooding. The River Trail continues along the Bluestone for another mile or so of level walking on a service road.

At the end of the service road is the park's second lodge, **Mountain Creek Lodge.** When you reach it, reward yourself with a tram ride up the hill, which takes about ten minutes and costs $4.00 for adults and $3.00 for children under twelve. (*NOTE:* The tram is open mid-May though October only. Inquire at the Main Lodge before you start your hike or you may have to retrace your steps.) The tram is really fun: It sways just enough to be pleasantly scary, and the views of the mountain and gorge below are fantastic.

At the top of the tram ride, at **Canyon Rim Center,** there are several gift shops, including one that sells the beautiful crafts of Appalachia. Look for carved wooden boxes and "collapsible" baskets, tooled leather goods, woven baskets, and pots of honey and jam.

You can return to McKeever Lodge where you started your hike on the main park road. The 4-mile hike with tram ride takes about two hours. Double that time if the tram is not running or you choose to walk back up the hill.

DINNER: **The Bluestone Dining Room** on the seventh floor of McKeever Lodge (304–466–1800, ext. 360) serves a buffet of regional beef, chicken, and fish dishes, and there will be at least one pasta dish for vegetarians. There is also a large salad bar. The view from the dining room is spectacular; try to schedule dinner so you can watch the sun go down behind the mountains. Moderate. Fancier fare is available in the **Mountain Creek Lodge Dining Room** at Pipestem, and, there, reservations are necessary.

LODGING: You have many choices of accommodations at Pipestem, including camping; two-, three-, and four-bedroom luxury cabins; and spacious rooms and suites at the resort's two lodges. Be sure to call ahead for reservations, especially during autumn, which is a particularly popular time at Pipestem; (304) 466–1800 or (800) 225–5982; www.pipestem resort.com. Lodge rooms are $59 to $89 a night; suites are $74 to $165; cottages are $83 to $177. Cottages must be rented by the week in the summer. Rates start at $766. Pipestem also has eighty-two campsites, which rent for $15 to $23 a night.

Evening

After dinner, stroll over to the **outdoor amphitheater.** There are educational programs and slide shows on weeknights and theatrical and musical performances on weekends.

Day 2 / Morning

BREAKFAST: For breakfast, the Bluestone Dining Room leans toward bacon, eggs, pancakes, fruit, and cereal.

After breakfast, you have plenty of options at Pipestem. There are horses and miles of bridle trails, an eighteen-hole golf course, a par 3 golf course, a driving range, lighted tennis courts, and indoor and outdoor swimming pools. At Long Branch Lake in the park, you can fish for largemouth bass, bluegill, crappie, and channel catfish. You can also rent a canoe or a paddleboat.

The park also offers archery, shuffleboard, Ping-Pong, a game room, a reading room, miniature golf, a nature center, an arboretum, and, of course, lots more trails to hike, as well as some trails where mountain biking is permitted. During the winter, there is a sled run, and several of the trails are open for cross-country skiing.

LUNCH: Depending on where you are in the park, grab a quick lunch at the **Black Bear Snack Bar** in McKeever Lodge or at the **Mountain Creek Lodge Dining Room** in the lodge at the bottom of the canyon. Both offer a wide range of moderately priced, family-friendly sandwiches, soups, and salads.

Afternoon

After lunch, take a short 9-mile drive north on WV 20 and check out another wonderful park, **Bluestone State Park;** (304) 466–2805; www.bluestonesp.com. Because the park sits adjacent to Bluestone Lake, West Virginia's third largest body of water, water-related activities are the primary recreational choices. You can enjoy boating and fishing and a large swimming pool. But there are also hiking trails, shuffleboard, croquet, badminton, volleyball, Ping-Pong, horseshoes, and a softball field. If you forgot to bring your Frisbee, you can rent one at Bluestone for 50 cents an hour.

DINNER: Oak Supper Club, Indian Ridge Road just off WV 20 near Pipestem (look for the signs); (304) 466–4800. It's known for its steaks, prime rib, chicken, trout, generous servings, and casual farmhouse setting; open for dinner only. Moderate.

The **Pipestem Drive-in Theater,** on WV 20 a few miles south of the park, shows first-run family movies. Admission is adults $5.00, children $2.00; Sunday is $10.00-a-car night. Call (304) 384–7382 to see what's playing.

LODGING: Pipestem Resort State Park.

Day 3 / Morning and Afternoon

Get up very early and drive directly to the Fayetteville-Lansing area on the **New River,** where you'll meet your guides, change into river gear, and prepare for a **white-water rafting** trip. Don't worry about breakfast; they'll almost certainly include breakfast and lunch as part of your rafting adventure. To get to the New River recreational area, take WV 20 south about 7 miles to Interstate 77 (West Virginia Turnpike). Then take I–77 north 34 miles to exit 48 and U.S. Highway 19 north another 14 miles to Fayetteville, the hub of white-water rafting activity on the New River. Lansing, where several of the outfitters have their shops, is another couple of miles up the road.

There are numerous rafting companies that provide equipment and guides for a trip down the New River. The guides travel with you, so even children and first-timers can safely have a wonderful time on the river. All you need is advance reservations (see There's More for a listing of outfitters) and proper attire. In warm weather wear a swimsuit or shorts, T-shirt, sunglasses, sunblock, visor hat, and a windbreaker. If you go in the spring or fall, a wet suit is advised, as well as a waterproof jacket and wool clothing. (Wet suits can be rented at most rafting facilities.)

Beginners and families should consider a trip on the Upper New River, which has gentle rapids that don't require much maneuvering. Most of the larger outfitters in the area offer a four- to six-hour beginning rafting trip, which includes breakfast and a picnic lunch. Expect to pay $40–$100 per adult (half that for children) for the trip.

If you're looking for more adventure, try a full-day trip on the Lower New River. After your outfitter buses you to the river and provides you with a flotation vest and safety helmet, you'll jump into an oversize inflatable "boat" and begin your wild and wet four- to six-hour roller-coaster ride over Class III to Class V rapids.

With the help of your guide, you learn to surf the waves, maneuver around exposed boulders, soar over ledges, and shoot rapids with names like "Surprise," "Double Z," and "Miller's Folly." At the end of the run, you'll be soaking wet, tired to the bone, and totally exhilarated. You might even want to add an extra day to your trip and sample the nearby Gauley River, ranked among the top ten rivers in the world (and among the top

Rafting on the New River

two in the United States) for rafting. Lower New River trips cost $70 to $180 per person.

DINNER: After your rafting adventure, refresh yourself with dinner at **Sedona Grille,** 106 East Maple Street, Fayetteville; (304) 574–3411. Sedona attracts rafters, hikers, and just plain tourists, who all seem to enjoy the crab cakes or the moderately priced Southwestern specials.

Be sure to stop at the **Canyon Rim Visitors Center** on US 19 on the north side of the river as you're driving back to Pipestem. The center includes a boardwalk through the woods to give you the best look at the magnificent New River Gorge below. The bridge, the world's largest single steel-arch bridge, is pretty impressive as well.

At Canyon Rim Visitors Center, there is also a very nice small museum with pictures, films, text, and artifacts depicting the history of the New River and the gorge. There you can see the extraordinary transformation of the area from a wilderness paradise to an industrial center back to the forested recreational area that it is today. Open daily 9:00 A.M. to 5:00 P.M., until nightfall in summer. (304) 574–2115; www.nps.gov/neri.

LODGING: Pipestem Resort State Park.

Day 4 / Morning

BREAKFAST: After breakfast at the Bluestone Dining Room in the McKeever Lodge and a last hike, pack your car and begin your trek home. If you're not in a hurry, consider a half-hour detour west on I–64 to Beckley, where you can while away a couple of hours at **Tamarack,** a regional shopping and entertainment complex whose dazzling array of West Virginia art and crafts draws a half million visitors a year. The fine-arts gallery features the work of several dozen contemporary West Virginia artists, photographers, printmakers, and sculptors. Or you might catch a dance ensemble or a storyteller at the Tamarack Theater. Located just off I–64 and the West Virginia Turnpike; (304) 256–6843 or (888) 262–7225; www.tamarackwv.com. Tamarack is open daily from 8:00 A.M. to 8:00 P.M. April through December and from 8:00 A.M. to 7:00 P.M. January through March.

LUNCH: By all means, pause for lunch at the **Taste of West Virginia Food Court at Tamarack.** The food court is managed by the Greenbrier Resort, and you can get some of the resort's famous chili, fried green tomato sandwiches with Swiss cheese and raspberry honey mustard, and bread pudding with vanilla sauce. Prices at the food court are moderate.

Afternoon

After lunch return home from Beckley via I–64 east, I–81 north, and I–66 east. Allow five to six hours.

There's More

White-Water Rafting. There are a score of rafting outfitters in the area. Among them are Class VI River Runners in Lansing, (304) 574–0704 or (800) 252–7784, www.800class-vi.com; Rivers Whitewater Rafting Resort in Lansing, (304) 574–3834 or (800) 879–7483, www.riversresort.com; New River Scenic Whitewater Tours in Hinton, (304) 466–2288 or (800) 292–0880, www.newriverscenic.com; and Ace Adventure Center in Oak Hill, (304) 469–2651 or (888) 223–7238, www.aceraft.com. For more information about white-water rafting, contact the Southern West Virginia Convention and Visitors Bureau at (304) 252–2244 or (800) 847–4898; www.visitwv.org.

Canoeing. If you're looking for a gentler water adventure, several companies rent canoes for paddling around on rivers closer to Pipestem. Try

Bluestone Marina, WV 20 below Bluestone Dam, Hinton; (304) 466–2628. You can rent a canoe for up to eight hours for $25.

Golf. Glade Springs Resort has a challenging eighteen-hole course that many consider one of the best courses in the state. Located at 200 Lake Drive, Daniels; (304) 763–2050 or (800) 634–5233; www.gladesprings .com. Eighteen holes of golf at Glade Springs will cost you $70 to $80. A round of golf at Pipestem Resort State Park will cost you $30 to $50 with cart rental; Pipestem's par 3 course costs $30. (304) 466–1800.

Theatre West Virginia. Broadway musicals and other entertainment at an outdoor amphitheater north of Beckley at Grandview State Park; (304) 256–6800 or (800) 666–9142; www.theatrewestvirginia.com.

Historic Fayette Theatre. Bluegrass bands, traditional Irish folk songs, country and western, rock, storytelling, plays, and other postrafting entertainment. Located at 115 South Court Street, Fayetteville; (304) 574–4655; www.historicfayettetheatre.com.

Special Events

March. Appalachian Heritage Weekend. Arts, crafts, and music at Pipestem State Park. (304) 466–1800 or (800) 225–5982.

May–September. Pipestem State Park Outdoor Amphitheater play and music series with performances on Saturday nights. (304) 466–1800 or (800) 225–5982.

July–August. West Virginia State Water Festival. Parades, pageants, events, and activities throughout the area. (304) 466–5332.

October. New River Gorge Bridge Day Festival. West Virginia's largest single-day festival; rafting, chili cook-off, music, and more. (304) 465–5617 or (800) 927–0263; www.officialbridgeday.com.

Other Recommended Restaurants

Pipestem Area

Brandon's at Nostalgia Inn, Indian Ridge Road; (304) 466–9110. Barbecue restaurant with traditional menu; ribs, chicken, steaks, fish sandwiches, kid's menu. Very near the park entrance. Inexpensive to moderate.

Kirk's Restaurant, WV 20 about 12 miles north of Pipestem; (304) 466–4600. Casual restaurant overlooking the New River. Kirk's serves family-style meals at dinner; also open for breakfast and lunch. Inexpensive to moderate.

Beckley

Ryan's Family Steak House, 1320 Eisenhower Drive; (304) 252–0522. Hand-cut steaks, hundred-item salad bar. Moderate.

The Cafe at Glade Springs Resort, US 19, 6 miles south of Beckley in Daniels; (304) 763–2900. Casual dining with a spectacular view of the golf course. Moderate.

Doughnuts: Elliott's Family Food Deli, 2122 Ritter Drive, Daniels; (304) 763–4003.

New River Gorge Area

Breeze Hill Restaurant, east on Lansing Road, just north of the New River Gorge Bridge; (304) 574–0436. Fancier than most of the rafting-resort restaurants; menu selections include black Angus filet stuffed with Boursin cheese, and trout and summer vegetables steamed in wine and garlic butter. Moderate.

Smokey's on the Gorge, Ames Height Road, Lansing; (304) 574–4905. Rafting-company eatery that's great for breakfast or for the weekend buffets that feature New American cuisine (roast lamb with zinfandel marinade; snapper baked in salt) and many vegetarian choices (herbed bean ragout; barley with toasted cumin seeds and mint; corn and cheese grits). Moderate.

Dirty Ernie's Rib Pit, 310 Keller Avenue, Fayetteville; (304) 574–4822. Hot wings, cheese sticks, soup, salad, chicken, pasta, and, of course, baby-back ribs. Moderate.

Other Recommended Lodgings

Pipestem Area

Bluestone State Park, WV 20 south of Hinton; (304) 466–2805 or (800) 225–5982; www.bluestonesp.com. Bluestone has twenty-five deluxe cabins and eighty-seven campsites. Cabin rates are $70 to $142; weekly rates are $440 to $886. Campsites are $13 to $20.

Nostalgia Inn Bed and Breakfast, just across the road from Pipestem State Park; (304) 466–0470 or (888) 888–6905; www.nostalgiainn.com. Six bedroom suites, all with private bath and 12-foot ceiling; spacious grounds; large country breakfast served. Rates: $85–$140.

Walnut Grove Inn, Broadway Road just off WV 20, 1.5 miles north of Pipestem State Park; (304) 466–6119 or (800) 701–1237. Conveniently located hundred-year-old farmhouse with five guest rooms. Biscuits and gravy or similar hearty fare for breakfast. Rates: $75–$85.

Beckley Area

Glade Springs Resort, 200 Lake Drive, Daniels (on US 19 about 6 miles south of Beckley); (304) 763–2000 or (800) 634–5233; www.glade springs.com. Full-scale resort with suites, villas, and cottages; tennis, horseback riding, indoor and outdoor pools, golf course. Rates: $152–$432.

New River Gorge Area

The Woodcrest, Jenkins Fork Road, Lansing; (304) 574–3870 or (866) 222–7238; www.thewoodcrest.com. Nicely restored farmhouse with five guest suites; amenities include a screened porch, hot tub, and swimming pool; coffee, tea, and fruit for breakfast. Rates: $98–$115. A separate four-bedroom rustic cabin rents for $150 to $250 per night.

Ace Adventure Center, Oak Hill; (304) 469–2651 or (888) 223–7238; www.aceraft.com. You can camp for $10; rent a tent for $39; stay in a cabin for $119; choose a one- or two-bedroom lakeside chalet for $119 to $219; or stay in a three-bedroom, three-bath lodge once used by Harry Truman for $329; or choose one of two log cabins from $229 to $329.

For More Information

West Virginia Division of Tourism and Parks, 90 MacCorkle Avenue Southwest, South Charleston, WV 25303; (304) 558–2200 or (800) 225–5982; www.wvtourism.com.

Southern West Virginia Convention and Visitors Bureau, 200 Main Street, Beckley, WV 25801; (304) 252–2244 or (800) 847–4898; www.visitwv.com.

New River Convention and Visitors Bureau, 310 Oyler Avenue, Oak Hill, WV 25901; (304) 465–5617 or (800) 927–0263; www.newrivercvb.com.

PENNSYLVANIA
ESCAPES

Philadelphia

Birthplace of Independence / 2 Nights

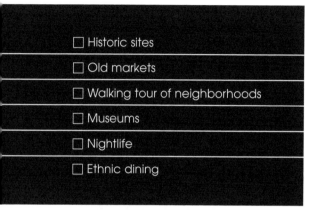

☐ Historic sites

☐ Old markets

☐ Walking tour of neighborhoods

☐ Museums

☐ Nightlife

☐ Ethnic dining

Philadelphia is a delicious mélange of contrasts, from the joyful frenzy of the Italian Market to the solemn dignity of Independence Hall, from the Mummers Parade to fine jazz—with a huge city park, hundreds of museums and galleries, the Liberty Bell, and Philly's famous cheesesteaks thrown in for good measure. Couple that with Philadelphia's well-deserved reputation as one of America's friendliest cities, and the charm of 200-year-old brick streets and horse-drawn carriages, and you begin to appreciate what the City of Brotherly Love has to offer.

Although Philadelphia's precious landmarks of American independence (Independence Hall and the Liberty Bell) are reason enough to visit, your quick escape to the city also includes a walking tour of the historic area and adds the Philadelphia Museum of Art and the Rodin Museum, shopping and gawking in funky South Street, a pasta feast in Little Italy, and late-night jazz. It's almost an insult to Philadelphia to pack it all into three too-short days.

Day 1 / Morning

It is about a three-hour drive to Philadelphia from Washington on Interstate 95. Continue on I–95 until you reach Interstate 676 just north of the downtown area and take I–676 to the North Fifteenth Street exit. Drive a few blocks south, and you're in the heart of downtown Philadelphia.

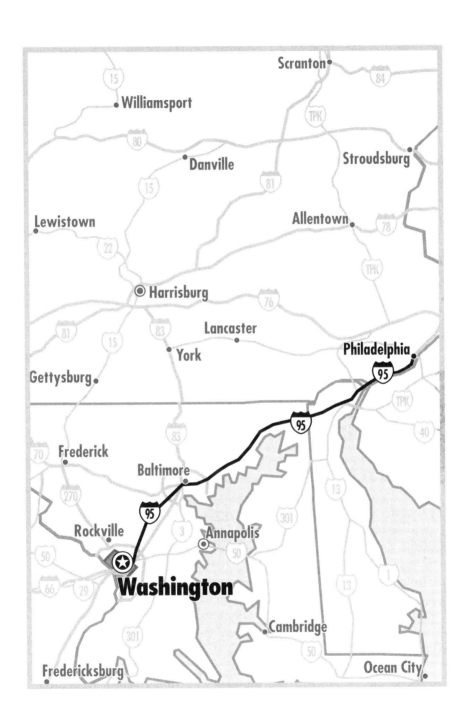

Given that most people consider Philadelphia a food-lover's mecca, it's a must to get on the road in time to make it for lunch. Philadelphia offers a world of choices, but the best way to meet the city is to eat your way through the **Reading Terminal Market.** Home to dozens of small grocery and food stalls, with plenty of places to sit and eat, the market offers such Pennsylvania Dutch fare as "chicken and waffles," scrapple, and homemade soft pretzels (sold by shy Mennonite girls in sober dress). You'll also find Italian specialties, Southern fried catfish and barbecued ribs, hoagies of all sizes and flavors, and Asian takeout. In between are butcher shops, espresso bars, fish stands, flower sellers, and African import stalls. Located at Twelfth and Arch Streets; (215) 922–2317; www.readingterminalmarket .org. Open Monday through Saturday 8:00 A.M. to 6:00 P.M.

LUNCH: For a real Philadelphia lunch, try a cheesesteak sandwich with provolone, onions, peppers, and sauce at **Rick's Philly Steaks** (formerly called Olivieri's Prince of Steaks) in Reading Terminal Market; (215) 925–4320. Open Monday through Saturday 10:00 A.M. to 4:00 P.M.; inexpensive. Top it off with a cup of coffee and a cream cheese and chocolate chip cannoli at **Termini Brothers Bakery;** (215) 629–1790.

Afternoon

Before leaving the downtown area, be sure to drive by the ornate **City Hall,** topped by a bronze statue of city father William Penn, the Quaker humanist and libertarian. Guided tours of the interior are available weekdays at 12:30 P.M., and the Observation Deck is open weekdays noon to 4:30 P.M. for a splendid view of the city. Located at Philadelphia City Hall, Broad and Market Streets; (215) 686–9074.

Then it's on to the historic district, where you'll drop your bags and your car at **Thomas Bond House,** a restored eighteenth-century bed-and-breakfast inn located in Independence National Historical Park, 129 South Second Street between Chestnut and Walnut Streets; (215) 923–8523 or (800) 845–2663; www.winston-salem-inn.com/philadelphia. The twelve guest rooms in the two-centuries-old house have all been carefully restored in the colonial style, and all have a four-poster bed, fireplace, and private bath. Room rates vary from $105 to $190 and include breakfast, afternoon wine and cheese, an evening brandy in winter, and complimentary coffee, tea, and soda all day long.

After you've checked in, embark on a walking tour of old Philadelphia. Start your trek at **Independence National Historical Park**'s visitor center, South Third and Chestnut; (215) 965–2305; www.nps.gov/ inde; open daily from 8:30 A.M. to 5:00 P.M. Park rangers are extremely helpful and not only will give you maps, but, once they know your particular interests, will also note appropriate stops on the route. A gift shop on the premises is loaded with books and souvenirs, and a half-hour film provides an excellent introduction to Philadelphia's role in the birth of the United States of America.

Independence National Historical Park is 17 blocks of arguably the most important historic buildings in the United States. The attractions are all free of charge, authentic, noncommercial, and interesting. The park itself is leafy, green, and quiet, with plenty of benches under big shade trees when you need a rest on your walking tour.

Long lines may look daunting, but be sure to make **Independence Hall** a priority. Here, in the "cradle of liberty," the Declaration of Independence was debated and eventually approved on July 4, 1776. Eleven years later, the Constitutional Convention met in the Assembly Room, argued, compromised, and drafted the Constitution of the United States of America. A thirty-minute tour starts every fifteen minutes or so, and it's worth the wait. Located on Chestnut Street between South Fifth and South Sixth Streets; (215) 965–2305. Open daily 9:00 A.M. to 5:00 P.M., sometimes later in summer months. Tours are free, but—to reduce long waits in line during peak season (March through December)—you can make a reservation for a tour at a specific time by calling (800) 967–2283 or by visiting http://reservations.nps.gov. Reservations by phone or Internet cost $1.50 for everyone over age two; no charge for infants.

Flanking Independence Hall are **Congress Hall,** where the U.S. Congress met from 1790 to 1800 when Philadelphia was the capital of the United States, and **Old City Hall,** the original meeting place of the U.S. Supreme Court. Both are must-sees.

A block north of Independence Hall is the modern glass and marble pavilion housing the **Liberty Bell,** which can be seen from the outside even when the building is closed. The fact that the bell is mobbed with tourists (many from abroad) testifies to its enduring attraction as the preeminent symbol of American independence. Located on Market Street between Fifth and Sixth Streets; (215) 965–2305. Open daily 9:00 A.M. to 5:00 P.M., sometimes later in summer months.

Other places of interest within a couple of blocks of the park are **Declaration House,** where Thomas Jefferson wrote the first draft of the

Declaration of Independence (open daily 9:00 A.M. to noon; Seventh and Market Streets; 215–965–2305); **Christ Church,** where Washington and Franklin often worshiped (open Monday through Saturday 9:00 A.M. to 5:00 P.M., Sunday 1:00 to 5:00 P.M.; Second Street, just north of Market Street; 215–922–1695); and the **Betsy Ross House,** where the famed seamstress may or may not have lived and may or may not have sewn the first American flag—neither debate keeps the tourists away (open Tuesday through Sunday 10:00 A.M. to 5:00 P.M. November through March, daily 10:00 A.M. to 5:00 P.M. April through October; 239 Arch Street; 215–686–1252).

When you are walked out, return to the Thomas Bond House for a glass of sherry and a biscuit, compliments of the inn. On cooler days there might be a fire in the parlor, which is a great place to put your feet up before going out for the evening.

DINNER: Head downtown for one of the best Chinese meals of your life at **Susanna Foo,** 1512 Walnut Street; (215) 545–2666. Start with the dim sum appetizers, then sample one of the French/Chinese/California fusion specialties like tea-smoked duck breast with grilled Asian pears, sautéed broccoli rabe, and potato dumplings. Expensive.

After dinner, head over to **Zanzibar Blue,** for coffee and dessert or a drink and, not incidentally, some of the best jazz in Philadelphia. Located at 200 South Broad Street; (215) 732–4500.

LODGING: Thomas Bond House.

Day 2 / Morning

BREAKFAST: The Thomas Bond House serves freshly squeezed orange juice, muffins, and coffee on weekdays and a full breakfast on weekends.

After a leisurely breakfast, head across town to the **Franklin Institute Science Museum,** 222 North Twentieth Street; (215) 448–1200; www.fi.edu. The Franklin Institute is really several museums in one building, and you could spend several days there. In the Science Center, there are four floors of hands-on exhibits, including a Baldwin locomotive; a 20-foot-high, walk-through human heart; and exhibits on aviation, electricity, and mechanics. The Tuttleman IMAX Theater presents science-oriented action movies on its 40-foot-high, 180-degree screen with fifty-six sound speakers. The Fels Planetarium is one of America's oldest, but it has been updated with the latest in projection equipment, and there are laser presentations on Friday and Saturday evenings.

One of the most popular exhibits is the **SkyBike,** which allows visitors to ride a bicycle 60 feet along a 1-inch diameter cable 28 feet above the atrium floor. It's scientifically impossible to fall, but most visitors choose to just watch. The bike is balanced by a 250-pound counterweight, and the museum straps riders onto the bike with a locked harness. You can even sway back and forth and try to fall, but the counterweight holds the bike in place. Museum personnel gleefully explain the scientific principles involved as everyone in the audience stands watching, mouths agape. The Franklin Institute's SkyBike is one of only two in the United States.

The museum is open daily from 9:30 A.M. to 5:00 P.M.; the Tuttleman IMAX Theater and the planetarium stay open until 9:00 P.M. on Friday and Saturday. The basic all-day museum admission charge is $13.75 for adults, $11.00 for senior citizens and students four to eleven; children under four are admitted free. Add $5.00 to attend the theater. SkyBike rides are $2.00.

LUNCH: A fun lunch stop is **City Tavern,** 138 South Second Street (215–413–1443), a five-story historic tavern frequented by Washington, Adams, Jefferson, and Franklin. Its ten dining rooms have been restored with period furniture, and the menu offers authentic colonial-era dishes, including lobster potpie, salmon and corn cakes, braised rabbit, and mushroom bisque.

Afternoon

After lunch, stroll about a half mile south on Second Street, and you'll be introduced to a completely different side of Philadelphia. Hip, bustling, witty **South Street** is approximately 9 blocks of shops (150-plus), restaurants (75-plus), galleries, and coffee bars. With its vintage clothing shops, bookstores, street musicians, and gorgeous men on skates, South Street is the place to find stores with such names as Condom Kingdom and Greasy Waitress Vintage Clothes. It's not all counterculture, either. South Street has antiques stores, jewelry stores, bookshops, and much more.

No pilgrimage to Philadelphia would be complete without a tribute to the Mummers. So collect your car, and head for the **Mummers Museum** in South Philly, 1100 South Second Street; (215) 336–3050; www.mummersmuseum.com. Open Tuesday through Saturday 9:30 A.M. to 4:30 P.M., Sunday noon to 4:30 P.M. October through April; Tuesday 9:30 A.M. to 9:30 P.M., Wednesday through Saturday 9:30 A.M. to 4:30 P.M., Sunday noon to 4:00 P.M. May through September. Admission is $3.50 for adults and $2.50 for seniors, students, and children under twelve.

Mumming is an ancient Christmas ritual in England. In Philadelphia it's a 200-year-old tradition that culminates every year in the famous New Year's Day Mummers Parade. It's a sort of Italian-German-Caribbean Philadelphia Mardi Gras in which 25,000 men dress up in extraordinary creations of feathers and glitter (some weighing more than one hundred pounds) and parade through town picking banjos to the delight of thousands of locals and visitors alike.

If you aren't lucky enough to catch their act on New Year's Day (or at several concerts given later in the year), the Mummers Museum has loads of information and Mummer paraphernalia.

Finish your afternoon at the city's famous **Italian Market,** 5 pungent, noisy, wonderful blocks of outdoor grocery stalls in the heart of Little Italy. Philadelphians go there to shop for fresh fish, homemade pasta, and freshly butchered meat. With its sidewalks crammed with vendors shouting back and forth, customers haggling, children dodging and racing, and tourists admiring, it's another slice of Philadelphia life. It's located on South Ninth Street between Christian and Dickenson Streets. Vendor hours vary, but most are open Monday through Saturday from 9:00 A.M. to 4:00 P.M. (215) 334–6008.

DINNER: Little Italy is home to lots of great restaurants. For a real treat, opt for America's first and Philadelphia's favorite Italian restaurant, **Dante's and Luigi's,** 762 South Tenth Street; (215) 922–9501. It's a no-frills place with Formica tabletops, glass-block windows, and pink painted walls. The extensive menu includes classic Italian-American favorites and much more. The osso buco, twenty-ounce veal chops, and seafood dishes are particularly good, but be sure to get a side of pasta with "tomato gravy," as they call marinara sauce in South Philly. Open for lunch Sunday through Tuesday, lunch and dinner Wednesday through Saturday. Moderate.

You might end your evening at the theater or concert hall. Philadelphia is truly a cultural center, with a world-class orchestra, three opera companies, several dance companies, and nearly a dozen theaters presenting musicals, comedy, and drama. From September through May the **Philadelphia Orchestra** performs at the Kimmel Center, Broad and Spruce Streets; (215) 893–1900; www.philorch.org. During the summer, performances are held at the Mann Music Center in West Fairmount Park; (215) 567–0707.

LODGING: Thomas Bond House.

Italian Market

Day 3 / *Morning*

BREAKFAST: After breakfast at the Thomas Bond House, head for the Fairmount Park area of town, where many of the art museums are located.

A good place to start your tour is at the wonderful **Rodin Museum,** Twenty-second Street and Benjamin Franklin Parkway; (215) 568–6026; www.rodinmuseum.org. This shrine to the great sculptor features the largest collection of his works outside of France. There's *The Thinker* as you enter the grounds, and the horrifying *Gates of Hell* at the doorway to the building. The *Burghers of Calais* dominates the main gallery, and other Rodin studies are arranged along the walls. Open Tuesday through Sunday 10:00 A.M. to 5:00 P.M.; a $3.00 donation is requested.

Next stop is a climb up the stairs made famous in the movie *Rocky,* to the gigantic **Philadelphia Museum of Art,** Twenty-sixth Street and Benjamin Franklin Parkway; (215) 763–8100; www.philamuseum.org. On

weekends, the terrace area is aswarm with helmeted in-line skaters working out, hanging out, or leaping perilously up and down the crumbling
stone steps. Inside, the museum has more than a hundred galleries with a
fabulous collection, featuring medieval and early Renaissance art, Near
Eastern and Asian art, four wings of European art, and magnificent collections of American, early-twentieth-century, and contemporary art.

Rather than try to take in the whole place at one gulp, you might
hone in on a particular period. A good choice would be the collection of
Impressionists, with dozens of paintings by Manet, Degas, Cézanne,
Cassatt, and Renoir. Enjoy the exquisite privilege of seeing van Gogh's
Sunflowers. Note also the pink and blue Matisse mural above the entrance
in the lobby. Open Tuesday through Sunday 10:00 A.M. to 5:00 P.M. and
Friday evenings until 8:45 P.M. Admission is $12.00 for adults; $9.00 for
seniors, $8.00 for full-time students, and children thirteen to eighteen;
children under thirteen are admitted free.

LUNCH: For a spectacular brunch or lunch, drive a couple of miles to
the **White Dog Cafe,** 3420 Sansom Street; (215) 386–9224; www.white
dog.com. At weekend brunch, your choice will range from brioche French
toast with orchard fruit compote to black pepper seared beef, blue cheese,
and portobello mushroom salad. For weekday lunch try the salmon burger
on a bagel, or the Waldorf-style chicken, fruit, and pecan salad with rosemary dressing. Moderate.

Afternoon

During your last few hours in town, you have several options. You can sit
and admire the wonderful Alexander Stirling Calder–designed bronze
Swann Memorial Fountain with its spouting turtles and joyfully writhing
nudes at **Logan Circle** at Nineteenth Street and Benjamin Franklin
Parkway.

You can also visit **Rittenhouse Square,** Walnut Street between
Eighteenth and Nineteenth Streets. The neighborhood around the square
is Philadelphia's classiest, and there are several shops and restaurants where
you can get a cup of coffee or a cool drink.

Best of all, take a stroll or a drive through **Fairmount Park,** located
west and north of downtown; (215) 685–0000. A gigantic swath of green
running along the Schuylkill River, Fairmount Park is the nation's largest
landscaped city-owned park. The park includes more than 4,000 acres of
natural beauty, with a forested gorge, a Japanese garden, a covered bridge,

tennis courts, ball fields and playgrounds, several early-American homes, and more than 200 pieces of outdoor sculpture. Kelly Drive is a particularly pleasant place to stroll or bike.

Your drive home to Washington on I–95 will take about three hours, just enough time to plan your next quick escape to Philadelphia.

There's More

Benjamin Franklin Bridge. At night, the Ben Franklin Bridge is not just a route to South Jersey; it's a pulsating light show stretching across the Delaware River.

African American Museum in Philadelphia. 701 Arch Street; (215) 574–0380, ext. 230; www.aampmuseum.org. Built in 1976 for the Bicentennial, the museum offers exhibits on black history, art, literature, and culture. It also has an excellent bookstore and gift shop. Open Tuesday through Saturday 10:00 A.M. to 5:00 P.M., Sunday noon to 5:00 P.M. Admission is $8.00 for adults; $6.00 for seniors, the physically disabled, and students five to eleven; children under five are admitted free.

Philadelphia Zoo. Thirty-fourth Street and Girard Avenue; (215) 243–1100; www.philadelphiazoo.org. America's first zoo. Home to Mopey, the 500-pound Galapagos tortoise; a family of Brazilian golden lion tamarin monkeys; and a four-ton white rhinoceros. Open daily 10:00 A.M. to 4:00 P.M. in December and January, 10:00 A.M. to 5:00 P.M. other months. Admission is $16.95 for adults and $13.95 for children two to eleven; children under two are admitted free.

Please Touch Museum. 210 North Twenty-first Street; (215) 963–0667; www.pleasetouchmuseum.org. One of the first museums designed especially for children under age seven. It's still a huge hit with the younger set, especially the full-size bus, toddler-size supermarket, and Maurice Sendak exhibit of *Wild Things.* Open daily 9:00 A.M. to 4:30 P.M., extended to 5:00 P.M. in summer. Admission is $9.95.

Eastern State Penitentiary. This was the model penal structure more than 160 years ago; more than 300 prisons around the world were built to its specifications. It's huge—at the time it was built, it was the largest construction project in U.S. history—and it's ghastly. But it's definitely worth seeing. Open daily 10:00 A.M. to 5:00 P.M. (last entry at 4:00 P.M.) April through November. Admission is $9.00 for adults, $7.00 for students and seniors, and $4.00 for children seven through twelve. No tours for children under seven. Located at 2124 Fairmount Avenue; (215) 236–3300; www.easternstate.org.

Rosenbach Museum and Library. This magnificent collection of rare books and manuscripts includes the manuscript of James Joyce's *Ulysses* and a major original collection of art by Maurice Sendak. The museum also has a fine collection of decorative arts. Open Tuesday and Thursday through Sunday 10:00 A.M. to 5:00 P.M., Wednesday 10:00 A.M. to 8:00 P.M. Admission is $8.00 for adults, $5.00 for seniors and children five to seventeen; children under five are admitted free. Located at 2010 DeLancey Place; (215) 732–1600; www.rosenbach.org.

Special Events

January 1. Mummers Parade, an all-day event centering on a parade of costumed string bands from Broad Street in South Philadelphia to City Hall. (215) 336–3050; www.mummers.org.

March. Philadelphia Flower Show, probably the world's largest indoor flower show. Philadelphia Convention Center, Thirty-fourth Street and Civic Center Boulevard. (215) 988–8800; www.theflowershow.com.

June. Rittenhouse Square Fine Arts Annual. America's oldest and largest outdoor juried art show, featuring paintings and sculpture by more than one hundred Delaware Valley artists. Rittenhouse Square, Eighteenth and Walnut Streets. www.rittenhousesquarefineartshow.org.

July. The Freedom Festival includes several days of events culminating in fireworks on the Fourth of July. (215) 636–1666.

August. Philadelphia's Folk Festival is the nation's largest folk music event. Music, food, crafts, and lots of folk dancing at Old Poole Farm in Schwenksville, northwest of Philadelphia. (215) 242–0150 or (800) 556–FOLK; www.pfs.org/PFF.php.

Other Recommended Restaurants

Striped Bass, 1500 Walnut Street; (215) 732–4444; www.stripedbassrestaurant.com. Glamorous, all-seafood restaurant that many consider to be Philadelphia's top restaurant. Try the sea bass served with chorizo, clams, shrimp, and saffron mussel broth. Expensive.

Friday, Saturday, Sunday, located just off Rittenhouse Square in a tiny town house at 261 South Twenty-first Street; (215) 546–4232; www.frisat sun.com. For more than thirty years, this has been one of Philadelphia's most romantic restaurants, serving excellent seafood, lamb, beef, poultry, and desserts. Moderate to expensive.

Jack's Firehouse, 2130 Fairmount Avenue; (215) 232–9000; www.jacksfire house.com. Really located in an old firehouse, Jack's does "back of the stove" Southern cooking such as black-eyed pea and ham hock soup and New American cuisine such as steamed wild salmon with sticky rice and wasabi vinaigrette. There's light jazz or live piano music. Moderate to expensive.

Le Bec Fin, 1523 Walnut Street; (215) 567–1000; www.lebecfin.com. One of America's premier restaurants. Everything about it—the dining room, the service, the exquisitely prepared food—is elegant. You can order snails in a hazelnut-champagne-garlic-butter sauce for a starter followed by roasted squab, figs poached in red wine, and almond and sautéed arugula salad. Expect to pay about $300 for dinner for two or $100 for lunch.

Alma de Cuba, 1623 Walnut Street; (215) 988–1799; www.almadecuba restaurant.com. Classy Cuban restaurant that draws large crowds. Menu sample: black-bean soup with creamy rice croquettes for appetizers; *lechon asada* (crispy twice-roasted pork with sweet plantain) for an entree. Moderate to expensive.

Cedars Restaurant, 616 South Second Street; (215) 925–4950; www.cedars restaurant.com. Casual, family-owned Middle Eastern favorite with excellent food and moderate prices.

Overtures Restaurant, 609 East Passyunk Avenue; (215) 627–3455. Elegant continental restaurant consistently rated one of the top twenty eating spots in the city. Expensive.

Rembrandt's, 741 North Twenty-third Street; (215) 763–2228, (215) 763–2229, or (800) 736–2726; www.rembrandts.com. New American cuisine, romantic setting. Good choice for Sunday brunch in the museum area—you can enjoy classical piano and viola music with your Belgian waffles. Moderate.

Delilah's at the Terminal, Twelfth and Arch Streets; (215) 574–0929. Southern fried chicken, Cajun catfish, collard greens, and (Oprah says) the best macaroni and cheese in the country. Inexpensive to moderate.

Ray's Cafe and Tea House, 141 North Ninth Street; (215) 922–5122. Small, inexpensive vegetarian Chinese restaurant where everything is prepared by hand to order. Worth a visit in the summer for its delicious iced coffee (cold water drips slowly through fine-ground coffee and ends up tasting like coffee ice cream). Inexpensive.

Best doughnuts in the area: Beiler's Bakery, Reading Terminal Market; (215) 351–0735.

Other Recommended Lodgings

La Reserve, also called Center City Bed & Breakfast, 1804 Pine Street; (215) 735–1137 or (800) 354–8401; www.lareservebandb.com. A very well-preserved and well-maintained town house with eight rooms and suites ranging in price from $89 to $159. Breakfasts are bountiful, and you can amuse yourself by playing the century-old Steinway concert piano or borrowing a book from the library.

Penn's View Hotel, 14 North Front Street; (215) 922–7600 or (800) 331–7634; www.pennsviewhotel.com. Near Independence Park, this forty-room inn is nicely furnished with colonial reproductions. All rooms have a view of the Delaware River, and many have fireplaces and Jacuzzis. Rates: $120–$255.

Shippen Way Inn, 416–418 Bainbridge Street; (215) 627–7266 or (800) 245–4873; www.shippenway.com. Restored inn with nine rooms, all with private baths, phones, and air-conditioning. Continental breakfast; afternoon wine and cheese or tea. Rates: $105–$150.

Best Western Independence Park Hotel, 235 Chestnut Street; (215) 922–4443 or (800) 624–2988; www.independenceparkinn.com. Small (thirty-six rooms), pleasantly decorated Victorian hotel near Independence Park. Rates: $150–$259, including continental breakfast.

The Gables, 4520 Chester Avenue; (215) 662–1918; www.gablesbb.com. Pleasant bed-and-breakfast near the University of Pennsylvania has ten guest rooms, most with private baths. Wraparound porch, gardens, fireplaces; full breakfast served. Rates: $95–$155.

The Omni Hotel at Independence Park, 401 Chestnut Street; (215) 925–0000 or (800) 843–6664. Deluxe hotel (150 rooms) just blocks from the park and South Street shopping. Fitness center, pool, gourmet restaurant, and twenty-four-hour room service. Rates: $139–$250.

For More Information

Philadelphia Convention and Visitors Bureau, 1700 Market Street, Suite 3000, Philadelphia, PA 19102; (215) 636–3300; www.philadephiausa .travel.

Once you are in Philadelphia, visit the Independence National Historical Park Visitors Center, South Third and Chestnut Streets; (215) 597–8974 or (800) 537–7616. The center has an extensive array of maps, guidebooks, and information about Philadelphia and the surrounding areas, as well as information about the park itself.

Lancaster County

Pennsylvania Dutch Country / 2 Nights

Lancaster County, Pennsylvania, is home to some of America's largest Amish and Mennonite communities. A trip to beautiful southeastern Pennsylvania permits the visitor a glimpse into the lives of these quiet,

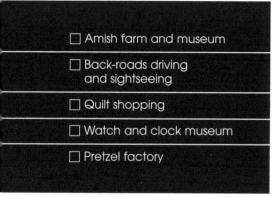

☐ Amish farm and museum

☐ Back-roads driving and sightseeing

☐ Quilt shopping

☐ Watch and clock museum

☐ Pretzel factory

unworldly families, who live today much the same as their ancestors did when they fled Europe in the eighteenth century to escape persecution for their religious beliefs.

Don't be in a hurry; the best part of your visit to Lancaster County may well be the drive along backcountry roads, where you will see bearded Amish men at work in their lush fields with horse-drawn plows and reapers. Amish and Mennonite women and girls, with their hair always covered by a net cap or cotton bonnet, sell produce from their gardens at roadside stands; little boys glide by on old-fashioned, foot-powered scooters; and horses pulling buggies and carriages trot along the road, seemingly oblivious to the roar of the modern world all around them. And you won't have any trouble identifying Amish farms: They are absolutely plain—no shutters, no decorations, no trim, and no power lines.

Unfortunately, there is a great deal of commercialism in the heart of Pennsylvania Dutch country, and many of the towns tend to be jammed with tourists. Your itinerary keeps you off the kitschy strip along U.S. Highway 30 as much as possible and includes some of the nicest ways to experience Mennonite and Amish culture, food, and crafts.

You'll have an opportunity to tour a typical Amish farm (now run commercially by others), to visit a farmers' market, to conduct a treasure hunt for the perfect quilt, and to sample authentic Pennsylvania Dutch cooking at its best.

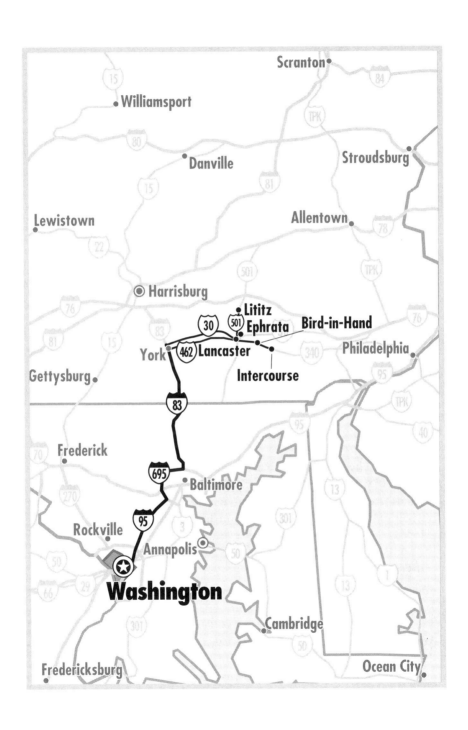

You'll also tour the historic Cloister in Ephrata, shop at the Mennonite-run Ten Thousand Villages store and a very modern complex of upscale art boutiques, and still have time for stops at a pretzel factory, a bakery, and a fascinating watch and clock museum.

Day 1 / Morning

Although Lancaster County is only about 110 miles from Washington, traffic and back-roads driving can make it a three-hour trip. Get an early-morning start so you can arrive by lunchtime. The best route is to take Interstate 95 to the Baltimore Beltway (Interstate 695), follow the beltway west and north to Interstate 83 (exit 24), take I–83 north 40 miles to York, Pennsylvania, and take traffic-laden US 30 east about 20 miles to U.S. Highway 222, which you can follow south a couple of miles to downtown **Lancaster.** If possible, park near the center of town (Penn Square, where King and Queen Streets intersect).

If you're interested in taking a walking tour of Lancaster, you can pick up a brochure at the **Lancaster Visitors Information Center** at 100 South Queen Street (717–397–3531). Do pick up a map of the general area; it's essential for navigating the back roads of Lancaster County, and the friendly guides will help you plan your trip in detail. You'll want to at least stop at the **Central Market,** the nation's oldest publicly owned farmers' market, where you can buy Amish baked goods and fresh meat and produce. It's located less than a block northwest of the square on Market Street.

LUNCH: The Pressroom Restaurant, 26-28 West King Street (717–399–5400; www.pressroomrestaurant.com), just off the square, makes for a quick and pleasant lunch stop. It serves thick deli-style sandwiches, French onion soup, and large salads (including a very nice Caesar salad). Moderate.

Afternoon

You could spend a whole day in the town of Lancaster, but the real beauty of Lancaster County is in the countryside. So gather up your map and brochures and drive east on King Street (Pennsylvania Highway 462) until you reach Pennsylvania Highway 340, the Old Philadelphia Pike. Follow PA 340 east a few miles to the heart of Lancaster County, the neighboring towns of **Intercourse** and **Bird-in-Hand,** located about 5 miles apart on PA 340.

There you'll find lots of commercialism, but you will also get to see something of authentic Amish life. Horses and buggies are plentiful in these towns, and Amish men and women do their shopping at the local stores, just like everybody else. Mennonite women and girls in sober dresses, aprons, and head coverings work in many of the establishments, and their clothes aren't some kind of tourist gimmick. If you listen quietly, you can hear some Mennonite and Amish speaking Pennsylvania Dutch, a dialect of German.

A good place to start your inquiry about Amish and Mennonite life is **The People's Place** in Intercourse, the more eastern of the two towns. It has a beautiful display of Amish quilts on the walls, and a slide show that offers a respectful description of Amish and Mennonite life. Located at 3513 Old Philadelphia Pike, Intercourse; (717) 768–7171 or (800) 390–8436; www.thepeoplesplace.com. Open Monday through Saturday 9:30 A.M. to 5:00 P.M. The affiliated **Old Country Store** just across the street has a very large selection of quilts, quilted pillows and place mats, wooden toys, Amish dolls, and other gifts. Open Monday through Saturday 9:00 A.M. to 8:00 P.M. June through October and 9:00 A.M. to 5:00 P.M. other months. The **People's Place Quilt Museum,** located upstairs, has beautiful displays of Amish and Mennonite quilts and wall hangings, and is definitely worth a visit. Open Monday through Saturday 9:00 A.M. to 5:00 P.M. April through October. (800) 828–8218; www.ppquiltmuseum.com. Free admission.

When you've had a chance to look to your heart's content, drive back west a few miles on PA 340 to Bird-in-Hand, where you'll find another fine quilt shop. **Fisher's,** 2713A Old Philadelphia Pike (717–392–5440), has some unusually interesting quilts and wall hangings in the dark and vivid colors and plain block patterns that are the hallmark of Amish design, as well as the pastel-colored pieced and appliquéd quilts that are more popular with tourists. Open Monday to Saturday 9:00 A.M. to 5:00 P.M.

A word about quilt prices: All of the quilts at the stores mentioned here are handmade. Considering the hundreds of hours that went into making them, their prices—in the $600 to $1,300 range, depending on the size—are a real bargain, but to customers more used to factory-made goods, they may seem high. Just remember that when you buy a handmade quilt, you are buying an original work of art!

As you leave Fisher's, stop downstairs at the **Bird-in-Hand Bakery** (717–768–8273) and pick up some local treats, like sticky buns, cream-filled "whoopie pies," and sticky molasses shoofly pies.

Amish buggy

To get to your final destination of the day, where you'll dine and spend the night, you can take PA 340 and US 30 west back to Lancaster and then Pennsylvania Highway 501 north 10 miles to Lititz. But also consider consulting the area map you picked up at the information center and devising your own circuitous back-roads drive to Lititz. Prosperous farms, plump cattle, flower and vegetable gardens, and rolling hills and valleys are all around. Keep your eyes open for more horse-drawn buggies and Amish stands by the roadside selling fresh fruit and baked goods.

DINNER AND LODGING: The **General Sutter Inn,** located at the intersection of PA 501 and Pennsylvania Highway 772 in downtown Lititz, is a beautiful old inn, in operation since 1764, when it was founded by the Moravian Church. Its lobby is furnished like a Victorian parlor, complete with a large ornate birdcage, with noisy inhabitants inside. The inn's **1764 House** dining room features expensive offerings (duck, medallions of elk, seafood coquilles); the tavern offers pub fare at moderate prices.

The General Sutter Inn's sixteen guest rooms and suites are all furnished with antiques, and there is a coffee shop for lunch and dinner, in addition to the formal dining room. Located at 14 East Main Street, Lititz; (717) 626–2115; www.generalsutterinn.com. Rates: $63–$160.

Day 2 / Morning

BREAKFAST: **Glassmyers Restaurant,** 23 North Broad Street, Lititz; (717) 626–2345. One of the best bargains in town: For $2.95 you will get scrambled eggs, hash browns, and toast in a pleasant environment with friendly service. Closed Sunday.

Follow breakfast with a walking tour of **Lititz.** It's small enough to see in an hour or two, and you'll enjoy the historic buildings, pretty tree-lined streets, and attractive shops. Don't miss **Sturgis Pretzel House,** 219 East Main Street, Lititz (717–626–4354; www.sturgispretzel.com.), where you can tour the oldest commercial pretzel bakery in America and watch pretzels being baked in 200-year-old ovens. The soft pretzels are baked to order and are divine. Open Monday through Saturday 9:00 A.M. to 5:00 P.M. The tour costs $4.00 for adults, $3.50 for seniors, and $2.00 for children three to twelve; children under three are free. The **Wilbur Chocolate Company's Candy Americana Museum and Store,** 48 North Broad Street, Lititz (717–626–3249 or 888–294–5287; www.wilburbuds.com), does not have as much hoopla as Hershey, but the displays from the old chocolate factory are fun. Open Monday through Saturday 10:00 A.M. to 5:00 P.M. No admission charge. And right across the street is **The Kowerski Gallery,** a showplace for local artists who do photography, watercolors, and folk art (49 North Broad Street; 717–664–2088 or 877–509–2879; www.kowerskigallery.com).

Follow your tour of Lititz with a back-roads drive through Lancaster County's lovely countryside. You will be looking for the little town of New Holland, where some of the area's finest Amish quilts are to be found. To get there, take PA 772 (East Main Street) east and south about 6 or 7 miles to Pennsylvania Highway 23, turn left, and follow PA 23 through Leola to New Holland. As you approach the town on West Main Street, keep your eyes open for quilts tossing in the breeze over a clothesline. That will be **Witmer's Quilts,** 1070 West Main Street, New Holland; (717) 656–9526. The "shop" opens at 8:00 A.M. Monday through Saturday and closes at 6:00 P.M. (except on Monday and Friday, when it stays open until 8:00 P.M.).

Emma Witmer not only has scores of spectacular quilts, but she also gives you a tour of them, which will turn you into as big a quilt fan as she is. The quilts are sold from a little brick house on the Witmer farm, where the family also runs a large buggy-wheel shop. You just walk in and look for the three rooms that are stuffed to the ceiling with ravishing quilts. Mrs. Witmer doesn't make all the quilts herself. She commissions them from Amish women in the area and sells them in her small shop. She also has some Laotian refugee women needling for her, and some of their unique pleated and appliquéd handicraft are incorporated into the quilts that she designs.

For customers to view the quilts, Mrs. Witmer needs a helper to stand on the opposite side of a big double bed to help her throw back each one and reveal the next. When a new quilt comes into view, Mrs. Witmer calls out its name—which in some cases she made up herself. There are dozens of variations on traditional patched designs, and even more beautiful appliquéd quilts in astonishingly lovely patterns.

Mrs. Witmer also has old and used quilts, and some genuine antiques. A gorgeous silk "crazy quilt" made from old neckties in the late 1800s recently sold for $800. Prices on the modern quilts are among the best in the area. Appliqués in queen and king size are in the $600 to $1,300 price range, and pieced quilts significantly less. But even if you don't intend to buy, Mrs. Witmer's is a wonderful stop. Her love for the quilts is infectious, and you just might end up taking one home after all.

Your lunch stop and afternoon adventures are in the town of **Ephrata,** north of New Holland. From the quilt shop, drive east into New Holland on PA 23. In the center of town, take a left on Railroad Avenue and drive 2 miles north to Pennsylvania Highway 322; then turn left and follow PA 322 into Ephrata. In Ephrata, turn right on Pennsylvania Highway 272 and drive a few blocks to your lunch stop, on the left.

LUNCH: Nav Jiwan International Tea Room, located within Ten Thousand Villages Gift Shop, has an attractive, low-cost menu featuring different foods of the world every week. One day, when Native American food was featured, the menu included stuffed pumpkin, oyster-potato cakes, fry bread, and succotash. Another week you might find the cuisine of Mexico, Indonesia, or Nigeria served here. No matter what your tastes, the International Tea Room is a quiet place to get off your feet and have a cup of tea or coffee with a dessert. Located at 240 North Reading Road (PA 272), Ephrata; (717) 721–8418. Open Monday through Saturday 10:00 A.M. to 3:00 P.M. (Friday until 8:00 P.M.). Inexpensive.

Afternoon

After lunch, stick around for some shopping. Established by the Mennonite Central Committee as a nonprofit shop, **Ten Thousand Villages** (formerly Selfhelp Crafts of the World) sells high-quality handicrafts from dozens of countries in Asia, Latin America, Africa, and the Middle East. Most of the store's help is volunteer, and the shop has made a commitment to paying the craftspeople good wages for their products. When you purchase brass items, textiles, baskets, rugs, carved boxes, jewelry, and Christmas ornaments here, you can be sure no child labor was used in their production, and that the purchase helps generate income in poor countries. Open Monday through Saturday 9:00 A.M. to 5:00 P.M. (Friday until 9:00 P.M.). (717) 721–8400.

If you can tear yourself away from Ten Thousand Villages, the town of Ephrata has much to offer. Plan to spend at least an hour at the **Ephrata Cloister,** one of America's earliest communal societies. There, an eighteenth-century community of religious celibates lived in complete austerity, with narrow benches for beds and wooden blocks for pillows. Yet, for all their asceticism, the cloister residents created original music and engaged in significant printing and publishing operations. Today, some ten of the original buildings have been restored on the grounds. Even though no one lives there now, the serenity and spiritualism of the cloister's residents pervade the entire restoration. It is a fascinating encounter with the past, and not to be missed on your visit to the area. Located at 632 West Main Street, Ephrata; (717) 733–6600; www.ephratacloister.org. Open Monday through Saturday 9:00 A.M. to 5:00 P.M., Sunday noon to 5:00 P.M. Closed most holidays and Monday in January and February. Admission is $7.00 for adults, $6.50 for seniors, and $5.00 for children six to seventeen; children under six are admitted free.

End your afternoon with a stop at **The Artworks at Doneckers.** This four-story complex is jam-packed with galleries and studios selling jewelry, oil paintings and watercolors, handcrafted furniture and woodcrafts, crystal, and much, much more. Sometimes you can watch the artists at work in their studios. There are also upscale clothing stores for men and women at Doneckers, and you're certain to see many things that you'd like to buy somewhere in the complex. Located at 100 North State Street, Ephrata; (717) 738–9500; www.doneckers.com. Open Monday, Tuesday, Thursday, and Saturday 10:00 A.M. to 5:00 P.M.; Friday 10:00 A.M. to 8:00 P.M.

DINNER: Splurge at the handsome **Log Cabin Restaurant,** 11 Lehoy Forest Drive, Leola; (717) 626–1181; www.logcabinrestaurant.com. Open for dinner only. Reservations necessary. You have to look for the Log Cabin, as it is tucked away in a residential neighborhood on the outskirts of Leola. Follow PA 272 south 5 miles from Ephrata and turn right on Rosehill Road. From there, it's a matter of following the signs through the woods, over a covered bridge, and through more woods. But don't give up—it's worth it.

You'll know you've arrived when you see an interesting and attractive group of low buildings hung on the outside with dozens of paintings. Is that a Picasso? A Miró? Could it possibly be? No, it's not, just the owner having a good time. An artist himself, he playfully made reproductions of some well-known works and hung them outside his restaurant.

Inside, the decor is casual and pretty at the same time, with lots of original eighteenth- and nineteenth-century art on the walls of the seven distinct dining rooms. Menu, service, and prices are distinctly classy, so this is a meal for a special occasion. Entrees are in the $20 to $40 range and include steaks, lamb chops, veal, lobster, and duckling. The desserts are baked on the premises.

Ask at the Log Cabin for directions back to Lititz, which is only 5 miles away via the shortcut. Or drive back down Rosehill Road, take PA 272 north 1 mile, turn left, and take PA 772 about 7 miles to Lititz.

LODGING: The General Sutter Inn.

Day 3 / Morning

BREAKFAST: The General Sutter Inn's **Sutter Cafe** offers generous breakfast at moderate prices. Particularly good are the eggs Florentine and the grilled cinnamon buns.

It's your last day in Lancaster County, but there's much more to see and do. After breakfast, drive south on PA 501 about 6 miles to US 30. Follow the motel- and outlet-laden strip east about 3 miles to the **Amish Farm and House,** 2395 Route 30 East, Lancaster; (717) 394–6185; www.amishfarmandhouse.com. Open daily from 8:30 A.M. to 5:00 P.M. (6:00 P.M. in summer, 4:00 P.M. in winter). Admission is $7.25 for adults, $6.50 for seniors, and $4.75 for children five to eleven; children under five are admitted free.

If you are really interested in learning about the Amish, the best way to do so would be to stay with an Amish or Mennonite family for a while. But if you only have a few days, the Amish Farm and House may be the best alternative. It is a commercial enterprise, and you won't see any conservative Amish on the premises. But it was once the home of an old-order Amish family, and both the house and farm have a certain authenticity about them.

Try to arrive in time for the first tour of the house, at 9:00 A.M., because crowds get large, particularly in the summer, and can be distracting from the peaceful and simple surroundings. On the tour, you'll get to see the very plain clothing and furnishings of the old-order Amish; these items have changed very little over the last 300 years. There is no electricity, and newly bought appliances like electric sewing machines have been modified so that they can be run by foot treadle. You'll also learn something of the group's culture and values. Religious services are in family homes and last for three and a half hours, with worshipers sitting on hard benches. Singing, which lasts for thirty-five minutes without interruption, is in German, as is Bible reading.

The life of the old-order Amish seems austere when you see the bare walls and severe clothing (women's aprons are pinned on with straight pins—buttons are thought to be decorative and are avoided). At the same time, one senses the commitment to community and family that is the source of Amish strength and joy.

If you managed to get to the Amish Farm and House early, you might also manage to beat the lunch crowds at noon. Sundays present even more of a problem because many of the restaurants in the area are closed. But if you're willing to brave the crowds for a real Pennsylvania Dutch smorgasbord, opt for Miller's, about 1 mile east of the Amish Farm on US 30.

LUNCH: Miller's Smorgasbord Dinner, US 30, 1 mile east of Pennsylvania Highway 896 (717–687–6621 or 800–669–3568; www.millers smorgasbord.com), is open daily for "dinner" from noon to 8:00 P.M. If your idea of a great dinner includes ham, chicken, roast beef, turkey, and going back for seconds, you've come to the right place. Miller's has been dishing up all-you-can-eat meals since 1929. If you're not in a buffet mood, Miller's specialty is chicken and waffles. Moderate.

Afternoon

Your final destination on the road home is the **National Watch and Clock Museum** in Columbia. You can reach it by backtracking on US 30 west for 3 or 4 miles to PA 462 and then proceeding west through Lancaster and on another twenty minutes to Columbia. Located at 514 Poplar Street; (717) 684–8261, ext. 234; www.nawcc.org. Open Tuesday through Saturday 10:00 A.M. to 5:00 P.M.; also open Sunday noon to 4:00 P.M. April through December. Admission is $7.00 for adults, $6.00 for seniors, $4.00 for children six to twelve; children under six are admitted free. A family admission is $16.

This little-known gem of a museum, established about twenty years ago, contains a collection of some 12,000 timepieces, from beautifully intricate gold pocket watches to a whole roomful of stately old grandfather clocks. There are cuckoos, chimes, and a water clock, as well as ancient sundials and other timekeepers. The museum's adjoining rooms are quiet and cool, and all around you are clocks, ticking like heartbeats.

A highlight is the Stephen Engle Monumental Clock. Built in 1878, this enormous, room-size clock includes a procession of apostles (which occurs at 9:55, 11:55, 1:55, and 3:55), two barrel organs, and pirouetting Revolutionary War soldiers. The apostolic procession is stunning; stick around for it if you can.

Your return trip from Lancaster County via US 30 to York, I–83 to the Baltimore Beltway (I–695), and I–95 from Baltimore to Washington should take you less than two and a half hours.

There's More

Hans Herr House. Tours of the oldest house in Lancaster County, which has been restored in the Colonial Mennonite fashion, are available Monday through Saturday 9:00 A.M. to 4:00 P.M. April through November. Located at 1849 Hans Herr Drive (off US 222), about 6 miles south of Lancaster; (717) 464–4438; www.hansherr.org. Admission is $5.00 for everyone over twelve, $2.00 for children seven to twelve; children under seven are admitted free.

Buggy Rides. Several enterprises offer buggy rides through the country in authentic Amish and Mennonite carriages. Aaron and Jessica's Buggy Rides (717–768–8828; www.amishbuggyrides.com) is located on PA 340 between Intercourse and Bird-in-Hand. Abe's Buggy Rides (717–392–1794 or 717–394–4422; www.abesbuggyrides.com) is just west of Bird-in-Hand on PA 340. Expect to pay about $10.00 per adult and $5.00 per child for a twenty- to thirty-minute ride.

Outlet Shopping. Most of the outlet stores in the area are located on US 30 on a 5-mile strip just east of Lancaster, although several are on PA 896 south of US 30. You can shop for just about anything, from rugs and china to shoes and name-brand clothes.

Special Events

April. Quilter's Heritage Celebration. Annual Lancaster event at which quilts are displayed and sold. (717) 299–6440.

June–July. Kutztown Pennsylvania German Festival. Popular Pennsylvania Dutch folklife festival. More than a thousand quilts for sale. (888) 674–6136; www.kutztownfestival.com.

August. Annual music fest at town square in Lancaster. Also food and crafts. (717) 291–4758.

August–October. Pennsylvania Renaissance Faire. Re-creation of sixteenth-century English country fair on the grounds of the Mt. Hope Estate and Winery, 15 miles north of Lancaster on Pennsylvania Highway 72. Food, crafts, minstrels, jousting matches. Open weekends only. Admission is $26.95 for those twelve and older, $9.95 for children five through eleven; children under five are admitted free. A two-day pass is $39 for adults, $15 for children. (717) 665–7021; www.parenfaire.com.

Other Recommended Restaurants

The Stockyard Inn, 1147 Lititz Pike (on PA 501 just south of US 30), Lancaster; (717) 394–7975. Former home of President Buchanan, converted into an inn in 1900. Steak, prime rib, seafood in a historic setting. Moderate to expensive.

Lombardo's Italian-American Restaurant, 216 Harrisburg Pike, Lancaster; (717) 394–3749; www.lombardosrestaurant.com. Open since 1946, this family-owned local favorite is noted for its veal, pasta, and desserts. Moderate.

Belvedere Inn, 402 North Queen Street, Lancaster; (717) 394–2422; www.belvederepa.com. Upscale casual restaurant with excellent beef and seafood entrees and creative appetizers. Moderate to expensive.

Groff's Farm Restaurant, 650 Pinkerton Road, Mount Joy; (717) 653–2048. Praised by the likes of James Beard and Craig Claiborne as perhaps the best of Pennsylvania Dutch fare, Groff's has fancied up its menu and is now open only for Friday and Saturday dinner. But you can still get its famous Chicken Stoltzfus (chunks of chicken in cream sauce on buttery pastry squares) followed by cracker pudding for dessert. Moderate to expensive.

Stoltzfus Farm Restaurant, 1 block east of Intercourse on PA 772 East; (717) 768–8156. Excellent homemade sausage, ham loaf, and fried chicken served family-style on the farm. Moderate.

Good'n Plenty Restaurant, PA 896, Smoketown; (717) 394–7111; www .goodnplenty.com. Family-style dining with pork and sauerkraut guaranteed to be on the table; large crowds. Moderate.

Akron Restaurant, PA 272, Akron; (717) 859–1181. Extensive sandwich selection, but try the baked oyster pie if you visit on Friday or chicken potpie on any other day of the week. Moderate.

The Restaurant at Donecker's, 333 North State Street, Ephrata; (717) 738–9501. Upscale ambience; French cuisine; fantastic desserts; expensive. Casual dining and moderate prices in the Tavern at the same inn.

Doughnuts: Achenbach's Bakery, 375 East Main Street, Leola; (717) 656–6671. Free tours of the huge bakery followed by a warm doughnut! Twenty-plus choices, including strawberry-and-cream-filled doughnuts. Bread, sticky buns, whoopie pies, and other Pennsylvania Dutch treats also available.

Other Recommended Lodgings

Swiss Woods B&B, 500 Blantz Road, Lititz; (717) 627–3358 or (800) 594–8018; www.swisswoods.com. Swiss chalet; seven rooms with private baths, some with Jacuzzis. Large garden; full breakfasts. Rates: $125–$190.

Alice's Manheim Manor, 140 South Charlotte Street, Manheim; (717) 664–4168 or (888) 224–4346; www.manheimmanor.com. An 1856 Victorian with six guest rooms and one suite, all with air-conditioning, cable TV, and private bath; full-course breakfast served. Rates: $89–$149 for the rooms, $214 for the suite.

The Railroad House Restaurant and B&B, 280 West Front Street, Marietta; (717) 426–4141; www.therailroadhouse.com. Romantic eight-room inn with exposed-brick walls, antique furnishings, private baths, Oriental rugs, gardens; full breakfast included. Restaurant on premises. Rates: $99–$179.

The Inns at Doneckers, 318–324 State Street, Ephrata; (717) 738–9502 or (800) 377–2206; www.doneckers.com. Classy, four-building inn with rooms ranging from $65 to $210 a night. The more expensive rooms might have a balcony and a Jacuzzi next to the marble fireplace.

Cameron Estate Inn, 1855 Mansion Lane, Mount Joy; (717) 492–0111 or (888) 422–6376; www.cameronestateinn.com. Two-hundred-year-old mansion on fifteen acres with eighteen guest rooms, each with private bath, phone, and canopy bed. Excellent restaurant on the premises. The $129 to $289 tariff includes a full breakfast.

The King's Cottage, 1049 East King Street, Lancaster; (717) 397–1017 or (800) 747–8717; www.kingscottagebb.com. Clean, friendly bed-and-breakfast with nine rooms, all with private bath. Rates: $135–$270.

1725 Historic Witmers Tavern and Inn, 2014 Old Philadelphia Pike, Lancaster; (570) 753–3884. The area's oldest continuously operating inn has seven guest rooms, two with private bath. Antiques in the rooms and for sale on the premises. Wood-burning stoves; continental breakfast. Rates: $70–$110.

For More Information

Pennsylvania Dutch Convention and Visitors Bureau, 501 Greenfield Road (Greenfield Road exit off US 30), Lancaster, PA 17601; (717) 299–8901 or (800) 723–8824; www.padutchcountry.com.

Downtown Lancaster Visitors Information Center, South Queen and Vine Streets, Lancaster, PA 17603; (717) 397–3531; www.lcci.com.

Laurel Highlands

Mountain Retreats / 3 Nights

Four hours from Washington, D.C., is an unspoiled recreational area in southwestern Pennsylvania known as the Laurel Highlands. When Washington's streets are slushy and one drab winter day blends into the next, it's time to break out of the weather-imposed claustrophobia and head for the hills, where you can ski, work out at a resort/fitness center, and swim in a heated indoor swimming pool.

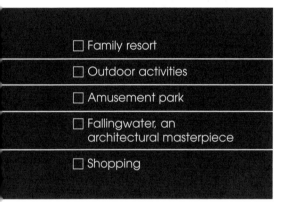

☐ Family resort

☐ Outdoor activities

☐ Amusement park

☐ Fallingwater, an architectural masterpiece

☐ Shopping

Winter isn't the only time to enjoy a long weekend escape to the Laurel Highlands. Hiking, biking, swimming, and white-water rafting are also available in this beautiful, secluded area of Pennsylvania, where temperatures will be at least ten degrees cooler than they are in Washington.

The weekend also includes a tour of Fallingwater, the cantilevered stone-and-glass home designed by Frank Lloyd Wright that many consider the premier masterpiece of American architecture. You'll also visit the town of Ligonier, which has lots of shops and restaurants, and a century-old amusement park built with tiny children in mind. Oh, and there's a place on the route where you can buy marvelous doughnuts.

Day 1 / Morning

Drive to Somerset, Pennsylvania, via Interstate 270 north to Interstate 70, I–70 west to the Pennsylvania Turnpike (Interstate 76), and the turnpike west to exit 10. The 180-mile drive will take about three and a half hours, so when you get to Somerset, you'll probably be ready for lunch.

LUNCH: Stop at the **Summit Diner,** a genuine, open-twenty-four-hours-a-day, old-time classic, with a menu to match. If a grilled cheese sandwich and a slice of pie—or scrambled eggs, hash browns, and toast any time of the day or night—are your idea of a good thing, you've come to the right place. The diner is located at 791 North Center Avenue (Pennsylvania Highway 985) in Somerset; (814) 445–7154. Inexpensive.

Afternoon

After lunch, drive to **Hidden Valley Four Seasons Resort** on Pennsylvania Highway 31, approximately 10 miles northwest of Somerset; (814) 443–8000 or (800) 458–0175; www.hiddenvalleyresort.com. The resort's address is 1 Craighead Drive, Hidden Valley, but just look for the signs on PA 31.

Once you're checked in at the resort, head for the great outdoors. If you go in winter, there are twenty-five ski slopes and eight lifts that operate daily from 9:00 A.M. to 10:00 P.M. There's a ski school with instructors who give individual and group lessons at all skill levels. There are also 30 miles of groomed cross-country ski trails that link up with another 20 miles in adjacent state parks and forests.

You can ski for nine hours (choose the daylight package that lasts from 9:00 A.M. to 6:00 P.M. or the twilight package that lasts from noon to 10:00 P.M.) for $40 for adults, $34 for seniors and children under twelve. If you're a night owl or you arrive really late, it's $20 if you wait until 4:00 P.M. to hit the trails. For general ski information phone (814) 443–2600. For the ski report hot line, phone (866) 443–7544.

You can rent skis, boots, and poles for $20. Snowboards rent for $20 a session. Private lessons will cost you about $50 an hour; group lessons, about $20 an hour. If your kids aren't old enough for the slopes, they might like snow tubing, igloo building, and sleigh rides. Or you can take advantage of the resort's child-care services for those under eight at $7.00 an hour per child. The kids get stories, movies, and snacks. There's also a special ski orientation school for three- to five-year-olds, which has half-day and full-day classes for $40 to $60.

Hidden Valley is also great fun in summer. There's a modern playground for kids, plus four heated swimming pools, three of them outdoors. There's also a small freshwater lake for fishing, sailing, kayaking, canoeing, or taking a leisurely paddleboat ride. At the Lake House equipment room, you can rent or borrow fishing poles, basketballs, volleyballs, and a croquet set. The lake is available for use from 10:00 A.M. to 6:00 P.M.; the outdoor swimming pools are open 8:00 A.M. to 10:00 P.M.

In spring, summer, or fall, you'll enjoy the 30 miles of well-marked hiking trails inside the resort, which connect with many more miles of trails in nearby state parks and forests. Resort guests get complimentary use of mountain bikes and helmets.

Hidden Valley's golf course sits on top of a mountain with a 3,000-foot peak and 30-mile vistas, and it's certainly one of Pennsylvania's most beautiful courses. Greens fees on the eighteen-hole, par 72 course are $32 to $45 a day; cart rental is included. Call (814) 443–8444 for tee times.

DINNER: Have dinner at Hidden Valley's **Snowshoe Lounge,** a casual pub that serves soups, salads, sandwiches, and pasta. Moderate.

LODGING: There are dozens of accommodation possibilities at Hidden Valley resort. There are studios and suites at the inn and one- to three-bedroom condominiums and town houses that you can rent. Lodging rates range from $95 to $450. During ski season, expect to pay 25 to 50 percent more. Call (888) 232–6554 to make a reservation.

Day 2 / *Morning*

BREAKFAST: The **Garden View Room** at Hidden Valley provides a complimentary continental breakfast of juice, coffee, bagels, cereal, and fruit.

Spend the morning at the **Sports Club,** Hidden Valley's health and fitness facility, complete with racquetball courts, indoor pool, weight room, modern exercise room, sauna, whirlpool, tanning bed, and massage room. There's also a video game room and a hair salon. The Sports Club is open daily from 8:00 A.M. to 10:00 P.M.

Or, weather permitting, head for the **Tennis Club,** which has six clay courts and four hard-surface courts. All of the courts are open dawn to dusk April through October; some are lighted for night play.

When you're ready for a break, take a thirty- to forty-minute drive into Ligonier (5 miles west on PA 31, about 12 hilly, scenic miles north on Pennsylvania Highway 381, and 3 miles west on U.S. Highway 30).

LUNCH: Have lunch at the **Ligonier Tavern,** a fun and funky old pink and turquoise Victorian home that was converted to a restaurant in 1935. The redecorated interior with several adjoining dining rooms is very pretty, and the menu is eclectic. Lunchtime favorites include chicken noodle soup, a hot meat loaf sandwich with gravy on ciabetta bread, or the grilled veggie platter. In warm months, you can eat outside on the screened front porch or on the upstairs balcony. The Ligonier Tavern is located at 137 West Main Street; (724) 238–4831; www.ligoniertavern.com. Moderate.

Afternoon

After lunch, wander around **Ligonier,** which has several gift, toy, clothing, and antiques shops clustered around the diamond in the center of town, where a gazebo sits on a patch of green. The Finishing Touch, 210 West Main Street, has Christmas collectibles. The Toy Box, 108 South Market Street, has puppets, puzzles, and educational toys. And Main Exhibit, 301 West Main Street, has contemporary art, jewelry, pottery, and sculpture.

Consider also a visit to **Fort Ligonier,** a full-scale, on-site reconstruction of the 1758 fort where the young George Washington fought with the British against the French. At the fort, there is a museum with period rooms, exhibits, dioramas, and a slide show. You might also catch a battle encampment or reenactment or an archaeological dig while you're there. Located at the intersection of US 30 and Pennsylvania Highway 711; (724) 238–9701; www.fortligonier.org. Open Monday through Saturday 10:00 A.M. to 4:30 P.M., Sunday noon to 4:30 P.M., May through October. Admission is $7.00 for adults and $4.00 for children six to fourteen; children under six are admitted free.

If it's summer and you have young children, don't miss **Idlewild and Soak Zone,** a child-oriented theme and amusement park about 3 miles west of Ligonier on US 30; (724) 238–3666 or (800) 432–9386; www .idlewild.com. Open Tuesday through Sunday 10:00 A.M. to dark, June through August, and some weekends in May. Admission is $23.95 for children and adults, $15.55 for seniors; children under two are admitted free. Idlewild first opened in 1878, and it claims to be the oldest continuously operated amusement park in the country. Many of the old rides are still there, but—faced with competition from parks with ever bigger and faster roller coasters—Idlewild today caters to the younger set.

Favorites at the park for the under-six crowd include the trolley ride through Mr. Rogers' Neighborhood of Make-Believe; the Story Book Forest, where children meet characters from nursery rhymes; the Jumpin' Jungle, a woodsy state-of-the-art playground; Hootin' Holler, a musical train ride through the Wild West; and Raccoon Lagoon, an area with amusement park rides for toddlers. Older kids will happily spend the whole day on the water slides at the Soak Zone and the roller coasters of Olde Idlewild.

DINNER: Unless you have a package plan at Hidden Valley that includes dinner, stop on the way back at **Ligonier Country Inn,** an attractive, moderately priced restaurant located on US 30 in Laughlintown, about 3 miles east of Ligonier; (724) 238–3651. There you can get a crab dip appetizer and a great lamb stew with puff pastry or choose from a dozen other steak, seafood, chicken, or pasta dishes. Everyone gets "flowerpot bread"— yeast bread baked on the premises in tiny clay flowerpots. Moderate.

Even if you don't stop in Laughlintown for dinner, you can't pass up the **Pie Shoppe,** US 30, Laughlintown; (724) 238–6621. In addition to pies of all flavors, they sell vegetarian pizzas (the spinach and tomato is great), sandwiches, and mouthwatering doughnuts.

Try the slopes at night or relax in one of Hidden Valley's lounges.

LODGING: Hidden Valley Four Seasons Resort.

Day 3 / Morning

BREAKFAST: After breakfast at the Garden View Room, head for **Fallingwater,** the former weekend home of Pittsburgh department store magnate Edgar J. Kaufman that was designed by Frank Lloyd Wright in 1936.

Fallingwater is about a half-hour drive from Hidden Valley. (Drive 5 miles west on PA 31 and 15 miles south on PA 381.) It is the only remaining home designed by America's greatest architect that includes the original furnishings, most of which were also designed by Wright. Voted by the American Institute of Architects in 1991 as the "best all-time work of American architecture," Fallingwater has to be seen to be believed. A miracle of concrete, flagstone, steel, and glass, the house is built in layers and cantilevered over a waterfall.

You can see the "perfect marriage between structure and nature" in the massive boulders built right into the house, the highly polished flagstone floors (which Wright meant to resemble the bottom of the riverbed), and the views of the ravine, woods, and waterfall from every angle of the house. Fallingwater cost the fabulous sum of $155,000 when it was built in 1936. Wright's fee for designing the house and furniture was $8,000. There is a wonderful hour-long guided tour of the house, and then you can spend as much time as you like on the forested grounds around it.

Finally, take a moment to visit the gift shop, which offers books and postcards, beautiful pottery and glass, and even a reproduction or two.

Fallingwater is located on PA 381, Mill Run; (724) 329–8501; www.fallingwater.org. Open Tuesday through Sunday 10:00 A.M. to 4:00 P.M. from mid-March through Thanksgiving weekend and weekends in December. Reservations for the tour are required. Admission is $16 for adults and $10 for students six through twelve. Children under six are not permitted on the tour; child care is available for $2.00 per child per hour. Photography is not permitted on regular tours, but there is a special $55 two-hour tour at 8:30 A.M., during which visitors are allowed to take still photographs.

LUNCH: Fallingwater Cafe, on the grounds, serves a very nice lunch of homemade soups, salads, sandwiches, and pastries. Many of the selections please vegetarians. If you eat there, you can spend an extra half hour admiring the building. But if you're in a hurry or you want to picnic at your next stop, they'll box the lunch to go. Inexpensive.

Afternoon

Just south of Fallingwater on PA 381 is **Ohiopyle State Park** (724–329–8591), the beautiful 18,000-acre state park that straddles the Youghiogheny River. (It's pronounced "Yock-a-gay-nee," but everyone calls it "the Yock.")

Ohiopyle is the site of the first commercial white-water rafting east of the Mississippi, and numerous rafting outfitters are located there. Among them are Laurel Highlands River Tours (724–329–8531 or 800–472–3846; www.laurelhighlands.com), White Water Adventurers (724–329–8850 or 800–992–7238; www.wwaraft.com), and Wilderness Voyagers (724–329–1000 or 800–272–4141; www.wilderness-voyageurs.com).

If you are a novice at white-water rafting (or have kids with you), you might want to start with a guided trip on the middle Youghiogheny. This 9-mile section of the river winds its way around Sugarloaf Mountain from Confluence to Ohiopyle and offers spectacular scenery and easy-to-navigate Class I and II rapids. The guided trip takes three to five hours and includes transportation to the launch site and a picnic lunch or snack. Expect to pay $20 to $40 per person for the guided tours.

If you want to launch out on your own, most of the outfitters will rent you a raft, canoe, kayak, or duckie (a rubber kayak) for use on the middle Yough.

Those with some white-water rafting experience will prefer the lower Yough, whose Class III and IV rapids are moderately difficult. The 7-mile trip from Ohiopyle to Bruner Run will take you three to five hours. Guided trips vary from $30 to $90 depending on season and day of the week.

For the veteran rafter, the upper Yough with its Class V-plus rapids—an hour or so south of Ohiopyle—is the place to be, although trips are usually scheduled only on weekdays, when water is released from the upstream dam. Rafting the upper Yough will cost you $100 to $150 for an all-day trip.

If white-water rafting isn't your sport, Ohiopyle State Park is also an ideal spot for hiking and picnicking. You can hike from park headquarters a mile or so to a beautiful spot where the waters of Cucumber Falls cascade into a waterfall bordered by a series of mountain peaks. Or you can cross the river and wander through Ferncliff Peninsula, a hundred-acre nature preserve formed by a horseshoe bend in the river.

Ohiopyle is also a great place to rent a mountain bike and go for a scenic spin along the river on the Allegheny Highlands Trail. The level, gravel bike trail stretches 11 miles upriver and 17 miles downriver to Connellsville. Nearly all of the rafting companies rent mountain bikes for about $16 a day.

The truly energetic can arrange a five- or six-hour "pedal and paddle" adventure by biking the 11 miles from Ohiopyle to Confluence and rafting or kayaking back down the middle Yough to the park.

If you rafted or biked to Confluence, you'll have noticed a picturesque, small cafe right on the bank of the river, and it's a great choice for dinner. To get there by car, drive east from Ohiopyle on Pennsylvania Highway 2012 for 8 miles, and then take Pennsylvania Highway 281 north one mile to Confluence.

DINNER: At **River's Edge Cafe,** 203 Yough Street, Confluence (814–395–5059), you can relax on the porch of the cafe and enjoy the beauty of the rippling Youghiogheny River a few feet away as you savor your chef-prepared pasta primavera or grilled chicken dinner and linger over coffee until the sun sets behind the mountains. Moderate.

LODGING: Hidden Valley Four Seasons Resort.

Day 4 / Morning

BREAKFAST: After breakfast at the Garden View Room, have a last ski, hike, mountain-bike ride, or swim before packing up for home. You can pick up sandwiches for the road at the **Snowshoe Lounge** in the main lodge or, if you're on the slopes, grab a burger at the cafe there.

Your drive back to Washington via PA 31 east, the Pennsylvania Turnpike east, I–70 east, and I–270 south will take four hours.

There's More

Additional Ski Slopes. The nearby Seven Springs Mountain Resort, just east of PA 711 near Champion, has seventeen cross-country trails and fourteen slopes for downhill skiing; (814) 352–7777. Nemacolin

Woodlands Resort, U.S. Highway 40 East, Farmington (724–329–8555 or 800–422–2736; www.nemacolin.com), has five downhill slopes and five cross-country trails. Ski rates at Nemacolin and Seven Springs are comparable to Hidden Valley Resort.

Golf. Seven Springs Mountain Resort (814–352–7777 or 800–452–2223; www.7springs.com) in Champion has a beautiful eighteen-hole golf course where the greens fees are $58 to $72. If you're looking for a challenge, drive down the road and try Nemacolin Woodlands' Links Course or the Peter Dye–designed Mystic Rock Course, now a regular stop on the PGA tour. Eighteen holes and a cart rental cost $55 to $84 on the links course, $84 to $150 for Mystic Rock. (724) 329–8555.

Kentuck Knob. Frank Lloyd Wright–designed home open for public touring is a hexagonal grid constructed entirely of red cypress and fieldstone. Mountainside location with a view of the Youghiogheny River; sculpture park on the grounds. Located near Ohiopyle State Park in Chalk Hill; (724) 329–1640; www.kentuckknob.com. Prearranged tours daily 9:00 A.M. to 4:00 P.M. March through December, 11:00 A.M. to 3:00 P.M. January and February. Admission is $15.00 for adults and $8.00 for children under eighteen. Children must be six years old to tour the house. A two-hour, in-depth tour offered at 8:30 A.M. and 4:15 P.M. costs $50.

Mountain Playhouse. Local theater company performs classic Broadway musicals and comedies at popular Green Gables Restaurant in Jennerstown; the company has been going strong since 1939; (814) 629–9201; www.mountainplayhouse.com. Performances mid-June through mid-October. Tickets run $10 to $35.

Special Events

March–April. Annual Pennsylvania Maple Festival in Meyersdale. Food, crafts, and music in Somerset County. (814) 634–0213; www.pamaplefestival.com.

September. Ligonier Highland Games. Games, parades, bagpipes and fiddles, dog shows, food, and more at various sites in or near Ligonier. (724) 851–9900; www.ligoniergames.org.

October. Springs Folk Festival. Annual crafts and music festival that draws artists and crowds from three states. Southeast of Ohiopyle State Park on Pennsylvania Highway 669 just off US 40. (814) 662–9202; www.springspa.org.

Fort Ligonier Days. Annual weekend event featuring food, crafts, a parade, and historical programs. (724) 238–4200; www.ligonier.com.

Other Recommended Restaurants

Oakhurst Tea Room, PA 31 west of Somerset; (814) 443–2897; www.oakhursttearoom.com. Large smorgasbord and dessert table; bring your appetite and burn off the calories on the slopes. Moderate.

Green Gables, PA 985, a half mile north of US 30, Jennerstown; (814) 629–9201, ext. 103; www.mountainplayhouse.com/gg. Regional American cuisine in a pleasant setting has made this restaurant popular since 1927. Moderate.

Falls City Restaurant and Pub, Garrett Street (just off PA 381), Ohiopyle; (724) 329–3000; www.fallscitypub.com. Rafting center restaurant that serves very good Italian and Mexican food and microbrews. Moderate.

Glisan's Restaurant, 4 miles east of Farmington on US 40; (724) 329–4636. No-frills, booth-filled diner that opens early for breakfast and bakes its own bread, rolls, and pies on the premises. Inexpensive.

The Sun Porch, US 40 East, Hopwood; (724) 439–5734. Dinner buffet with huge salad bar; chicken and biscuits every day. Inexpensive to moderate.

Chez Gerard, US 40 (Business Route), Hopwood; (724) 437–9001; www.chezgerard.net. You might not expect haute cuisine in the county where the Big Mac was invented, but Chez Gerard serves traditional French cuisine good enough to earn this small restaurant a statewide reputation. Don't go if you're on a diet; there are more than thirty selections on the cheese board and several thousand-calorie desserts. The prix fixe dinner is $48; the lunch, $22—but you can order from the a la carte menu and get by for less.

For additional listings see Other Recommended Lodgings.

Other Recommended Lodgings

Ligonier Country Inn, US 30, Laughlintown; (724) 238–3651; www.ligoniercountryinn.com. Homey inn with twenty-four guest rooms and three cottages, all with private bath, air-conditioning, TV, and telephone; swimming pool and restaurant on premises. Rates: $85–$170 for rooms, $165 for cottages.

Mountain View Inn, US 30 East, Greensburg; (724) 834–5300 or (800) 537–8709; www.mountainviewinn.com. Large, comfortable inn with eighty-nine guest rooms and suites furnished with brass beds and antiques. Pleasant gardens, gazebos, and pool; restaurant on premises serves first-rate regional fare. Rates: $72–$150 for rooms, $162–$250 for suites.

Seven Springs Mountain Resort, Champion; (814) 352–7777 or (800) 452–2223; www.7springs.com. Pennsylvania's largest resort, with accommodations for more than 5,000 people in its hotel, cabins, chalets, and condos. Five restaurants on the premises; five additional restaurants in the ski lodges during winter. (All are casual except Helen's, which serves continental cuisine and is expensive.) Accommodation rates range from $150 to $700 a night, but the many package deals can substantially reduce the price of a stay.

Nemacolin Woodland Resort and Spa, US 40 East, Farmington; (724) 329–8555 or (800) 422–2736; www.nemacolin.com. Attractive resort with hundred-plus units in the lodge, dozens of town houses, and the Chateau Lafayette Hotel (modeled closely after the Ritz in Paris). Amenities at the resort include a polo field, a shooting academy, a warm-water spa, mud baths, a billiards room, a regulation croquet court, and ten restaurants (three of which—Lautrec, the Golden Trout, and Seasons—are elegant and expensive). Lodging rates range from $150 to $650 a night for a double.

River's Edge Cafe Bed and Breakfast, 203 Yough Street, Confluence; (814) 395–5059. This small, delightful bed-and-breakfast on the banks of the fast-flowing Youghiogheny River has three guest rooms with private baths. Continental breakfast served. Rate: $75.

Ohiopyle State Park Campgrounds; (724) 329–8591 or—for reservations— (888) 727–2757. The park has 226 sites for tents and trailers, a couple of dozen of which are walk-in, tent-only sites. Rates: $14–$19.

For More Information

Laurel Highlands Visitors Bureau, 120 East Main Street, Ligonier, PA 15658; (724) 238–5661 or (800) 333–5661; www.laurelhighlands.org.

Pittsburgh

Great Museums in River City / 2 Nights

People have been saying for years that Pittsburgh is one of the most livable cities in the United States. Well, it's a great place to visit, too. This old river city shed its smokestack image long ago and is now bursting with art, culture, upscale shopping, new restaurants, Steelers fans, and delighted visitors.

One of the city's many draws is the beauty and variety of its architec-

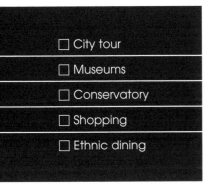

☐ City tour

☐ Museums

☐ Conservatory

☐ Shopping

☐ Ethnic dining

ture. In the downtown area, you'll see the glittering neo-Gothic spires of the PPG Place Building, the nineteenth-century Mellon Bank building (with its beautifully carved trim, looking like a lace handkerchief draped over the roof), the gigantic rust-red U.S. Steel building, and off in the distance behind a hospital, an angel with outstretched wings atop a church.

Old and new exist side by side all over Pittsburgh. There are old museums with new acquisitions, new restaurants in old neighborhoods, inns and shops springing up in once-blighted enclaves. There are famous attractions that have existed for a hundred years, like the Carnegie Museum of Natural History and the spectacular Phipps Conservatory. And the Frick Estate, built a century ago, is open for visitors to tour the grand home, grounds, and art gallery and museum.

Your tour won't be confined to the nineteenth century, however. The dazzling Carnegie Science Center on the Allegheny River was completed in 1991, and the Andy Warhol Museum opened in 1993 to showcase the works of this Pittsburgh native, the central figure of pop art. Shops and restaurants have opened up at the renovated Station Square along the waterfront. And there are hip and lively shopping districts near the University of Pittsburgh and Carnegie Mellon University, where coffee bars, ethnic restaurants, and upscale clothing and gift shops abound.

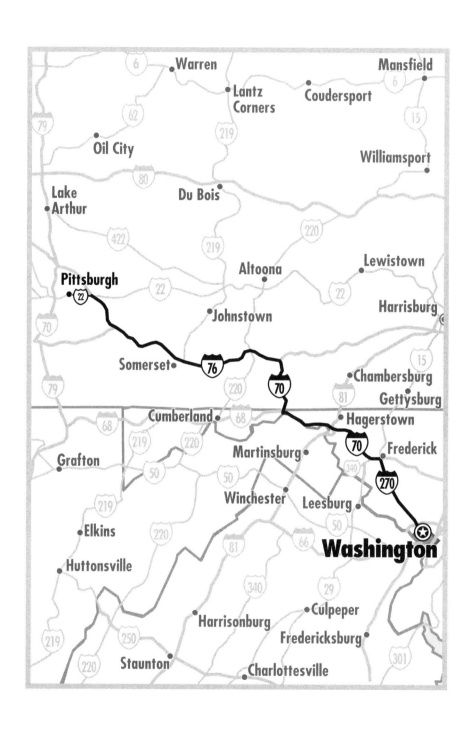

Your three-day weekend itinerary isn't long enough to do it all, but you'll see enough to fall in love with Pittsburgh and want to return again and again.

Day 1 / Morning

Get an early start—8:00 A.M., if possible—so you'll have a full afternoon in Pittsburgh. Pittsburgh is 220 miles from Washington, but it's a four-and-a-half to five-hour drive via Interstate 270 north to Interstate 70 west to the Pennsylvania Turnpike (Interstate 76) west. Take the turnpike's exit 6 and follow the parkway (Interstate 376 and U.S. Highways 22 and 30) west through the eastern suburbs for 16 miles to the center of the city.

Your first destination is the **Shops at Station Square,** a complex of stores and restaurants right along the Monongahela River directly across from the Golden Triangle, Pittsburgh's 11-by-11-block, spruced-up business district.

In many ways, the Shops at Station Square are a symbol of the "new" Pittsburgh. A century ago this fifty-acre site was the Pittsburgh and Lake Erie Railroad Yards, and, if the wind was right, the coal-burning, smoke-belching trains could cover downtown Pittsburgh with a dark cloud. Today Station Square is a renovated two-building indoor mall that includes boutiques, upscale apparel chain stores, bookstores, and more than a dozen places to eat. Special events are often held at Station Square or in the spacious parking lots. Station Square is located on West Carson Street; (412) 261–2811; www.stationsquare.com. Shops are open Monday through Saturday 10:00 A.M. to 9:00 P.M., Sunday noon to 5:00 P.M. Restaurant hours vary.

LUNCH: Upon arriving at the Shops at Station Square, your immediate objective is lunch, and there are several choices—from ribs, pizza, or sandwiches to raw bars or ethnic food. One good choice is the very popular **Sesame Inn,** which offers fine Chinese dining in the evening and $6.00 specials for lunch; (412) 281–8282.

Afternoon

After lunch, drive up the hill to the **Mount Washington** section of town. When you reach Grandview Avenue, park your car and stroll west.

Mount Washington itself is worth seeing, with its century-old Victorian homes, peaceful streets, old churches, and art galleries, but most people make the trip up the hill because Grandview Avenue has, well, a grand view.

You'll see the Allegheny and Monongahela Rivers meet to form the Ohio River. You'll see where tiny **Point State Park** juts right into the middle of the rivers' intersection, a patch of green with a spewing fountain. And, as you stroll along Grandview Avenue, you'll survey all of the Golden Triangle and the vibrant downtown business and commercial center of Pittsburgh.

As you head west on Grandview Avenue, just past the clutch of restaurants, you'll come to the **Duquesne Incline** station. Don't pass it by. Pittsburgh has two funiculars, or inclines: the **Monongahela Incline,** which climbs Mount Washington from Station Square to the foot of Grandview Avenue, and the Duquesne Incline, which climbs the mountain from a point just west of the Fort Pitt Bridge to the commercial heart of Grandview Avenue.

Take a moment to walk around inside the Duquesne Incline station, which has walls covered with old pictures and postcards of Pittsburgh in the past. And don't miss the view from the observation deck, where you can see at least sixteen of Pittsburgh's 720 bridges on the Allegheny, Monongahela, and Ohio Rivers.

And, of course, you'll want to ride down and up the Duquesne Incline itself in the original tram car that has been gliding up and down the hill since 1877. It's slightly scary, but that only makes it more fun. The view from the trams at night, when Pittsburgh is all lit up, is especially nice, and the Duquesne Incline has been considered among the most romantic night spots in Pittsburgh for more than a century. Both inclines operate from 5:30 A.M. to 12:45 A.M. every day except Sunday. Incline rides cost $1.75 (85 cents for children under twelve) each way. (412) 381–1665.

Now that you have the big picture and the topography of Pittsburgh mastered, it's time for a brief history lesson. Drive back down the hill from Grandview Avenue, recross the bridge, and head for the **Senator John Heinz Pittsburgh Regional History Center,** 1212 Smallman Avenue; (412) 454–6000; www.pghhistory.org. The center has an interactive and informative exhibit (Points in Time) that highlights significant events and trends in the more-than-two-century history of Pittsburgh. You'll learn about the early settlers and the military campaigns centered at Fort Pitt, rise of the steel industry and labor unions, great fire of 1845, polio and the Salk vaccine, Pittsburgh's role as the glass capital of America, and birth of a "new" high-tech Pittsburgh. Open daily 10:00 A.M. to 5:00 P.M. Admission: adults $7.50, seniors $6.00, students $5.00, children six to eighteen $3.50; children under six are admitted free.

The Gateway Clipper *and Point State Park*

When you finish your afternoon's introduction to Pittsburgh, check in at your evening digs, located across the Allegheny River from the Golden Triangle. Take the Ninth Street Bridge and you'll see Pressley Street after about 7 blocks. There you'll find **The Priory—A City Inn,** 614 Pressley Street; (412) 231–3338 or (866) 3PRIORY; www.thepriory .com. Built in 1888, this nicely restored European-style inn once was a way station for Benedictine priests traveling to Pittsburgh. The Priory has twenty-four rooms and suites, all of which are large, high-ceilinged, and quiet. Complimentary sherry, cheese, and crackers are served in the parlor in the afternoon, and there's a self-serve "honor" bar, too. Rates: $79–$210.

After sherry and a shower, take in a surprising local attraction that is just a couple of blocks from your hotel: the **Andy Warhol Museum,** 117

Sandusky Street; (412) 237–8300; www.warhol.org. Open Tuesday through Sunday 10:00 A.M. to 5:00 P.M., Friday open until 10:00 P.M., closed Monday. Admission is $10.00 for adults, $7.00 for seniors, and $6.00 for students and children over three.

Warhol was a Pittsburgh native who studied art at what is now Carnegie Mellon University. His images of Marilyn Monroe and Campbell's Soup cans became the icons of pop art, and his innovative photographic techniques transformed the modern-art world. This interesting gallery, which houses the largest single-artist collection in the world, is one of the Carnegie museums, in collaboration with the Dia Center for the Arts and the Andy Warhol Foundation.

DINNER: Pittsburgh has lots of nice restaurants to choose from, but for your first night, stay downtown and sample the osso buco, the linguine with fresh clams and mussels, or any of the seafood dishes at **Piccolo Piccolo Ristorante,** 1 Wood Street; (412) 261–7234. Don't overdo it at the complimentary antipasto salad table, because you also get a pasta course, an entree, and a salad course, and the servings are enormous. Expensive.

LODGING: The Priory Inn.

Day 2 / Morning

BREAKFAST: The Priory Inn serves a buffet continental breakfast that you can eat outdoors on the garden patio in seasonable weather.

After breakfast, drive to the east side of Pittsburgh for a morning exploring the wonders of the great **Carnegie Museum** complex. You can't miss the gorgeous century-old building that houses the original structure. Topped with statues, fronted with archways and pillars, and covering an entire city block, the classical Greek building now houses the Carnegie Library, the Museum of Natural History, the Museum of Art, and the Music Hall.

The immense building, expanded in 1903 so that it now covers fourteen acres, is even more wondrous inside than out. The lavish and gleaming foyer, with an arched gold ceiling and towering green marble pillars; the plaster reproductions in the Hall of Architecture and the adjacent Hall of Sculpture (which is modeled after the Parthenon); the brilliant **Music Hall,** with red velvet seats and a beautifully carved ceiling . . . well, you'll have to see them all for yourself.

The **Museum of Art,** which opened in 1896, was designed to bring to Pittsburgh exhibitions of contemporary paintings from Europe and the United States. Today, the Carnegie International (a six-week exhibition of art from around the world held in midwinter) is the biggest international art show in the United States, and the second oldest in the world. It includes old masters, decorative arts, and sculpture.

One complete wing of the Carnegie Museum building is devoted to natural history. The **Museum of Natural History** contains an extraordinary collection of dinosaur skeletons and fossils; a glittering hall of minerals and gems; anthropological treasures such as Egyptian mummies, jade artifacts, and Native American art; and much, much more. The museum cherishes living creatures, too. It is affiliated with a 2,200-acre natural sanctuary in the nearby Laurel Highlands that serves as the base for research on many species.

Be sure to leave time for a visit to the Natural History Museum Gift Shop, which is a treasure trove of posters, imported art objects, masks, dolls, and nature-oriented videos, books, and games.

The **Carnegie Library of Pittsburgh,** at the same location, has an outstanding science and technology collection, one of the nation's best music collections, and an excellent humanities collection. For more than a century it has been a pioneer in defining the true purpose of libraries.

The Carnegie Museum complex is located at 4400 Forbes Avenue; (412) 622–3131; www.carnegiemuseums.org. Both of these Carnegie museums are open Tuesday through Saturday 10:00 A.M. to 5:00 P.M., Sunday noon to 5:00 P.M. (open Monday in July and August). The Carnegie Library is open Monday through Thursday 10:00 A.M. to 8:00 P.M., Friday and Saturday 10:00 A.M. to 5:30 P.M., Sunday 1:00 to 5:00 P.M. Admission to the museums is $10.00 for adults, $7.00 for seniors, $6.00 for children three and up and for full-time students. (*NOTE:* The Carnegie has a six-level parking garage where you can leave your car for $4.00; be sure to have your ticket validated at the museum.)

LUNCH: When you're ready to get off your feet, head for the **Star of India,** a quiet, charming Indian restaurant at 412 South Craig Street, a short walk from the Carnegie; (412) 681–5700. The extensive menu has dozens of meat and vegetarian dishes, including tandoori chicken, lamb, shrimp, biryanis, curries, and wonderful breads, such as puffy pooris and onion naan. This is a "bring your own alcoholic drinks" restaurant, which charges 30 cents for the glass, but cups of hot spiced tea are readily available and are the perfect accompaniment to the spicy food. Don't forget dessert. The kulfee (cardamom-flavored ice cream) is wonderful. Moderate.

Afternoon

After lunch, stroll along South Craig Street in the pleasant **Oakland** neighborhood and shopping district. There you will see interesting import stores, ethnic restaurants, and coffee bars. Notice Macondo and History, two import stores with beautiful Haitian, African, and Asian arts and crafts, both in the 400 block of South Craig Street, just north of Forbes Avenue.

From South Craig Street, walk or drive a block east on Forbes Avenue to Boundary Street, turn right, and go a few blocks to the Schenley Park Bridge. There turn left and enter **Schenley Park,** an enormous expanse of green where bikers, walkers, and in-line skaters fly up and down the winding drive.

Schenley Park is also home to the **Phipps Conservatory.** The Phipps, built in 1893, has thirteen glass show houses (covering two and a half acres) featuring beautiful and exotic trees, plants, and flowers. Outdoors, there are shade trees, fountains, benches, and more gardens, including a Japanese courtyard. The conservatory is open daily 9:30 A.M. to 5:00 P.M. (until 9:00 P.M. Friday). Admission is $7.50 for adults, $6.50 for seniors, $5.50 for students, and $4.50 for children two to fourteen; children under two are admitted free. (412) 622–6914; www.phipps .conservatory.org.

From the Phipps, drive east about a mile and north about a mile and you'll be in **Shadyside,** another pleasant neighborhood, with an interesting shopping area along Walnut Street. There you'll find some fine antiques and clothing stores interspersed with familiar chain-store outlets. Don't miss the Four Winds Gallery at 5512 Walnut Street, which has a collection of Native American artwork, jewelry, pottery, and weavings for sale.

DINNER: Shadyside is also home to lots of ethnic restaurants. You can find Vietnamese, Japanese, Greek, and Italian within just a few blocks. A pleasant little Mexican restaurant is close by, too. **Cozumel,** 5507 Walnut Street (412–621–5100), is an unpretentious place with an enormous menu that includes old standbys and more adventuresome dishes, including lots of vegetarian selections. The enormous margaritas and nearly a dozen brands of Mexican beer increase Cozumel's appeal. Moderate.

After dinner you should explore what's going on at the **Carnegie Music Hall;** its chamber music series is likely to be featuring an internationally acclaimed group. Call (412) 622–3131 for tickets and program information. Alternatively, check out **Heinz Hall for the Performing Arts,** where the world-famous Pittsburgh Symphony Orchestra performs (412–392–4900; www.pittsburghsymphony.org), or the **Benedum Center for the Performing Arts,** home of the Pittsburgh Opera and the Pittsburgh Ballet (412–471–6070; www.pgharts.org/venues/benedum.aspx).

LODGING: The Priory Inn.

Day 3 / Morning

BREAKFAST: After breakfast at the Priory, take a walking or a driving tour of downtown Pittsburgh to get a closer look at its many beautiful buildings. (A walking-tour brochure is available at the visitor center and at most hotels.)

Worth a close look are the USX Tower on Grant Street, at 841 feet the tallest building between New York and Chicago; the Alcoa Building on William Penn Place, America's first aluminum skyscraper; Trinity Episcopal Cathedral and the First Presbyterian Church next door to each other on Sixth Avenue, two century-old churches with marvelous stained-glass windows; Kaufmann's Department Store on Fifth Avenue, with a large bronze clock that is Pittsburghers' favorite meeting place; and PPG Place, the castle of glass located between Third and Fourth Avenues.

About midmorning, head for the **Carnegie Science Center,** a huge museum with a four-story, domed Omnimax theater; a sophisticated interactive planetarium; a World War II vintage submarine; and 250 more exhibits that make this truly "an amusement park for the mind." You could and should spend days visiting the science center. There are special exhibits for preschoolers; three free theaters—the science stage, the kitchen theater, and the works theater—where minidramas illuminate everyday science; the largest science and sports exhibit in the world; an aquarium; an insect exhibit where you can let insects run up your hands and arms; a weather center; and a creative-technology center.

A favorite of visitors of all ages is the miniature railroad and village, which must rank among the top two or three miniature railroads in the world. Yes, there are trains—more than a dozen on the 30-by-90-foot platform. There are also automobiles, bridges, farms, factories, a stone quarry, a baseball field, and inch-high people. And they're nearly all moving. Except, of course when the lights dim to simulate nighttime, or winter comes and the snow begins to fall, or well, you get the point—when they're not supposed to be moving. It's not unusual to see a visitor standing transfixed through two or three rotations of the seasons, watching a tiny portion of the village for fifteen or twenty minutes.

The Carnegie Science Center is located at 1 Allegheny Drive; (412) 237–3400; www.carnegiesciensecenter.org. It's open Sunday through Friday 10:00 A.M. to 5:00 P.M., Saturday 10:00 A.M. to 7:00 P.M. General admission (the science exhibits, the sports center, the planetarium, and the submarine) is $14 for adults, $10 for seniors and children three to eighteen; children under three are admitted free. Tickets to the Omnimax theater are $5.00 extra.

Your last stop in Pittsburgh will be a visit to the **Frick Art and Historical Center,** which sits in an elegantly landscaped, six-acre complex at the edge of Frick Park, Pittsburgh's largest city park. The Frick complex is located at 7227 Reynolds Street in Pittsburgh's fashionable East End; (412) 371–0600; www.frickart.org. Open Tuesday through Sunday 10:00 A.M. to 5:00 P.M. Admission to the art gallery is free, but guided tours of the mansion cost $10.00 for adults, $8.00 for seniors and students; children under six are admitted free.

LUNCH: Begin your visit to the Frick with lunch at the **Cafe,** located in the middle of the complex. As you eat your sandwich, salad, and pastry, you'll have a panoramic view of the estate. (412) 371–0600. Moderate.

Afternoon

After lunch, start your tour of the Frick Art and Historical Center at the **Frick Art Museum,** with its beautiful collection of fourteenth-century icons and Italian, French, and Flemish paintings and examples of the decorative arts. Francesco Ubertini's *Madonna and Child with Saint Elizabeth and John the Baptist* will draw your eyes immediately, with its lush colors and beautifully rendered faces.

Elsewhere in the complex is **Clayton,** Henry Clay Frick's renovated estate, which you can tour if you make an advance reservation; (412) 371–0606. Crowd favorites on the docent-led tour are the leather high-chair, the miniature children's entrance, and the tiny sink and coat rack, which show that Clayton was a real family home as well as an elegant mansion where world leaders and wealthy industrialists were entertained.

Also visit the **Carriage Museum,** which displays the Frick's seventeen carriages and automobiles (including a 1914 Rolls Royce Silver Ghost); the **Greenhouse,** with thousands of exotic plants and flowers; and the **Children's Playhouse,** which now houses the visitor center and museum shop.

When you finish at the Frick, drive home via the parkway east to the Pennsylvania Turnpike (I–76), I–76 east to I–70, I–70 east to I–270, and I–270 south to Washington. The trip will take you about five hours.

You can stop for dinner on the way home at one of the many fast-food places or diners on, or just off, the Pennsylvania Turnpike. For a more relaxed meal, consider one of the Hagerstown restaurants listed in Maryland Escape Five.

There's More

Children's Museum of Pittsburgh. "Please touch" exhibits, climbing maze, fantastic puppet shows, crafts, a special infant play area with a rice table and peekaboo boxes, and exhibits from *Mr. Rogers' Neighborhood,* which was taped in Pittsburgh. Located at 10 Children's Way; (412) 322–5058; www.pittsburghkids.org. Open Monday through Saturday 10:00 A.M. to 5:00 P.M., Sunday noon to 5:00 P.M. Admission is $9.00 for adults and $8.00 for seniors and children two to eighteen; infants are admitted free.

Kennywood Park. One of the oldest amusement parks in the United States and a National Historic Landmark. It has some of the old historic rides, plus lots of gentle rides for little kids. It also has the Phantom's Revenge, which may be one of the world's fastest roller coasters. Located at 4800 Kennywood Boulevard, West Mifflin; (412) 461–0500; www.kennywood.com. Open daily 11:00 A.M. to midnight, mid-May through Labor Day. General admission is $28.95, and you can ride all day.

Pittsburgh Zoo and PPG Aquarium. Seventy-five-acre natural-habitat zoo with more than 5,000 animals in the African Savannah, the Asian Forest, and the Tropical Forest. The Pittsburgh Zoo also includes a children's zoo and an aquarium where you can see octopi, sea horses, and the nation's only Amazon River dolphin. Located in Highland Park on the Allegheny River about 7 miles east of downtown; (412) 665–3640 or (800) 474–4966; www.pittsburghzoo.com. Open daily 9:00 A.M. to 5:00 P.M., one hour later in the summer. Admission is $9.00 for adults, $8.00 for seniors, and $7.00 for children age two to thirteen; children under two get in free.

The National Aviary. Your opportunity to see some 450 exotic birds, from egrets to condors to piping plovers to blue-winged kookaburras, at the largest freestanding aviary in America. Located at Allegheny Commons West; (412) 323–7235; www.aviary.org. Open daily 9:00 A.M. to 5:00 P.M. Admission is $8.00 for adults, $7.00 for seniors, and $6.50 for children two to twelve; children under two are admitted free.

Gateway Clipper. Six huge riverboat-style cruise ships offer sightseeing cruises, dinner cruises, and family-oriented cruises. Operates from Station Square Dock. There are more than twenty different cruises; admission varies. (412) 355–7980; www.gatewayclipper.com.

Pittsburgh Center for the Arts. Pennsylvania's largest community art center has regional, national, and international exhibitions and sells the work of more than 500 local artists. Located at 6300 Fifth Avenue; (412) 361–0873; www.pittsburgharts.org. Open Tuesday through Saturday 10:00 A.M. to 5:30 P.M., Sunday noon to 5:00 P.M. Donations of $3.00 are requested.

Special Events

May. International Children's Festival. Week of children's performing arts and family activities. (412) 321–5520.

July–August. Three Rivers Regatta. Formula One powerboat racing, water sports, hot-air balloon rides, food, and entertainment at the nation's largest inland regatta. (412) 875–4841; www.pghregatta.com.

August. Shadyside Arts Festival. Weekend festival with paintings, sculpture, workshops, and evening jazz draws more than 200,000 people. (412) 681–8481.

November–December. Sparkle Season. Begins in November with "Light-Up Night," when all the lights in downtown Pittsburgh are turned on, and ends with "First Night" festival on New Year's Eve; numerous affiliated events. (412) 566–4190.

Other Recommended Restaurants

Poli, 2607 Murray Avenue, Squirrel Hill; (412) 521–6400. Legendary Italian restaurant that regularly competes for the "best seafood in town" label. Expensive.

Cliffside Restaurant, 1208 Grandview Avenue; (412) 431–6996. Longtime Mount Washington favorite with traditional continental menu and spectacular view of the city from almost every table. Expensive.

Mallorca Restaurant, 2228 East Carson Street; (412) 488–1818; www
.mallorcarestaurant.com. Popular restaurant on the South Side serving
Spanish and Portuguese cuisine. All entrees are served with rice, vegetables, and fried potatoes. Moderate.

Penn Brewery Restaurant, Troy Hill Road and Vinial Street; (412)
237–9400; www.pennbrew.com. Restored North Side brewery serving
German specialties and a dozen microbrews in a publike atmosphere.
Moderate.

1902 Landmark Tavern, 24 Market Square; (412) 471–1902. Tin ceilings,
tile floors, and hundred-year-old brick walls provide plenty of atmosphere.
Award-winning chef provides great food; Vodka Bar stocks more than
fifty brands of vodka and has thirty-three brands of beer on tap. It's a win-
ning combination. Moderate to expensive.

Max and Erma's, 630 Stanwix Street; (412) 471–1141. Ask locals where to
eat and this is likely to be their recommendation. The regional chain serves
ten-ounce burgers and thinly sliced onion rings. Inexpensive to moderate.

Eat'n Park, twenty-five locations in Pittsburgh; www.eatnpark.com. Breakfast
buffet; salad bar; burgers and other sandwiches; open twenty-four hours a day.
Inexpensive.

Best place for doughnuts: Balcer Bakery, 2126 East Carson Street; (412)
431–6193.

Other Recommended Lodgings

Shadyside Bed & Breakfast, 5516 Maple Heights Road; (412) 683–6501 or
(866) 613–9330. Very nice bed-and-breakfast with eight rooms, five with
private baths. Library with fireplace, billiards room, guest kitchen, and dining room; continental breakfast. Rates: $100–$145.

Shadyside Inn, 5405 Fifth Avenue; (412) 441–4444 or (800) 76–SUITE;
www.shadyside inn.com. East Side inn with one hundred suites; all have
kitchen, cable TV, and telephone. Rates: $99–$185.

Morning Glory Inn, 2119 Sarah Street; (412) 431–1707; www.gloryinn
.com. Convenient South Side bed-and-breakfast with five guest rooms, all
with private bath. Garden, porches, music room with grand piano; full
breakfast includes German baked eggs, biscuits, and fruit. Rates:
$139–$450.

The Inns on Negley, 703 South Negley Avenue; (412) 661–0631; www.the innsonnegley.com. Two elegant Shadyside Victorians with sixteen guest rooms and suites, all with private bath and beautiful furnishings. Rates: $150–$235.

Sheraton Hotel Station Square, 7 Station Square Drive; (412) 261–2000 or (800) 255–7488. Multistory hotel with 396 rooms. Convenient location, good view, indoor pool and fitness facilities; restaurants on premises. Rates: $114–$199.

Omni William Penn, 530 William Penn Place; (412) 281–7100; www.omniwilliampenn.com. Elegant, old downtown hotel with 630 rooms and suites and gracious service; the Palm Court has tea every afternoon. Rates: $105–$345.

For More Information

Greater Pittsburgh Convention and Visitors Bureau, Regional Enterprise Tower, 425 Sixth Avenue, 30th floor, Pittsburgh, PA 15219; (412) 281–7711, (800) 359–0758, or (877) 568–3744; www.visitpittsburgh.com.

DELAWARE
AND BEYOND
ESCAPES

Wilmington and the Brandywine Valley

Best Homes and Gardens / *2 Nights*

The Brandywine Valley, a heavily wooded, rolling stretch of green in Delaware and Pennsylvania, was home to some of America's greatest industrialists, art collectors, gardeners, and artists. A weekend escape here offers the visitor a wonderful range of experiences, from exploring homes and gardens of the very rich and famous to canoeing the placid Brandywine River.

☐ Mansions

☐ Garden

☐ Art museums

You see the imprint of Delaware's legendary du Ponts everywhere, from the enormous Italian Renaissance hotel they built in Wilmington to the mansions and gardens at nearby Nemours, Longwood, and Winterthur. Each one of these estates offers a different pleasure: A. I. du Pont's estate, Nemours, reveals the fascinating inventions and enthusiasms of its owner; Longwood Gardens boasts miles of flower trails, fountains, and trees; and Winterthur displays 300 years' worth of American decorative arts.

Interestingly, the Brandywine Valley also produced a great dynasty of local artists whose work is the aesthetic polar opposite of the du Ponts' gilded drawing rooms and crystal chandeliers. A highlight of the weekend is a visit to the Brandywine River Museum, which houses the country's greatest collection of works by the three generations of Wyeths—N. C., Andrew, and Jamie—and the landscape artists and illustrators who were their friends and contemporaries in this distinctive movement in nineteenth- and twentieth-century American art, known as the Brandywine School.

Day 1 / *Afternoon*

It's a two-and-a-half-hour drive to Wilmington and the Brandywine Valley; if you start in the late afternoon or right after work, you'll be there in time for dinner. Follow Interstate 95 north 110 miles to downtown

Wilmington. Leave I–95 at exit 7B (Delaware Highway 52 North), and drive north on Pennsylvania Avenue. After a couple of miles, Pennsylvania Avenue becomes Kennett Pike (but it's still DE 52). Drive 5 miles farther north on DE 52, and you'll reach your dinner destination in the tiny town of Centreville, Delaware.

DINNER: Buckley's Tavern, located in a house built in 1817, has been greeting and feeding travelers since 1951. Local people unanimously recommend it to visitors, and it is easy to see why. The intimate paneled bar and separate dining rooms are fragrant with wood smoke from the kitchen, and wait staff is friendly, quick, and casual.

Buckley's menu is creative and classy, with unexpected items like spinach, roast beet, pecan, and goat cheese salad appearing alongside classics like crab cakes and pork chops and sweet potatoes. Located at 5812 Kennett Pike (DE 52) in Centreville; (302) 656–9776. Moderate.

After dinner, continue north on DE 52 about 5 miles to U.S. Highway 1; turn left and drive 3 miles west (past Longwood Gardens) to Delaware Highway 82. Turn right on DE 82, and drive a little more than a mile north, then turn right on Pennsylvania Highway 926. If you feel as if you are out in the country, you're right. Your lodgings are on a farm, located at the third driveway on the left.

LODGING: Meadow Spring Farm Bed and Breakfast, 201 East Street Road (PA 926), Kennett Square, Pennsylvania; (215) 444–3903. Meadow Spring Farm is an extremely popular bed-and-breakfast with six comfortable guest rooms, all with antiques, television, and air-conditioning. It's a real farm with chickens, cows, and roosters. Kids love the animals— and the owner's doll collection, Santa collection, and cow collection. Adults love the peaceful perennial garden, the pool, and the hot tub. Rates: $85–$95 per night, two-night minimum on weekends.

Day 2 / Morning

BREAKFAST: Local residents claim that the Brandywine River Valley produces more than 90 percent of the mushrooms consumed in the United States, so it is appropriate that the breakfast specialty at Meadow Spring Farm Bed and Breakfast is a mushroom omelette. But you're also likely to get fruit pancakes or homemade jam and bread alongside, so pack your appetite.

After breakfast, reverse your drive of the night before and take DE 82 south and US 1 east. Within five minutes, you'll be at the estate of Pierre

Samuel du Pont, who served as chairman of the DuPont and General Motors Companies and who was the owner and architect of **Longwood Gardens.**

Said to be the nation's premier public display garden, Longwood Gardens provides visitors literally hours of enchantment with its 11,000 different kinds of plants in a beautifully landscaped park of more than 1,000 acres.

You really should return to Longwood many times, because it is so vast that you could never explore all of it in a single visit. There is a "flower walk" past enormous beds ranging from a deep purple group to the pink family and on to the reds and oranges. There is a garden with dozens of fountains, which on summer and some fall evenings are lit for a 9:00 P.M. fountain display, as well as an enormous indoor conservatory with orchids, tropical gardens, a fern grotto, growing houses, and bonsai. Longwood also has huge arching rose arbors, a topiary garden, waterlily ponds, statues, and a lake. Plan to spend the whole morning; there are plenty of benches that allow you to rest as you tour the gardens.

At the gift shop in the visitor center, shoppers can browse among books, flower prints, gardening tools, whimsical gifts, and live plants. Longwood Gardens is located on US 1 near Kennett Square, Pennsylvania; (610) 388–1000; www.longwoodgardens.org. Open daily from 9:00 A.M. to 5:00 P.M. January through March, 9:00 A.M. to 6:00 P.M. April and May. From June through August the gardens stay open to 10:00 P.M. on Tuesday and Saturday. Admission is $10.00 to $15.00 for adults, $6.00 for youth sixteen to twenty, and $2.00 for children six to fifteen; children under six are admitted free.

LUNCH: After you finish touring Longwood, stay for lunch at Longwood's **Terrace Restaurant,** which has a modestly priced cafeteria and a lovely sit-down dining room. Both dining areas have great views of the surrounding gardens. The Terrace's dining-room menu includes fancy sandwiches, rack of lamb, shellfish, pasta, Caesar salad, and much more. There are boutique beers (including several local brews), mineral water, and espresso to quench your thirst, and Viennese omelettes with marscapone for dessert. Dining-room prices are moderate.

The Terrace Cafeteria's prices are significantly lower, and the menu is child-friendly. On summer afternoons the cafeteria offers fresh fruit cobblers for afternoon tea from 2:00 to 4:00 P.M. (610) 388–6771.

Longwood Gardens

Afternoon

After lunch, drive a couple of miles east on US 1 and about 5 miles south on DE 52. Within ten minutes, you'll be at **Winterthur,** one of the great attractions in the area and—many think—the top decorative-arts exhibition in the United States. Winterthur's owner, Henry Francis du Pont, didn't just collect three centuries of priceless American antique furniture, ceramics, and textiles; he literally bought whole rooms—woodwork, plaster, ceilings, wallpaper, and all—and had them installed at his enormous estate.

Happily, his extraordinary 175-room home has been turned into a museum. Du Pont's collection is displayed in dozens of period rooms, showing how antique furniture, furnishings, china, crystal, silver, and textiles from Revolutionary War times to the Shaker period would have been used in daily life, with every detail as historically accurate as possible. A separate building houses galleries where you can take a closer look at treasures from the vast collection.

Because you cannot begin to see it all in one visit, the museum offers a number of ways to view Winterthur, including one-hour introductory tours, and one- or two-hour decorative-arts tours. (*NOTE:* Young children are welcome on introductory tours, but the more specialized decorative-arts tours are limited to visitors ages eight and up.) An introductory tour is $20 for adults and $18 for seniors and children. The decorative-arts tours cost $30 a person. General admission, which entitles you to tour the galleries, the Touch-It Room, and the 900-acre naturalistic garden, costs $15.00 for adults, $13.00 for seniors and students, and $5.00 for children two to eleven. The number of people on each tour is limited, so reserve as far in advance as you can. Located on Kennett Pike (DE 52) north of Wilmington; (302) 888–4600 or (800) 448–3883; www.winterthur.org. Open Tuesday through Sunday 10:00 A.M. to 5:00 P.M.

Before leaving, stop in at the museum's pretty seven-room gift shop, which has reproduction furniture, china, jewelry, books, and plants for sale. And do explore the garden; there's something in bloom nearly year-round.

After your Winterthur tour, drive south 5 miles to downtown Wilmington, where you can tour the original du Pont gunpowder factory or enjoy a sample of art from the Brandywine School. (See Day 3 for details.) But, by all means, end up at the **Hotel du Pont,** an enormous old downtown hotel. Built in 1913 and renovated in the early 1990s, the du Pont has the wonderfully luxurious feel of century-old Wilmington. The ceilings are heavily carved, the moldings are gilded, the music is discreetly classical.

DINNER: If you're in Wilmington on a weekend, you must dine in the Hotel du Pont's beautiful **Green Room.** A harpist plays on the balcony, the surroundings are glorious, and the menu exquisite (that is to say, expensive). Think French, as in escargots, pheasant, and elegant desserts—and splurge. Located at Eleventh and Market Streets in Wilmington; (302) 594–3154.

While you're at the hotel, poke your head into the Lobby Lounge, where a splendid afternoon tea is served from 3:00 to 5:00 P.M.

LODGING: Meadow Spring Farm Bed and Breakfast.

Day 3 / Morning

BREAKFAST: After a leisurely breakfast at Meadow Spring Farm Bed and Breakfast, drive about 5 miles east to the nearby **Brandywine River Museum,** US 1, Chadds Ford, Pennsylvania; (610) 388–2700; www .brandywinemuseum.org. Open daily 9:30 A.M. to 4:30 P.M. Admission is $8.00 for adults, $5.00 for seniors, students, and children older than six; children under six are admitted free.

The museum is housed in a nineteenth-century gristmill and has been designed so that on every floor you get a 180-degree view of the Brandywine River flowing below you. Quiet and unpretentious, the Brandywine River Museum presents a fine collection of nineteenth- and twentieth-century art, with an exceptional group of paintings and drawings by the Wyeth family and other artists and illustrators of the Brandywine School. Be sure to visit the gift shop, which has a large selection of prints, books, and gifts.

LUNCH: The cafeteria-style **Brandywine River Museum Restaurant** is open daily for lunch from 10:00 A.M. to 3:00 P.M., except for Monday and Tuesday from January through March. If the weather is nice, take your sandwich outside for a picnic by the river; otherwise find a table that looks out over the Brandywine and enjoy one of the entrees. Inexpensive.

Afternoon

After lunch, head for **Brandywine Battlefield Park,** a Revolutionary War treasure trove in Chadds Ford; (610) 459–3342; www.thebrandy wine.com/attractions/battle.html. To get there from the Brandywine River Museum, head just a half mile east on US 1 to the park.

The 10-mile Brandywine battle site saw the Revolutionary Army, led by Washington and including the teenaged Marquis de Lafayette, eventual war hero, meet the better-equipped British forces, led by Gen. William Howe. Brandywine would eventually see the largest one-day battle of the Revolutionary War. Because of Brandywine Valley's proximity to the country's new capital, Philadelphia, the Americans had to hold firm. The battle took place on September 11, 1777. Unfortunately for Washington's army, the British defeated them and marched on to Philadelphia, forcing Congress to abandon the city. However, we all know how the story ended up—our boys lost the battle, but won the war.

Now you can follow the footsteps of the battle's participants in one of three separate driving tours; the closest to the battle sequence is the aptly named Battle Driving Tour, and the others are the Straight-Ahead and

Cornwallis' Tours. Each tour lasts between one and two hours and can be arranged from the visitor center, which is where you should begin your visit.

Tucked in amid beautiful rolling hills and valleys, the visitor center includes displays of weaponry and war uniforms, and a movie is shown that helps to re-create the context of the battle within the larger British push for Philadelphia. The visitor center is open Tuesday through Saturday 9:00 A.M. to 5:00 P.M. and Sunday noon to 5:00 P.M.

The two main attractions among the battlefield sites are historic houses and headquarters: Benjamin Ring House, where Washington quartered and planned the battle, and Gideon Gilpin's farmhouse, which housed French hero Lafayette. Both houses require organized tours, leaving frequently from the visitor center. The Benjamin Ring House has been fully restored to its battle appearance, and Gilpin's House also looks the same, but for one big difference: look for the towering, 400-year-old sycamore nearby. Both the visitor center and parking are free, but admission to the historic houses costs $3.50 for adults, $2.50 for seniors, and $1.50 for children six to twelve.

To get back to Washington, go east on US 1 to US 202 South to I–95 South.

There's More

Hagley Museum and Eleutherian Mills. Original du Pont gunpowder factory, which launched the company that became the world's largest arms manufacturer. Also includes the original du Pont family estate and gardens. Located on DE 141 north of Wilmington in Greenville, Delaware (follow the signs); (302) 658–2400; www.hagley.lib.de.us. Open daily 9:30 A.M. to 4:30 P.M. mid-March through December, weekends 9:30 A.M. to 4:30 P.M. during the winter months. Admission is $11.00 for adults, $9.00 for seniors and students, and $4.00 for children six to fourteen; children under six are admitted free.

Delaware Art Museum. Renovated and expanded, the museum is home to an interesting collection of American art in the Brandywine tradition, and the largest pre-Raphaelite English collection in the country. Located at 2301 Kentmere Parkway, Wilmington; (302) 571–9590; www.delart.org. Open Tuesday through Saturday 10:00 A.M. to 4:00 P.M. (Wednesday until 8:00 P.M.), Sunday noon to 4:00 P.M. Admission is $10.00 for adults, $8.00 for seniors, $5.00 for students, and $3.00 for youth; children six and under are admitted free.

Canoeing. The gentle Brandywine River is great for canoeing, and rental shops are available at numerous sites, including one near Longwood Gardens: Northbrook Canoe Company, 1810 Beagle Road, West Chester, Pennsylvania; (610) 793–2279 or (800) 898–2279; www.northbrookcanoe .com. Expect to pay about $40–$50 for three to four hours of canoeing.

Chaddsford Winery. Pennsylvania's largest winery. 632 Baltimore Pike, Chadds Ford; (610) 388–6221; www.chaddsford.com. On US 1, halfway between the Brandywine River Museum and Longwood Gardens. The winery is anchored by a restored seventeenth-century barn and produces European-style dry whites and reds, as well as seasonal sweet wines. Chaddsford is open year-round for tours and hosts special events, such as wine tastings and dinners, but summer is when things really take off: The season is bracketed by the Brandywine River Blues Festival on Memorial Day weekend and the Labor Day Weekend Jazz Festival. In between, there's "Summer Nights Under the Stars" on Friday nights, featuring jazz and Big Band music. Admission to the winery is free.

Used Books. There are two excellent stores in the area. Baldwin's Book Barn, 865 Lenape Road, West Chester, Pennsylvania (610–696–0816; www.bookbarn.com), has more than 300,000 used and rare books, maps, prints, and paintings in a rustic stone barn. Open Monday to Friday 9:00 A.M. to 9:00 P.M., Saturday and Sunday 10:00 A.M. to 6:00 P.M. Thomas Macaluso Rare and Fine Books, 130 South Union Street, Kennett Square, Pennsylvania (610–444–1063; www.abcbooks.com/home/macaluso books), is a charming establishment with six showrooms of books and prints. Open Monday through Friday 11:00 A.M. to 6:00 P.M., Saturday 11:00 A.M. to 5:00 P.M.

Special Events

April–May. Acres of Spring. Spring wildflower exhibits at Longwood Gardens. (610) 388–1000.

June–September. Festival of Fountains. Illuminated fountain displays at Longwood Gardens. (610) 388–1000.

July. Ice Cream Festival at the Rockwood Museum, a Victorian English country estate with seventy acres of gardens. Food and crafts; ice cream; admission charged. Located at 610 Shipley Road, Wilmington. (302) 761–4340; www.rockwood.org.

September. Revolutionary Times. Reenactment of the Battle of Brandywine, Brandywine Battlefield Park. (610) 459–3342.

November–December. Yuletide at Winterthur. Enchanting display of
antique Christmas decorations. (302) 888–4600 or (800) 448–3883.

Other Recommended Restaurants

The Columbus Inn, 2216 Pennsylvania Avenue, Wilmington; (302)
571–1492; www.columbusinn.com. The perfect spot for a twenty-ounce
sirloin, prime rib with Yorkshire pudding, or rack of lamb with white bean
ragout. Moderate to expensive.

Ristorante Carucci, 504 Greenhill Avenue (Wawaset Plaza), Wilmington;
(302) 654–2333. Stylish Italian local favorite with artwork and vocal sere-
nades. Moderate to expensive.

Brandywine Brewing Company, 3801 Kennett Pike, Greenville Center
(DE 52 north of Wilmington); (302) 655–8000. Casual pub with fine sandwiches and a selection of beers brewed on the premises. Inexpensive to
moderate.

Mendenhall Inn, Pennsylvania Highway 52, Mendenhall, Pennsylvania;
(610) 388–2100; www.mendenhallinn.com. Candlelight dining in historic
mill. Pheasant, lobster, prime rib; harp and piano music. Expensive.

Hank's Place, intersection of US 1 and Pennsylvania Highway 100, Chadds
Ford, Pennsylvania; (610) 388–7061. Diner that is a hangout for artists and
staff from the Brandywine River Museum across the road. Pancakes,
chipped beef on biscuits, and a three-egg shiitake mushroom omelette that
won the praise of *Gourmet* magazine. Inexpensive.

Harry's Savoy Grille, 2020 Naamans Road, Wilmington; (302) 475–3000;
www.harrys-savoy.com. Prime rib and crème brûlée make this a favorite
of locals. Elegant and expensive.

Feby's Fishery Restaurant, 3701 Lancaster Pike (Delaware Highway 48),
Wilmington; (302) 998–9501. Good choice for lobster and seafood.
Moderate.

Dilworthtown Inn, 1390 Old Wilmington Pike, West Chester, Pennsylvania;
(610) 399–1390; www.dilworthtown.com. Duck terrine for starters, followed by baby spinach with shaved wild mushrooms, and then a
chateaubriand or saffron-infused lobster. Expensive.

Serpe and Sons, 1411 Kirkwood Highway, Wilmington; (302) 994–1868. Sells doughnuts for $5.00 a dozen.

Other Recommended Lodgings

Fairville Inn, Kennett Pike (PA 52), Chadds Ford, Pennsylvania; (610) 388–5900 or (877) 285–7772; www.fairvilleinn.com. Centrally located inn with fifteen individually decorated rooms. All have antiques and flowers; some have fireplaces. Complimentary breakfast and afternoon tea served. Rates: $150–$250.

Inn at Montchanin Village, DE 100 and Kirk Road, Montchanin; (302) 888–2133 or (800) 269–2473; www.montchanin.com. Luxurious Delaware inn with twenty-eight rooms and suites (all with private bath) in eleven buildings; gardens. Fireplace, coffeemaker, and newspaper in each room; upscale restaurant on the grounds. Rates: $169–$209 for rooms and $249–$375 for suites.

Brandywine River Hotel, intersection of US 1 and PA 100, Chadds Ford, Pennsylvania; (610) 388–1200 or (800) 274–9644; www.brandywineriver hotel.com. Renovated country Victorian hotel with forty-one guest rooms and suites; restaurant and fitness room on the premises. Large continental breakfast; complimentary wine and cheese in the afternoon. Rates: $125–$169.

Pennsbury Inn, 883 Baltimore Pike (US 1); Chadds Ford, Pennsylvania; (610) 388–1435; www.pennsburyinn.com. Two-hundred-year-old coach house with original fireplaces, uneven floors, and six renovated guest rooms, each with feather bed and antique furnishings; private bath, telephone and cable TV. Pleasant grounds; full country breakfast. Rates: $100–$260.

The Inn at Whitewing Farm, 370 Valley Road, Kennett Square, Pennsylvania; (610) 388–2664; www.whitewingfarm.com. Beautiful bed-and-breakfast on forty-three acres adjacent to Longwood Gardens; seven guest rooms and three suites. Tennis court and pitch-and-putt golf course; full country breakfast on the terrace; afternoon tea. Rates: $135–$289.

Bed and Breakfasts of Delaware, 2701 Landon Drive, Suite 200, Wilmington (302–479–9500; www.bbonline.com/de/), will make reservations for you at one of dozens of bed-and-breakfasts in the area. Rates range from $65 to $280 per night.

For More Information

Greater Wilmington Convention and Visitors Bureau, 100 West Tenth Street, Suite 20, Wilmington, DE 19801; (302) 652–4088 or (800) 489–6664; www.visitwilmingtonde.com.

Chester County Visitors Center, US 1, Kennett Square, PA 19348; (610) 388–2900 or (800) 228–9933; www.brandywinevalley.com.

Bethany Beach and Rehoboth Beach

Oceans of Fun / 2 Nights

One of the quickest and most complete escapes from Washington is "the beach," which to many city dwellers means Delaware's Bethany and Rehoboth Beaches.

These once-sleepy beach towns have experienced something of a boom in recent years, and Rehoboth, in particular, is home to an increasing number of upscale shops, restaurants, condos, and outlet malls. But an unspoiled stretch of national seashore is just a few miles away when you want to escape the crowds.

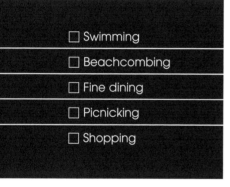

☐ Swimming

☐ Beachcombing

☐ Fine dining

☐ Picnicking

☐ Shopping

Your weekend escape to the shore is an enjoyable mix of old and new. You'll lunch on boardwalk fries and pizza, then have dinner at one of the fanciest restaurants at the beach. There will be a luxurious stay at a fine old inn that has lace curtains in the Victorian parlor and afternoon iced tea and cookies on the big front porch directly facing the ocean.

But the main reason for escaping to the Atlantic shore is the ocean itself, with the beautiful white-sand beaches of Delaware stretching before you. Spread out a beach blanket and watch the waves roll in and out and the kids whoop and tumble as they bodysurf the big ones. Walk next to the water as the sand slips away under your feet and the gulls shriek overhead. Then give in and joyously splash into the spray, while the sun warms and the water chills. It's the beach, and it's all yours, absolutely free of charge.

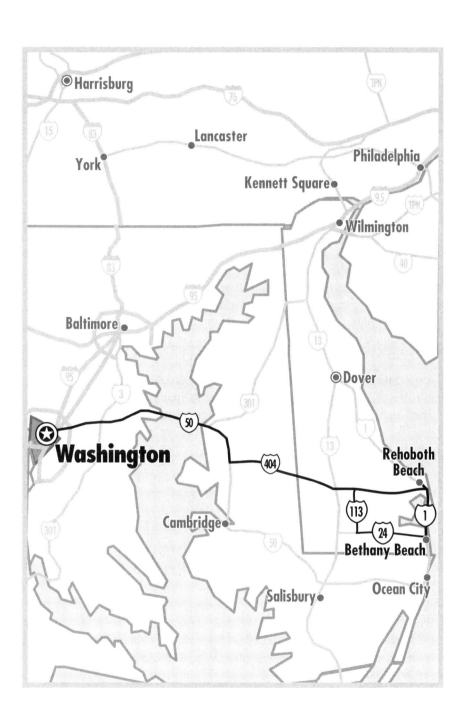

Day 1 / *Morning*

Leave Washington early, especially on a Friday or a Saturday, so you can beat the considerable weekend beach traffic. Although the ocean is only about 125 miles from Washington, count on a three-hour drive. Take U.S. Highway 50 east from Washington. About 16 miles after you cross the Chesapeake Bay Bridge, turn east on Maryland Highway 404, where the route becomes scenic and enjoyable. The terrain is flat and level, with fields of corn, roadside fruit stands, and pleasant little towns along the way. To avoid the worst of the beach traffic, just before you reach Georgetown, turn south on Delaware Highway 113 and drive 11 miles to Dagsboro, then east on Delaware Highway 20 a mile or so to Delaware Highway 24 east, which you follow about 10 miles to **Bethany Beach.** As you get close to the shore, you'll smell the sea and sense the change in the air even before you see the ocean.

Bethany Beach is a small and friendly town with a devoted summer crowd that returns every year. Garfield Parkway, the town's main drag, is lined with shops selling candy, T-shirts, and beach paraphernalia. There are also a number of casual restaurants on Garfield Parkway and on the short boardwalk, but a picnic is a better choice for lunch your first day.

LUNCH: **Di Febo's Restaurant,** 789 Garfield Parkway (302–539–4914; www.difebus.com), located on DE 24 about a mile before you reach the beach, is a first-class restaurant with an attached carryout. It has a great selection of deli sandwiches and Italian subs, as well as buffalo wings, cheesesteaks, and pasta specialties. If you're picnicking, be sure to take lots of cold drinks and napkins. Inexpensive to moderate.

Afternoon

One of Bethany Beach's charms is the **Addy Sea Bed and Breakfast,** a century-old house where you will be staying. You'll want to dump your suitcases and change into your swimsuit before your picnic, so check in as soon as you pick up provisions for lunch. The Addy Sea has thirteen rooms with curtains waving in the breeze in the open windows, and a lovely Victorian parlor with an antique pressed-tin ceiling. Rocking chairs on the porch face the sea, and in the afternoon there's sure to be a big pitcher of lemonade or iced tea. Located at the corner of Atlantic Avenue and Ocean View Parkway, 5 blocks north of Garfield Parkway; (302) 539–3707 or (800) 418–6764; www.addysea.com. Rooms range from $150 to $400

Bethany Beach

during the summer, $100 to $300 in the off-season. Call well in advance for summer weekend reservations.

The Addy Sea is slightly off the beaten track of Bethany's commercial area, and the beach in front of the inn is less congested than other sections of Bethany Beach. Once you're settled in, the first order of business, of course, is to race to the ocean for a long look at the waves and some deep gulps of clean, salty sea air.

If you're a walker, there are miles of immaculate white beach to explore—walk right along the water where it's hard packed, and watch the shorebirds skitter and race. Kids will love to collect the rounded stones and purplish bits of shells, rubbed smooth by the sand and water. If you're a water baby, this section of the Atlantic Ocean is perfect for floating and swimming, with waves just big enough to give you a good ride all the way up to the beach if you bodysurf them at the right moment.

After you get cleaned up back at the Addy Sea, take a short drive to Fenwick Island for dinner. Go 6 miles south on Delaware Highway 1, turn right (west) on Delaware Highway 54, and drive about 1.5 miles to a bright pink building just past the bridge.

DINNER: Your dinner destination is **Tom and Terry's.** Don't let the flamingo-colored exterior deter you. This is a beautiful, casual, upscale restaurant. Seafood is fresh, and all the classics are there: clams casino (with bacon and cheese), sea scallops, flounder topped with crab imperial, soft-shell crabs, catch of the day, and more. For those who prefer turf to surf, there are hand-cut Angus beef steaks char-grilled to order, as well as a handful of chicken and pasta selections. Even if the food at Tom and Terry's were only half as good, you should go anyway for the view. The pale pink walls indoors match the color of the sky as the sun sets over the marshy inlets of Assawoman Bay. It's a perfect end to a perfect day. Located on DE 54 in Fenwick Island; (302) 436–4161. Moderate.

LODGING: The Addy Sea Bed and Breakfast.

Day 2 / Morning

BREAKFAST: After a breakfast of homemade muffins, juice, and coffee at the Addy Sea, go for a morning dip or long walk by the ocean.

Midmorning, take a short drive to the nearby town of **Rehoboth Beach.** There, the 10-block boardwalk is lined with shops and fast-food stands, and the beach is crowded with umbrellas, bikinied and Speedo-clad sun worshipers gliding along the sand, toddlers in sun hats with their pails and shovels, and kids with boogie boards, racing for the waves.

LUNCH: If you want lunch before a swim, you won't have to go far. Do what everybody seems to do, and stroll up and down Rehoboth Avenue and the boardwalk, collecting junk food as you go. A favorite in the area is **Grotto Pizza,** where $2.50 will get you a greasy, pepperoni-studded slice of pure pleasure. (Grotto has eight locations in the Delaware beach towns, including three on the boardwalk in Rehoboth; 302–227–3278; www.grottopizza.com.) Then it's on to **Thrashers French Fries** for a large cupful of some of the best fries made anywhere. They're best straight from the deep-fat fryer, sprinkled with salt and vinegar. Stands are located at 7 Rehoboth Avenue and several other spots; (302) 227–8994.

Afternoon

Just in case you haven't had enough beach food, there's plenty more harm to be done. Rehoboth has made some concessions to the changing times: There are now espresso bars and Italian lemon ice shops. But the gigantic saltwater taffy sign that reads DOLLE'S SALTWATER TAFFY still hangs in the most prominent spot on the boardwalk. Located on the boardwalk at Rehoboth Avenue; (302) 227–0757.

As you cruise Rehoboth's extensive shopping area, don't limit yourself to the T-shirt shops along Rehoboth Avenue. Be sure to explore the flanking streets, Baltimore and Wilmington Avenues, and the short connecting side streets. Here you'll find several interesting stores, and renovated Cape Cod homes that have been painted in Crayola colors—melon with spruce trim, periwinkle with egg-yolk yellow trim, and purple everywhere.

While exploring Rehoboth, consider renting a bike or a hilarious "team trike," a cumbersome monster that will seat two people side by side. Team trikes rent for $6.00 to $8.00 an hour, regular bikes for $4.00 to $5.00 an hour at several beach locations.

Or take a short drive north to Henlopen Acres, the beautiful residential section of Rehoboth, and stop in at the **Rehoboth Art League,** 12 Dodds Lane, Henlopen Acres, just north of Rehoboth; (302) 227–8408; www.rehobothartleague.org. Open Monday through Saturday 10:00 A.M. to 4:00 P.M., Sunday noon to 4:00 P.M. You'll know it by the bizarre cement couch and matching archway in the yard, painted to resemble old-fashioned upholstery. The art league exhibition center is located in a quiet, cool clapboard home filled with juried works by local artists. There are watercolors, sculpture, oil paintings, and prints for sale.

DINNER: Plan to stay in Rehoboth for dinner at the **Blue Moon Restaurant,** a chic beach house decorated in myriad shades of blue. It's a serious competitor for best restaurant at the beach, located at 35 Baltimore Avenue; (302) 227–6515; www.bluemoonrehoboth.com. The Blue Moon, which has been earning kudos from the beach crowd for more than twenty-five years, specializes in Pacific Rim cuisine. Look for fresh-roasted vegetable ravioli or seared ahi tuna with ginger dipping sauce, wasabi mashed potatoes, and stir-fried tat soi. Expensive.

LODGING: The Addy Sea Bed and Breakfast.

Day 3 / Morning

BREAKFAST: After a light breakfast at the Addy Sea, take a long walk on the beach or a morning swim. If you're interested in a truly unspoiled beach area, drive a few miles north to **Delaware Seashore State Park** (302–227–2800) or a few miles south to **Fenwick Island State Park**

(302–227–2800; www.destateparks.com). Swimming, wave-jumping, and sand-castle building are even better there, because the crowds are smaller. And the sand is the same immaculate white quartz. Both state parks have showers and bathhouses for changing. An entrance fee of $8.00 a car ($4.00 for Delaware residents) is charged. The fee entitles you to enter any state park on the day of purchase.

LUNCH: When you're hungry, head back to Bethany and **Mango's,** Garfield Parkway and the Boardwalk; (302) 537–6621; www.mangomikes .com. You can fill up on appetizers (black bean hummus, steamed clams, flash-fried margarita-marinated calamari) or opt for one of the many seafood specials. Moderate.

As you head toward home, you might want to take an hour or so to explore some of the dozens of outlet shops that have sprung up just north of Rehoboth Beach. Most of the stores are open from 10:00 A.M. to at least 9:00 P.M. daily, except Sunday, when they close at 6:00 P.M.

The fastest route home from Rehoboth Beach is to take DE 1 about 8 miles north to U.S. Highway 9 heading west, which quickly runs straight into Delaware Highway 404. As you drive through the Delaware countryside, you will notice several barbecue-chicken signs, announcing roadside stands run by fire departments, civic organizations, and struggling entrepreneurs battling the fast-food giants. Most have picnic tables for the really hungry, or, better yet, rearrange your cooler and enjoy a late supper at home. After 20 miles or so, DE 404 becomes MD 404, which will take you to US 50 west, your route back to the Washington, D.C., area.

There's More

Amusement Rides and Arcade. At the corner of Delaware Avenue and the Boardwalk in Rehoboth, there are several amusement-park rides and arcades; the latter are especially crowded on rainy days.

Lake Gerar. A quiet spot on First Street, just 5 blocks north of the strip in Rehoboth Beach, where you can escape the crowds and feed the ducks and geese. Also a site for children's concerts in summer.

Surf Fishing. If you want to try your luck with a rod and reel, contact the Indian River Marina at Delaware Seashore State Park north of Rehoboth; (302) 227–3071. You can also spend up to six hours on the water for $25–$40, rods and bait provided.

Special Events

June–August. Summer concert series at the Bethany Beach Bandstand features free family entertainment. Call for scheduled events. (302) 539–8011. Similar series in Rehoboth, (302) 227–2233 or (800) 441–1329.

August–September. Boardwalk Arts Festival in Bethany Beach includes paintings, sculpture, pottery, photographs, and amazing sand castles. (302) 539–2100 or (800) 962–7873; www.bethany-fenwick.org.

October. Annual Sea Witch Halloween and Fiddler's Festival. Parade, entertainment, broom-throwing contests at Rehoboth Beach. (302) 227–2233.

Other Recommended Restaurants

Bethany Beach

Sedona, 26 Pennsylvania Avenue; (302) 539–1200; www.fusion-sedona.com. Bethany's top dining spot features new Southwest cuisine and desert decor. Expensive.

McCabe's Gourmet Market, York Beach Mall, DE 1, South Bethany; (302) 539–8550. Fresh-baked bread, cheeses, salads, specialty foods; great for picnic supplies.

Magnolia's Restaurant and Pub, 191 Cedar Neck Road, Ocean View; (302) 539–5671 or (888) 415–3474; www.magnoliasrestaurant.com. The restaurant's menu and ambience are Old South; seafood, prime rib, and corn muffins are featured. The pub has nice salads, hearty sandwiches, and a dance floor. Moderate.

Old Mill Restaurant and Crab House, Cedar Neck Road, Ocean View; (302) 537–2240. The best reason to choose this informal restaurant is the steamed crabs, and scores do so nightly. Moderate.

Gary's Beach Cafe, Marketplace at Sea Colony; (302) 539–2131. Casual spot and good choice for vegetarian fare; whole-grain breads and soy cheese featured. Inexpensive.

Cottage Cafe, DE 1 (across from Sea Colony); (302) 539–8710; www .cottagecafe.com. Popular spot for families and the place to go if you get the urge for pot roast or liver and onions at the beach. Inexpensive.

Best place for doughnuts: Griff's Bethany Beach Bakery, Lem Hickman Beach Plaza (DE 1), Bethany Beach; (302) 539–8879.

Rehoboth Beach

Camel's Hump, 21 Baltimore Avenue; (302) 227–0947. If sand makes you hungry for Middle Eastern food, you're in luck; the tabbouleh, hummus, and kebobs here are excellent. Moderate.

La La Land, 22 Wilmington Avenue; (302) 227–3887. Glittery California-style restaurant that is a favorite of locals and critics. Expensive.

Back Porch Cafe, 59 Rehoboth Avenue; (302) 227–3674. Excellent seafood, generous portions, outside dining. Expensive.

Sydney's Blues and Jazz, 25 Christian Street; (302) 227–1339. Dine on New Orleans specialties as you listen. Moderate.

Fran O'Brien's Beach House, 59 Lake Avenue; (302) 227–6121. A Rehoboth attraction for more than two decades. Steak and fresh seafood until 1:00 A.M. Many go for the piano bar. Moderate.

Other Recommended Lodgings

Bethany Beach

Blue Surf, Oceanfront at Garfield Parkway; (302) 539–7531; www.beach-net.com/bluesurf.html. No-frills oceanfront rooms and efficiencies ideal for families. All units have refrigerators and microwaves; some have full cooking facilities. Rates: $55–$240.

Bethany Arms, Oceanfront, a half block from Garfield Parkway; (302) 539–9603; www.beach-net.com/bethanyarms.html. Rooms and efficiencies on the beach. Rates: $50–$240, depending on season and view.

Cedar Breeze Bed and Breakfast, 334 Cedar Neck Road in Ocean View about 1 mile from Bethany Beach; (302) 537–7015; www.cedarbreeze.com. A nice alternative to being right on the water; three rooms and a suite, all with private bath; garden; hot tub; full breakfast, complimentary wine and cheese in the afternoon. Rates: $75–$175; suite, $150–$225.

Rehoboth Beach

The Bellmoor Inn and Spa, 6 Christian Street; (302) 227–5800 or (800) 425–2355; www.thebellmoor.com. Beautiful inn with seventy-eight rooms and suites, spa, indoor and outdoor pools, gourmet breakfast, afternoon tea. Rates: $115–$615.

The Delaware Inn Bed and Breakfast, 55 Delaware Avenue; (302) 227–6031 or (800) 246–5244; www.delawareinn.com. Pleasant seven-room inn open year-round. Beach chairs, bicycles, box lunches, continental breakfast. Rates: two nights $140–$240.

Royal Rose Inn, 41 Baltimore Avenue; (302) 226–2535; www.royal roseinn.com. Delightful seven-bedroom bed-and-breakfast close to the beach. You can get a room off-season on a weekday for as little as $60. Summer weekend rates: $110–$180; full breakfast included.

Corner Cupboard Inn, 50 Park Avenue; (302) 227–8553; www.corner cupboardinn.com. Sixteen guest rooms, comfortably furnished. Rates: $100–$250; breakfast included.

Camping. Delaware Seashore State Park, Indian River Inlet, between Rehoboth Beach and Bethany Beach; (302) 539–7202 or (877) 987–2757; www.destateparks.com. Bayside campground with 434 sites. No reservations accepted. Rates: $31–$35. Full service March through November.

For More Information

Bethany-Fenwick Area Chamber of Commerce, P.O. Box 1450, Bethany Beach, DE 19930; (302) 539–2100 or (800) 962–7873; www.bethany-fenwick.org. Located on DE 1 south of Bethany Beach on the ocean side of the road.

Rehoboth Beach–Dewey Beach Chamber of Commerce, 501 Rehoboth Avenue, P.O. Box 216, Rehoboth Beach, DE 19971; (302) 227–2233 or (800) 441–1329 (outside Delaware); www.beach-fun.com.

DELAWARE AND BEYOND ESCAPE THREE

Lewes and Cape May

Victorian Secret / 2 Nights

A funny thing about the reign of good Queen Victoria in the final sixty years of the nineteenth century: The dictionary refers to the era that bears her name as prudish, repressed, narrow-minded, and exceedingly fastidious. Yet the Victorian era was also a time of exuberant artistic expression, best reflected in architecture that was as colorful, lush, and playful as Queen Vicky (in her stiff black satin and jet beads) was not.

- ☐ Victorian house tour
- ☐ Ferry ride
- ☐ Shopping
- ☐ Biking
- ☐ Ocean beaches

There is no better way to explore the delights of the Victorian era than to visit Cape May, New Jersey, a beautifully preserved and restored little town right alongside the Atlantic Ocean. In the nineteenth century, Cape May was the summer playground of the Philadelphia rich. Today it's a village that is bent on pleasing its doting visitors. Its inns, tea shops, and magnificently restored Victorian homes are strewn through town as thickly as currants in an English scone.

When you combine some 600 candy-colored, extravagantly beautiful Victorian homes with the fresh, cool breezes off the ocean, and add superb restaurants to linger in, flower gardens to admire, a gorgeous beach, and the surf to play in, you have the makings for a heavenly weekend escape.

Being so small, Cape May is easy to explore, and its unique attractions—the Victorian "painted lady" homes—are impossible to miss. The itinerary outlined here contains some hints, though, about how to see and do the most if you have only a few days to spend in Cape May and in the delightful town of Lewes, Delaware, where you'll catch the ferry to Cape May.

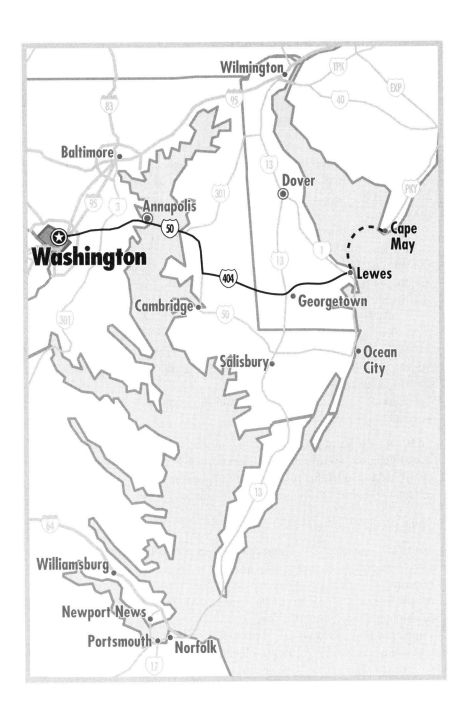

Be sure to bring your camera, because the whole area is so special that you'll want some proof when you brag about it later. And don't forget swimsuits; the beach is clean and inviting. As for picture hats, flowing skirts, lace handkerchiefs, handlebar mustaches, waistcoats, and pocket watches—that's up to you!

Day 1 / *Morning*

As always when heading for the Atlantic Ocean from Washington on a weekend, an early start is a smart start. Pack a thermos of coffee and a bag of doughnuts, and hit the road before 8:00 A.M. if you can, especially in the summer.

To get to Lewes from Washington, take U.S. Highway 50 east. Twenty-eight miles after you cross the Bay Bridge, take Maryland Highway 404 east through Maryland into Delaware. Just before you reach the ocean, follow the signs (and U.S. Highway 9) east to **Lewes.** The 125-mile trip will take you nearly three hours even if traffic is light.

Lewes has the feel of a real fishing town and has fewer Victorian trappings than Cape May. But you will find some shopping opportunities, especially in the attractive historic area along Second Street and Market Street. There are antiques shops, art galleries, and gift stores, as well as coffee bars, bakeries, and restaurants.

After an hour or so of strolling and shopping, stop at one of Lewes's many pleasant restaurants for lunch.

LUNCH: La Rosa Negra, 1201 Savannah Road (302–645–1980; www .larosanegrarestaurant.com), has a menu filled with tasty delights. You can easily make a splendid meal of the focaccia and soup or salad, or opt instead for one of the sophisticated pasta dishes. Moderate.

Afternoon

Lewes has one must-see: **Cape Henlopen State Park,** just east of the ferry terminal on US 9; (302) 645–8983; www.destateparks.com. This beautiful state park has 4 miles of unspoiled beaches that are much less crowded than the beaches to the south. Here, the "walking" sand dunes (including Great Dune, the largest sand dune between Cape Cod and Cape Hatteras) are loved and protected, and several areas of the park are set aside as sanctuaries for nesting birds.

A map that you can pick up at the entrance to the park will show you where to find marked trails through the dunes and brush. There's also the ocean beach for strolling and swimming, as well as a nature center and a World War II observation tower for a great view of the whole area. Open daily 8:00 A.M. to sunset. Admission varies by season, but it is usually $5.00 a car for out-of-staters and $2.50 for Delaware residents.

As you leave the park, you'll see the ferry dock, which is located about a half mile east of downtown Lewes, almost immediately. The **Cape May–Lewes Ferry** makes six to fifteen trips a day between 6:00 A.M. and 9:30 P.M., depending on season and day of the week. For ferry schedule information call (609) 889–7241 or log on to www.capemaylewesferry.com. To make a reservation, call (800) 643–3779. Reservations can also be made online. (*NOTE:* Reservations may not be accepted on many busy weekends; instead, the ferry operates on a first-come, first-served basis. On those weekends, count on a two-hour wait.) The one-way fare for a car and driver is $23 November through March, $29 April through October, and an additional $3.50 to $9.50 for each passenger over six years old; children under six ride free. It will cost you $7.00 to $9.50 if you go on foot or travel by bike. The ferry ride itself is a very pleasant seventy-minute trip across the Delaware Bay.

When you arrive in Cape May, you will find yourself instantly drawn to the historic area of town. If you arrive before 5:00 P.M., head first for the **Cape May Welcome Center,** at the corner of Lafayette and Bank Streets, where you can obtain additional information about most of the area's attractions, lodgings, and restaurants. There are lots of evening activities in Cape May; if you are interested in theater or chamber music, you can pick up a calendar of events while you're there. (609) 884–9562.

Then, check in at the **Queen Victoria,** the bed-and-breakfast inn where you will be staying, to relax for a while and change for dinner. The inn serves a very nice complimentary tea that will perk you up after your day's travel.

The Queen Victoria is near the top of everyone's list of most beautiful and romantic bed-and-breakfasts in the country. There you will find classical music, quilts on the beds, ceiling fans, a cozy fireplace, a player piano, a popcorn maker, a library, a game room, bicycles you can borrow, and juice and soda available all day. The Queen is really two buildings with fifteen guest rooms (each with a private bath) and six suites. Located at 102 Ocean Street; (609) 884–8702; www.queenvictoria.com. Rates: $115–$255; suites, $165–$485.

The Queen Victoria's proprietors also own the **House of Royals** across the street, a completely renovated historic home with eleven guest rooms and modern amenities. Rates $100–$300. Contact the Queen Victoria for reservations.

DINNER: One of Cape May's attractions is its many fine restaurants. Among the best is **410 Bank Street,** located at 410 Bank Street; (609) 884–2127. It's a very pretty little Victorian restaurant with mint green trim, ceiling moldings, and a tiny lamp with a pink frosted globe on every table. Here the specialty is French, New Orleans, and Caribbean cuisine, and the offerings might include baby rack of lamb with demi glaze and foie gras or bayou pan-seared oyster stew. Rasta (bread) pudding is a crowd favorite for dessert. Expensive. (*NOTE:* Most of Cape May's restaurants do not have liquor licenses and operate as "bring your own bottle" establishments.)

Follow dinner with one of the plays or concerts in town, or turn in early after a long day.

LODGING: The Queen Victoria.

Day 2 / Morning

BREAKFAST: The Queen Victoria serves a bounteous buffet breakfast that includes fruit, cereal, an egg dish, pastries, and plenty of coffee.

There are many good ways to tour Cape May. If you walk up and down the streets running perpendicular to the ocean boardwalk, from Windsor to Howard, and the cross streets between them in a 10-by-4-block area along the ocean, you will see most of the beautiful Victorian houses. Alternately, you can borrow a bike from your bed-and-breakfast or rent a bicycle, a tandem, or a four-person bicycle surrey at any of a half dozen convenient shops or stands in town. Bikes rent for $4.00 an hour or $10.00 a day, surreys for about $30.00 a day.

But perhaps the best way to see the town is to head for the east end of the Washington Street Mall Information Booth at Ocean Street, where you can purchase a combination ticket that allows you to take a forty-five-minute guided trolley tour of the downtown residential area and spend an equal amount of time touring the beautiful Emlen Physick estate. Proceeds from ticket sales ($14.00 for adults, $7.00 for children three to twelve) benefit the Mid-Atlantic Center for the Arts (MAC), which conducts the tour. (609) 884–5404 or (800) 275–4278; no reservations accepted for individual tickets.

No matter how much you have heard about the more than 600 "painted ladies" of Cape May, nothing quite prepares you for your first visit. With their pastel colors, exquisitely elaborate porches, gingerbread trim, and stained-glass windows, the Victorian homes are absolutely ravishing. Each inn seems to be trying to outdo the others with its beautiful colors and trim, and even modest private homes are decked out in sherbet colors and have flowers peeping from window boxes.

As you creep along through the tree-lined streets of Cape May on the jolly red MAC trolley, you'll see Gothic cottages, Italianate villas, and mansard and Stick Style homes. Keep your eyes open for cupolas and captain's walks, wide verandas, gazebos, fancy wrought-iron fences, horse ties and carriage steps, and beautiful stained-glass windows. You'll want to keep your camera handy.

Cape May residents are proud of the little town's uniquely decorative architecture. Even a tiny, portable kiosk that sells church bingo tickets recently was painted three shades of lavender, with lots of fancy gingerbread trim. And the tiny 12-by-24-foot **Cape May Firemen's Museum** at the corner of Washington and Franklin Streets looks like an overgrown Victorian dollhouse. Children will love the gleaming, vintage American La France fire engine inside; admission is free.

At the end of the trolley tour, you get to tour the marvelous **Emlen Physick House and Estate,** located at 1048 Washington Street; (609) 884–5404; www.capemaymac.org. In many ways, the Emlen Physick House is Cape May's most authentically restored house. Designed by renowned architect Frank Furness and built in 1879, the fifteen rooms of the Stick Style house have all been restored to their original grandeur. The house also contains Cape May's most extensive collection of Victorian furniture, clothing, toys, tools, and artifacts. MAC also sponsors special seasonal exhibits, such as "A Physick Family Christmas," portraying Victorian life.

Take a few minutes while you're at the Physick Estate to visit the two museum shops there. The Sun Porch Museum Shop has books, cards, Victorian home furnishings, and thousands of Victorian-style Christmas ornaments. The Carriage House Gallery Shop specializes in teapots and tea accessories. Should you need a restorative, there is a tearoom that serves tea sandwiches and scones.

The Physick Estate offers tours from 10:00 A.M. to 3:00 P.M. daily from mid-May through October 31. During the off-season, tours are offered two or three days a week. Call (609) 884–5404 or (800) 275–4278 for information and reservations. Admission is $8.00 for adults and $4.00 for children three through twelve; children two and under are admitted free.

Before lunch, try to fit in a visit to a second beautiful Cape May mansion, the **Mainstay Inn,** 635 Columbia Avenue; (609) 884–8690. Originally built as a gambling club in 1872 for $7,000, the inn is famous today for its elegant interior, although the exterior, with its gleaming white columns, extra-wide veranda, and 13-foot-high windows, is pretty spectacular as well. Only the downstairs is open for touring (and only from 11:00 A.M. to 1:30 P.M.); the upstairs houses the inn's guests. But you can see the grand parlor with its several sofas and love seats, Oriental carpets, gleaming chandeliers, and ornate ceiling. You can also see the luxurious dining room and library with their walnut furnishings. Many consider the Mainstay to be the most lovingly and beautifully restored period house in America. The self-guided tour costs $3.00, which goes to support the Mid-Atlantic Center for the Arts.

LUNCH: Have a late lunch at the **Mad Batter,** 19 Jackson Street; (609) 884–5970; www.madbatter.com. This marvelous restaurant somehow manages to be young, Victorian, decadent, and health conscious all at the same time, and it could easily become your favorite place to eat in Cape May. For lunch try the blackened grouper sandwich or the vegetarian crustless quiche. Wash lunch down with a fresh fruit smoothie or one of the special blends of coffee. And take seriously the sign outside that says LIFE IS UNCERTAIN . . . EAT DESSERTS FIRST! Desserts at the Mad Batter are fabulous (try the triple chocolate cake), and the sumptuous choices on the menu are augmented with daily specials. Moderate.

Afternoon

After lunch, spend the rest of the afternoon shopping. The **Washington Street Mall** is a 2-block pedestrian shopping mall in the heart of Cape May between Perry Street and Decatur Street. There, several nice shops offer chocolates, antiques, jewelry, and gifts. **Swede Things in America,** 307 Washington Street Mall (609–884–5811; www.swedethings.com), has beautiful Scandinavian crystal and pottery and lots of Christmas selections. **The Toy Shop of Cape May,** 510 Washington Street Mall (609–884–0442 or 609–884–0272), has kites, beach toys, travel games, and children's arts-and-crafts kits.

After your shopping, give your feet a rest and enjoy tea or a soda on the porch of the Queen Victoria. If you've had a late lunch, you might want to plan a late dinner as well; it would be in keeping with Victorian tradition.

DINNER: For a special experience, try **Black Duck on Sunset,** 1 Sunset Boulevard; (609) 898–0100; www.blackduckonsunset.com. The ambience is casual; the food is fancy. You can start with a Napoleon of asparagus, yellow and red heirloom tomatoes, crab, and lobster, covered by

Emlen Physick House, Cape May

a dab of pesto sauce and Parmagiano-Reggiano cheese, and follow it with roast duck over sweet potato risotto, rib-eye steak with potato pancakes, or any of a half dozen seafood specials. Expensive.

LODGING: The Queen Victoria.

Day 3 / Morning

BREAKFAST: After breakfast at the Queen Victoria, take a long, leisurely stroll up and down the promenade along the beach. There you'll find some elegant shops and more amazing Victorian homes and inns. If you've brought your suit, spend the morning playing on the oceanfront. The narrow beach is clean and pretty, and it's dotted with umbrellas, children with sand pails, and couples strolling by the water's edge. There is a beach admission charge of $4.00 for those twelve or older.

LUNCH: **Zoe's,** located right on the beach at 715 Beach Drive (609–884–1233), has generous fresh-roasted turkey or roast beef sandwiches, burgers, hoagies, salads, vegetarian specials, cheese fries, potato salad, coleslaw, and desserts. If you skipped the beach scene and want to get an early start home, Zoe's will pack your lunch to go. Inexpensive.

Afternoon

Before you leave the area, consider a visit to the **Cape May Lighthouse** at Cape May Point State Park; (609) 884–2159. There you can climb the 199 steps of this structure, built in 1823, and get a panoramic view of the whole area, including, on a clear day, the Delaware coast. The lighthouse is still in the process of reconstruction, but it has been repainted in its original colors, and the lantern has been finished. (Restoration of the grounds and rebuilding of the privies is next up on the refurbishment schedule.) The Mid-Atlantic Center for the Arts conducts living-history events at the lighthouse, and you're sure to learn much about the lighthouse's history and the lives of its keepers on your visit. Open 9:00 A.M. to 5:00 P.M. daily from April through November, weekends only December through March. Admission is $5.00 for adults, $1.00 for children five through twelve; children under five are admitted free.

To return to Washington, you can retrace your route, using the ferry and driving home through Delaware. Or you can take New Jersey Highway 47 north about 50 miles to Millville, New Jersey; New Jersey Highway 49 west 40 miles to Interstate 295; I–295 west a few miles across the Delaware Memorial Bridge to Wilmington; and Interstate 95 south to Washington. Either option will take a little more than four hours.

There's More

Ocean Cruise. The Cape May Whale Watcher offers one- or two-hour cruises on the ocean in search of either whales or dolphins, depending on the season. Three trips daily March through December. The one-hour whale- and dolphin-watch cruise costs $35 for adults and $20 for children age seven to twelve; children under seven ride free. The two-hour dolphin-watching cruise is $5.00 to $10.00 cheaper. Sightings are guaranteed on all cruises. Located at Miss Chris Marina, Second Avenue and Wilson Drive; (609) 884–5445 or (800) 786–5445; www.capemaywhalewatcher .com.

Historic Cold Spring Village. Nineteenth-century farm village with country store, restaurant, bakery, and daily craft demonstrations of pottery, basketry, ironware, and more. Located at 720 U.S. Highway 9, about 3 miles north of downtown Cape May; (609) 898–2300; www.hcsv.org. Open Tuesday through Sunday 10:00 A.M. to 4:30 P.M. mid-June through August; weekends 10:00 A.M. to 4:30 P.M. in early June and early September. Admission is $8.00 for adults, $7.00 for seniors, and $5.00 for children three to twelve; children under three are admitted free.

Wildwood. Just north of Cape May is the widest and among the most popular beaches in New Jersey. Wildwood has a mile-and-a-half-long boardwalk with four amusement piers, hundreds of souvenir and novelty shops, and tons of saltwater taffy.

Special Events

March–April. Annual Delaware Kite Festival. Kite-flying at Cape Henlopen State Park; festival events at the park and in Lewes; area attraction since 1968. (302) 645–8073.

April. Cape May Jazz Festival. Regional and national artists perform at the ferry terminal. (609) 884–7277; www.capemayjazz.com.

May–June. Annual Cape May Music Festival. Chamber music, jazz, opera, and pops. (609) 884–3860.

October. Victorian Week. With all the tours, craft shows, food, and entertainment, everyone has so much fun that Victorian Week now lasts ten days. (609) 884–5508 or (800) 275–4278.

December. Christmas Season in Cape May. Candlelight house tours, holiday crafts fair, gingerbread house workshops, heated trolley tours with complimentary wassail punch. (609) 884–5508 or (800) 275–4278.

Other Recommended Restaurants

Cape May

Axelsson's Blue Claw, 991 Ocean Drive (north of downtown); (609) 884–5878; www.blueclawrestaurant.com. Seafood, beef, veal; piano bar; waterfront dining. Moderate to expensive.

Dock Mike's Pancake House, South Jersey Marina (on Lafayette Street 1 mile north of downtown area); (609) 884–2855; www.dockmikes.com. First choice for huge, inexpensive breakfasts.

Louisa's Cafe, 104 Jackson Street; (609) 884–5882. Small, upscale restaurant specializing in innovative vegetarian and seafood entrees and great desserts; open for dinner Wednesday through Saturday. Moderate to expensive.

Gecko's, Carpenter's Square Mall (downtown); (609) 898–7750. Casual downtown restaurant featuring Southwestern fare for breakfast, lunch, and dinner. Moderate.

The Lobster House Restaurant, on Fisherman's Wharf; (609) 884–8296; www.thelobsterhouse.com. Ultrafresh seafood (they have their own fleet of boats). Make the catch of the day your choice after you've had a bowl of the crab soup. Moderate to expensive.

Fresco's, 412 Bank Street; (609) 884–0366. Attractive, upscale Italian restaurant that serves both old and new Italian cuisine. Try the four-cheese lasagna, the osso buco, or the veal chops with crabmeat, asparagus, and garlic. Expensive.

Best place for doughnuts: Cape May Bakers, 482 West Perry Street; (609) 884–7454.

Lewes

Rose & Crown Restaurant and Pub, 108 Second Street; (302) 645–2373. Sandwiches and pub food for lunch; seafood, pasta, poultry for dinner; large selection of beers. Moderate.

The Lighthouse Restaurant, Savannah Street and Anglers Road, by the Drawbridge on Lewes Harbor; (302) 645–6271; www.lighthouselewes .com. Seafood and great view make for a pleasant breakfast, lunch, or dinner spot. Moderate.

Gilligan's Restaurant, Front and Market Streets; (302) 645–7866. New American seafood and more; dine inside or outside. Moderate to expensive.

Other Recommended Lodgings

Cape May

Angel of the Sea, 5 Trenton Avenue; (609) 884–3369 or (800) 848–3369; www.angelofthesea.com. One of Cape May's most popular inns, with twenty-six guest rooms, all with private bath. Close to the beach; full breakfast, complimentary afternoon tea, use of bicycles and beach equipment. Rates: $95–$315, depending on season and size of the room.

The Mainstay Inn, 635 Columbia Avenue; (609) 884–8690; www.main stayinn.com. Exquisite Italianate villa considered by many to be the top bed-and-breakfast in Cape May; has thirteen guest rooms, all with private bath. Beautiful grand parlor, spacious veranda with swings and hammocks; full breakfast served. Rates: $155–$345.

Ashley Rose Victorian Inn, 715 Columbia Avenue; (609) 884–2497 or (800) 601–7673; www.victorianroseinn.com. Former tearoom, now a romantic bed-and-breakfast with eight guest rooms, four suites, and a cottage. Most of the rooms have private baths; the suites and cottage have fully equipped kitchens. The inn has a large porch with rockers, and a rose garden. The $125 to $250 tariff for the rooms and suites includes a full breakfast. The cottage rents for $1,400 a week in summer. The restored Victorian Main House runs $425–$1,400 nightly and $2,000–$5,700 weekly.

Carroll Villa, 19 Jackson Street; (609) 884–5970 or (877) 275–8452; www .carrollvilla.com. Family-run 1882 bed-and-breakfast hotel with twenty-two guest rooms. Private baths, air-conditioning, phones, period antiques; full breakfast at the Mad Batter next door. Rates: $75–$200.

The Brass Bed Inn, 719 Columbia Avenue; (609) 884–2302; www.brass bedinn.com. Lace curtains, wall coverings, Oriental rugs, and brass beds adorn the nine airy guest rooms in this nicely restored 1872 home; full breakfast served. Rates: $100–$225.

The Abbey, 34 Gurney Street at Columbia Avenue; (609) 884–4506 or (866) 884–8800; www.abbeybedandbreakfast.com. Very pleasant inn with fourteen large, antiques-filled rooms, all with private bath. The draw here is the owners, who entertain you with songs, hats, and snappy patter. Rates: $85–$250. Minimum two-night stay on weekends.

Lewes

Zwaanendael, Second and Market Streets; (302) 645–6466 or (800) 824–8754; www.zwaanendaelinn.com. Nicely restored inn with twenty-three elegant guest rooms and suites and lots of warm hospitality; continental breakfast included. First-rate restaurant on premises. Rates: $50–$280.

Inn at Canal Square, 122 Market Street; (302) 644–3377 or (888) 644–1911; www.theinnatcanalsquare.com. Downtown inn on the canal with twenty-four rooms. All the rooms are large and tastefully furnished; all have a private bath, phone, and cable TV, and nearly all have a balcony overlooking the scenic canal. Continental breakfast is served. Rates: $105–$300.

Cape Henlopen State Park, US 9; (302) 645–2103; www.destateparks
.com, has 156 campsites near the ocean. Rates: $22–$30.

For More Information

Lewes Chamber of Commerce and Visitors Bureau, P.O. Box 1, Lewes,
DE 19958; (302) 645–8073 or (877) 465–3937; www.leweschamber.com.

Chamber of Commerce of Greater Cape May, P.O. Box 556, Cape May,
NJ 08204; (609) 884–5508 or (800) 275–4278; www.capemaychamber
.com.

Cape May County Department of Tourism, P.O. Box 365, Cape May
Court House, NJ 08210; (609) 884–5508, (609) 884–9562, or (800)
275–4278; www.beachcomber.com/capemay/capemay.html.

For more information visit www.capemay.com.

INDEX

About the Authors

John Fitzpatrick teaches political science and is the Director of the State University of New York at Brockport's Washington Semester Program. John is a graduate of Georgetown University and has a Ph.D. from the State University of New York at Buffalo. He worked as a Congressional staffer for ten years and ran a political consulting firm for eight years.

Holly J. Burkhalter is advocacy director of Physicians for Human Rights, an international human rights monitoring organization. Holly is a graduate of Iowa State University and a recipient of one of its Distinguished Young Alumni awards. She is the author of numerous articles and op-ed pieces, and she frequently appears on radio and television discussing foreign policy. She is also the author of a cookbook/memoir, *Four Midwestern Sisters Christmas Book* (Viking Penguin, 1991).

John and Holly have been married since 1984. They have two daughters, Grace Bofa Fitzpatrick and Josie Bao-Ngan Fitzpatrick.